*for*
*The Shakespeare Institute*

*Shakespeare's Political Drama*

# Shakespeare's Political Drama

## THE HISTORY PLAYS
### AND
## THE ROMAN PLAYS

## Alexander Leggatt

*London and New York*

First published 1988
by Routledge
11 New Fetter Lane, London EC4P 4EE

Simultaneously published in the USA and Canada
by Routledge
29 West 35th Street, New York, NY 10001

First published in paperback 1989
Reprinted 1992, 1994

Typeset by AKM Associates (UK) Ltd
Printed and bound in Great Britain by
the University Press, Cambridge

*British Library Cataloguing in Publication Data*
A catalogue record for this book is available from the British Library

*Library of Congress Cataloging in Publication Data*
A catalog record for this book is available from the Library of Congress

ISBN 0-415-00655-4 (hbk)          ISBN 0-415-03888-X (pbk)

# Contents

# Acknowledgements

There is an oral tradition behind this book. Papers arising from my work on these plays have been read at McGill University, the State University of New York at Buffalo, Yale University, the International Shakespeare Conference at Stratford-upon-Avon, the Shakespeare Association of America meeting at Nashville, the University College Symposium (Toronto), the New Jersey Shakespeare Festival, and the Stratford Festival of Ontario. I am grateful to all those who made these occasions possible, and to the audiences who helped me test my ideas. Chapters 3 and 9 contain, in considerably revised form, material that first appeared in '*Henry VIII* and the Ideal England', in *Shakespeare Survey* 38, and 'A Double Reign: *Richard II* and *Perkin Warbeck*', in *Shakespeare and his Contemporaries: Essays in Comparison*, ed. E. A. J. Honigmann. I am grateful to Cambridge University Press and Manchester University Press respectively for permission to reproduce this material.

For help and encouragement of various kinds, and for the sharing of ideas, I wish to thank Hardin Aasand, Northrop Frye, R. Chris Hassel, Jr, Harriet Hawkins, G. R. Hibbard, Maureen Hill-Elder, Martha Kurtz, R. B. Parker and Susan Snyder. I am particularly grateful to William Blissett and T. W. Craik, who read the final manuscript with great care and saved me from many errors and infelicities. The flaws that remain are my own responsibility.

Early stages of this work were made possible by travel grants from the University of Toronto and the Social Sciences and Humanities Research Council of Canada. I owe special thanks to the University of Toronto for allowing me to take a sabbatical to complete the work, and to the John Simon Guggenheim Memorial Foundation, not only for awarding me a Fellowship, but for the very civilized and efficient way in which the Fellowship was administered.

*Alexander Leggatt*
*University College*
*University of Toronto*
*July 1987*

viii

# *Preface*

I should begin by stressing the limits of this study. There is, of course, political interest everywhere in Shakespeare. *Macbeth* and *Hamlet* are concerned with kingship, *Measure for Measure* with law, *The Tempest* with power. *Cymbeline* has surprising things to say about war, peace, and international relations generally. Everywhere there are rulers, laws, contracts, questions of authority and obedience. The range widens if, as frequently happens these days, the term 'political' is defined to include any act with a social dimension. In this light there is a political dimension in the relations of the sexes in *The Taming of the Shrew* and *As You Like It*, or of parents and children in *Romeo and Juliet* and *A Midsummer Night's Dream*. But if everything is political then nothing is, for the word has lost its edge. I want to concentrate on what is political in a more narrow, traditional sense: the ordering and enforcing, the gaining and losing, of public power in the state. And I want to concentrate on those plays of Shakespeare's that are most directly concerned with that, rather than with more private emotional, moral, or spiritual issues. A simple test is to observe the different weights given to England in *Richard II* and to Scotland in *Macbeth*: both matter, of course, but England matters more. At the end of *Richard II* the business of the play is only half done, for though Richard is dead England is still in disorder. At the end of *Macbeth* the business is fully done, for that business was to explore the fate of the hero. Scotland has been restored, but we do not feel compelled to think further about its fate, any more than we think of Cyprus under Cassio. With this kind of distinction in mind, I have chosen to study Shakespeare's English history plays and his Roman plays – which are also history plays, though the term is not so often used of them.

It is now customary for a critic dealing with the English histories in particular to begin with a ritual attack on E. M. W. Tillyard's *Shakespeare's History Plays* (1944). I think we have had enough of this.

ix

We have established that to see Shakespeare as a propagandist for the Tudor Myth, the Great Chain of Being, and the Elizabethan World Picture will not do. So far so good. But in fairness to Tillyard it should be said that his book contains much that is wise and sensitive, and that he himself makes the reservations about his main argument that most of us would like to make. More important, we should notice that Tillyard, though persistently attacked, will not go away. Other books of that period are forgotten; his is not. Tillyard on the histories, like L. C. Knights on Restoration comedy or Edmund Wilson on Ben Jonson, remains a perpetual irritant because there is something in what he says. Shakespeare does in fact deal in political myths, stylized images of good (or bad) order that go beyond the conditions of history realistically appraised. Nor will it do to set up against Tillyard's myth a myth of our own. There is a current tendency to see society as a structure of oppression and exploitation, and to read Shakespeare accordingly.[1] We will get at part of the truth in that way, but only part. Here as elsewhere Shakespeare is exploratory, not prescriptive. He examines power and its implications realistically, and beside the official view that order is a good thing and that God is watching over England there are always minority reports. But he allows us to feel the excitement, even the longing, that the dream of good order produces, for that too is part of our political life: no fully realistic view can leave it out of account, and no fully responsible view can dismiss it as mere illusion. We may not agree that the good life can be made, Tudor-fashion, by a strong central power. But if we stop believing that it can be made at all we are lost.

In the chapters that follow I shall try to see Shakespeare not as the propagandist for a myth of order, nor as a cynic who sees only deception and oppression and calls this realism. He is concerned both with things as they are and with things as they ought to be, and his depiction of public life includes clear appraisals of the one and powerful images of the other. It is the interplay of the two that makes the drama. It is worth extending this investigation into the Roman plays, for they too concern the interplay between myth and reality, centred less on the state and more on the great individuals who dominate public life and whose tragedies have public implications that weigh more heavily than is usual in tragedy. In this way we will also see what, in Shakespeare's view, changes when one moves from a monarchy to a republic, and what remains the same. If we are to get a full view of Shakespeare as a political writer we need to see him examining both models.

I have tried to see each play as a fresh experiment, so that what emerges is not a single, homogeneous view of Shakespearian politics but a series of explorations of differing material, asking the same questions but not always getting the same answers. There are two principal questions. One has already been touched on: what is the relation between the stylized, myth-making view of political life and the realistic one that reports the unsatisfying reality? The second is a consequence of the first: how does Shakespeare's medium, which is drama, shape his political thinking? For Shakespeare does think about politics; but he thinks in the way a playwright thinks. He works through a form that deals not in theory but in practical demonstration,[2] and his medium is the actor. Painters or sculptors can create purely heroic images, for they have absolute control over what we see. Dramatists can also deal in the heroic, but their concepts will be embodied in ordinary human figures. Shakespeare not only accepts that fact but exploits it. At the same time his medium works swiftly and economically; however much realism it allows, it also requires simplification and stylization. It is by its very nature artificial. (This is true even of the drama that is called realistic: there are soliloquies in Chekhov.) This artifice means that actors are both liberated and tied down by the roles they play. They can experience through their own being a nature other, perhaps larger than their own; yet they are bound as no one is in reality to a set routine of words and movements. Shakespeare is interested in his characters as role-players, at once freed and limited by their parts. The historian's assessment of political characters will come down in the end to the changes they made to the community they worked in, and to what they left behind them. Shakespeare watches, moment by moment, the way his political figures impress others, and themselves, the means they use to do so, and the price they pay.

We have two testimonies from Shakespeare's time to the effect of putting famous people and events into popular drama. These testimonies are in conflict. Thomas Nashe, in *Pierce Penilesse*, speculates as follows:

> How would it have joyed brave *Talbot* (the terror of the French) to think that, after he had lain two hundred years in his tomb, he should triumph again on the stage, and have his bones new embalmed with the tears of ten thousand spectators at least (at several times) who, in the tragedian that represents his person, imagine they behold him fresh bleeding![3]

Against this report from the beginning of Shakespeare's career we may set Sir Henry Wotton's, from the end:

> The Kings Players had a new Play called *All is True*, representing some principal pieces of the Reign of Henry 8. which was set forth

with many extraordinary circumstances of Pomp and Majesty, even to the matting of the stage; the Knights of the Order, with their Georges and Garter, the Guards with their embroidered Coats, and the like: sufficient in truth within a while to make greatness very familiar, if not ridiculous.[4]

This is not just a contrast between Elizabethan romanticism and Jacobean scepticism; both are possibilities latent in the theatre all the time. It brings legends to life and makes us believe in them; it brings them down to earth and makes us examine them. Its economy both intensifies and diminishes. We shall see Shakespeare drawing on both these powers as he examines the famous men and women of English and Roman history.

A few more practical questions should be disposed of here. One concerns two notable omissions from the list of plays. *Titus Andronicus* is a Roman tragedy no less than the others, and its first act in particular is full of political interest. But its focus from Act II onwards is, I think, more private than that of the other Roman plays: it is more about pain than about politics. If I were writing about Shakespearian tragedy I would not dream of omitting it; but I have omitted it here. *King John* presents a more difficult case. It is a fascinating if untidy play, and if my theme were, say, the problem of legitimacy *King John* would be indispensable. But given my present approach there is little I could say about it that is not shown as well or better in other plays. I have discussed it extensively elsewhere,[5] and have little to add now; under those circumstances it seemed best to omit it.

Two critical questions, on which I have made assumptions that may be controversial, call for comment. The first is authorship, affecting *Henry VI* and *Henry VIII*. I have assumed that *Henry VI* is Shakespeare's play, and that the three parts were written in their natural chronological order. It used to be widely held that this was a committee play, and the idea that Part 1 was written last is still current. The latter question is not of much concern: whatever the order of composition, the trilogy as we find it in the Folio is, I think, a finished and coherent piece of work and can be discussed as such. It is also, despite its limitations, controlled and intelligent in a way in which the committee plays of the period frequently are not. Though full of variety, it is not merely episodic, its style and attitudes are consistent throughout, and, if a committee wrote it, it was a very well-organized committee. My decision to treat *Henry VIII* as simply Shakespeare's may be more debatable. The critics who support Fletcher as part-author are a formidable group, in numbers and in quality. Yet there is no external evidence for Fletcher's role, as there is for *The Two Noble Kinsmen*, and (more to the point) I find the differences between those two plays striking. Even if we did not have title-page evidence for the divided authorship of *The Two Noble Kinsmen*, we would notice startling changes in manner between one scene and another. *Henry VIII* seems to me a much more unified work; in my discussion of it I have observed splits of style and attitude, but they cut across the authorship division generally accepted by the Fletcher party. The shifts in this play, some of which are striking, go not just from scene to scene but from line to line. I would not rule out the possibility of some Fletcherian influence, or even collaboration in a small way. But I have referred to the author of this play as 'Shakespeare', partly for convenience but mostly because that is where I think the balance of probability lies. If it were proved otherwise this would not change my reading of the play: it is what it is no matter who wrote what. It would not greatly change my view of Shakespeare as a political dramatist, for I see *Henry VIII* merely as his last political play, not his climactic one. What it would do is increase considerably my respect for his ability to work with a collaborator, an ability *The Two Noble Kinsmen* leaves very much in doubt.

Another controversy that affects the English history plays in particular is the question of whether to read each play on its own, or as part of a larger unit formed by the series as a whole. The latter approach, associated with Tillyard, is currently out of favour, and there are so many inconsistencies between one play and the next that the notion of treating the sequence from *Richard II* to *Richard III* as a single great work, developed over the years but meant to stand together, deserves to be viewed with suspicion. At the same time there are many points at which the plays consciously refer to each other. The two tetralogies (*Henry VI* to *Richard III* and *Richard II* to *Henry V*) need on the whole to be kept separate, but to keep each play separate is to reject quite explicit invitations in the texts – invitations to remember, to make connections. The best approach is the pragmatic one: not to force connections, but to be ready to acknowledge them if they can add something to our understanding. There is also a difference, I think, between the three-part *Henry VI* and the two-part *Henry IV* (though in the chapters on these plays I have taken the parts together for the sake of convenience and economy). Each part of *Henry VI* ends with the introduction of a new action that will be picked up in the next play; the technique is that of the cliffhanger, demanding that the audience keep coming back. The two parts of *Henry IV* are, I think, free-standing by comparison, though much of Part 2 presupposes an audience familiar with Part 1. There is enough evidence in the texts themselves to suggest that Shakespeare meant the audience of one play to call up, on occasion, memories of its predecessors. It could be objected that sustained attention of this kind is possible only to a special audience like that of Bayreuth.[6] But we have enough recent examples in successful films that spawn sequels to know that similar demands can be made on a popular audience. Shakespeare was never afraid to make such demands if there was something to be gained by them. I have already stressed my interest in seeing each play as a fresh experiment; but each experiment is part of an ongoing investigation.

# Note on the texts

All references to Shakespeare are to the Arden editions, published in London by Methuen. The principal texts are: *Henry VI*, Parts 1, 2, and 3, ed. Andrew S. Cairncross (1962; 1957, revised 1962; 1964); *Richard III*, ed. Antony Hammond (1981); *Richard II*, ed. Peter Ure (1956, revised 1961); *Henry IV*, Parts 1 and 2, ed. A. R. Humphreys (1960, revised 1961; 1966); *Henry V*, ed. J. H. Walter (1954); *Julius Caesar*, ed. T. S. Dorsch (1955); *Antony and Cleopatra*, ed. M. R. Ridley (1954); *Coriolanus*, ed. Philip Brockbank (1976); and *Henry VIII*, ed. R. A. Foakes (1957, revised 1964).

*Malcolm.* ... Comes the King forth, I pray you?
*Doctor.* Ay, sir. There are a crew of wretched souls
　　　That stay his cure. Their malady convinces
　　　The great assay of art; but at his touch –
　　　Such sanctity hath heaven given his hand –
　　　They presently amend.

　　　　　　　　　　　　　　　　*Macbeth*


*Gloucester.* O, let me kiss that hand!
*Lear.* Let me wipe it first; it smells of mortality.

　　　　　　　　　　　　　　　　*King Lear*

# 1

# *Henry VI*

The first scene of the *Henry VI* trilogy is a formal ceremony, the funeral of Henry V. Bedford's opening speech dignifies the occasion with a note of cosmic tragedy – 'Hung be the heavens with black, yield day to night!' (I.i.1) – and goes on to rebuke 'the bad revolting stars, / That have consented unto Henry's death' (I.i.4–5). He later imagines Henry, now a star himself, combating 'with adverse planets in the heavens' (I.i.54) to preserve the welfare of England. His life on earth is already acquiring the status of myth. Gloucester declares:

> His brandish'd sword did blind men with his beams:
> His arms spread wider than a dragon's wings:
> His sparkling eyes, replete with wrathful fire,
> More dazzled and drove back his enemies
> Than mid-day sun fierce bent against their faces.
> What should I say? His deeds exceed all speech:
> He ne'er lift up his hand but conquered.      (I. i. 10–16)

This not only recalls Marlowe's Tamburlaine but anticipates later Shakespearian heroes who transcend the human – Coriolanus, in particular. But, as in *Tamburlaine*, the price for attributing all this grandeur to one man is that when he dies there is nothing left. Exeter brings us down to flat mortality: 'Henry is dead and never shall revive. / Upon a wooden coffin we attend' (I.i.18–19). As the scene proceeds, with the coffin still onstage,[1] messengers bring news of English losses in France. In history nothing happens as fast as that; but the economy of the theatre allows a tight connection between the death of the hero and the collapse of his achievements.

Before the end of the scene we are introduced to a new hero as the hopes of the English turn to Lord Talbot. But Talbot is not a king. In fact the first half of *1 Henry VI*, like the Roman plays, is set in a kingless world. The infant Henry VI is unseen and rarely mentioned; the French

1

have only a Dauphin, who behaves as first among equals. With the supernatural (and kingly) hero dead and transformed to myth, Shakespeare turns our attention to a remarkable man: one who can generate legends but is himself nothing more, or less, than a good field commander operating in the normal conditions of war. With Henry V as a giant shadow in the background, Shakespeare gives us a full and realistic appraisal of Talbot, the myth and the reality. The messenger who brings news of the Battle of Patay describes an epic hero operating in a state of military confusion:

> No leisure had he to enrank his men;
> He wanted pikes to set before his archers;
> Instead whereof sharp stakes pluck'd out of hedges
> They pitched in the ground confusedly
> To keep the horsemen off from breaking in.
> More than three hours the fight continued;
> Where valiant Talbot, above human thought,
> Enacted wonders with his sword and lance:
> Hundreds he sent to hell, and none durst stand him.    (I. i. 115–23)

This description of Talbot suggests a need to imagine a hero on the scale of Henry. But he is not, as Henry is, invincible. When the messenger announces a fight between Talbot and the French, Winchester anticipates the outcome – 'Wherein Talbot overcame, is't so?' – only to be told, 'O no: wherein Lord Talbot was o'erthrown' (I. i. 107–8). The account of Talbot's scrambling desperation evokes the practical realities of war. We hear the same note of desperation when during the English rout at Amiens Talbot cries, 'My thoughts are whirled like a potter's wheel; / I know not where I am, nor what I do' (I. v. 19–20).[2] When he is winning, on the other hand, all a common English soldier has to do is cry 'A Talbot!' and the French run away in comic fear (II. i. 77SD–81).

Talbot shows at times an exalted sense of his own heroic identity: we first see him standing on a turret, exalted above us, describing how he refused to be exchanged with a prisoner of lower rank. But in battle he is usually more practical than this. During the siege of Orleans he is contrasted with Bedford, for whom everything depends on one man. Bedford, at the late king's funeral, declared, 'arms avail not, now that Henry's dead' (I. i. 47),[3] and now he wants to fall in line behind the new hero. Talbot has other ideas:

> *Bed.* Ascend, brave Talbot; we will follow thee.
> *Tal.* Not all together; better far, I guess,

> That we do make our entrance several ways,
> That if it chance the one of us do fall,
> The other yet may rise against their force. (II. i. 28–32)[4]

Success in battle is the achievement of the group, not the individual; hero-worship must not interfere with tactics. The importance of this idea is emphasized when we first hear of Talbot: though he fought, as we have seen, with supernatural courage, he lost the Battle of Patay because of the desertion of Sir John Falstaff (I. i. 130–5).

Given the strong message that with Henry's death the English are finished, the recapture of Orleans is Talbot's most impressive achievement; he turns what had looked like the inevitable tide of history. In the aftermath of that victory Shakespeare sets forth the nature of Talbot's greatness in one of those stylized set pieces he uses throughout the history plays to bring key ideas into focus. The Countess of Auvergne invites Talbot to her castle. His friends jocularly tell him to prepare for a love encounter (II. ii. 44–58), but the challenge to his manhood takes a different form. The Countess's messenger raises the real question when he asks, 'Which of this princely train / Call ye the warlike Talbot . . .?' (II. ii. 34–6). Octavius Caesar will try the same insulting ploy on Cleopatra: 'Which is the Queen of Egypt?' (*Antony and Cleopatra*, V.ii.112). There is nothing in the character's appearance to match his reputation. The Countess herself makes it clear that while her purpose is to capture Talbot she also wants to satisfy her curiosity about him: 'Fain would mine eyes be witness with mine ears / To give their censure of these rare reports' (II. iii. 9–10). She professes herself disappointed:

> I thought I should have seen some Hercules,
> A second Hector, for his grim aspect
> And large proportion of his strong-knit limbs.
> Alas, this is a child, a silly dwarf!
> It cannot be this weak and writhled shrimp
> Should strike such terror to his enemies. (II. iii. 18–23)

The question is one of shadow and substance. The physical body of Talbot is a disappointment in view of his great reputation, just as the appearance of the actor himself may not live up to the legend of the character he is portraying; behind the challenge to Talbot, Shakespeare is dealing with one of the fundamental problems of historical drama, characteristically calling attention to the difficulty rather than smoothing it over.[5] No actor could look like the Henry V described in the opening scene; the actor playing Talbot does not have to, for his ordinariness is just the point. As the Countess interprets the shadow–

3

substance theme, Talbot's picture embodies his legend, and both are shadows; the real thing is the little man in front of her:

> Long time thy shadow hath been thrall to me,
> For in my gallery thy picture hangs;
> And now thy substance shall endure the like.   (II. iii.  35–7)[6]

Talbot replies that she has it backwards. The man himself is the shadow; Talbot's substance lies in his army, which he summons by winding his horn:

> How say you, madam? Are you now persuaded
> That Talbot is but shadow of himself?
> These are his substance, sinews, arms, and strength.
>
> (II. iii.  60–2)

In the Roman plays the relations between the hero's shadow and his substance will not be resolved in this way. Talbot's appraisal of his greatness is self-deprecating and realistic; for once we are not challenged to believe that the great legend is literally true. But the final note of the scene is paradoxical: while Talbot asks the Countess to feast his soldiers as well as himself, she persists in honouring the single hero: 'With all my heart, and think me honoured / To feast so great a warrior in my house' (II.iii.80–1). Perhaps she has accepted his argument and the words 'so great a warrior' are meant to include them all; but I rather think she still has eyes for Talbot alone. His demonstration of his power was theatrically exciting: he sounded his horn and the stage filled with soldiers. And the realism of his insistence that his greatness depends on others is itself impressive. He is the sort of great man, like Washington and Wellington, whose legend includes tales of modesty.[7]

But where Talbot is great he is also vulnerable, as the single hero is not. While Coriolanus alone can take on a city, Talbot needs enough of what Wellington called 'that article', the common soldier, and he is destroyed at Bordeaux when the wrangling York and Somerset deny him men.[8] Not only destroyed, but in the bitter words of Lucy, who is trying to shame the quarrelling lords into action, 'bought and sold' (IV. iv. 13), a chivalric hero finally and fatally dependent on the mundane, brought down by politicians whose arguments are arguments for doing nothing. The long rhymed sequence Talbot shares with his son John expresses their values of honour and piety in a manner that is slow and frigid to modern taste. But Nashe testifies to its power for its original audience,[9] and it has the effect of stylizing the idealism of the Talbots to sharpen the contrast with the crass and fussy excuses we hear from York and Somerset. Talbot, like Henry, is expanded into a legend as he dies, and in the process we get a double view of him. As he challenges Bordeaux, the French general defending the city greets him:

> Lo, there thou stand'st a breathing valiant man
> Of an invincible unconquer'd spirit:
> This is the latest glory of thy praise,
> That I, thy enemy, due thee withal;
> For ere the glass, that now begins to run,
> Finish the process of his sandy hour,
> These eyes, that see thee so well coloured,
> Shall see thee wither'd, bloody, pale and dead.
>
> *Drum afar off.*
> (IV. ii. 31–8)

Shadow and substance again: the reality of the hero dissolves into the picture of his corpse. The power of the speech comes from its quiet, its gentleness, and its eerie certainty of doom, confirmed by the distant drum. There is a more extravagant effect later when Lucy asks for Talbot, taking twelve lines to list all his titles, and Joan replies, 'Him that thou magnifiest with all these titles, / Stinking and fly-blown lies here at our feet' (IV.vii.60–76).[10] But, like the long sequence with John, this at least fixes Talbot for our contemplation, making him a vivid double image of greatness and mortality. What follows is more subtly disturbing. Too late to save their own hero, the English unite to capture and kill Joan; but this achievement is wiped out by the larger movement of history as, before the English can consolidate their victory, a peace is signed that allows the French a useful breathing space. As history goes on, Talbot, whose name was on every tongue while he lived, is forgotten. King Henry's argument for peace –

> I always thought
> It was both impious and unnatural
> That such immanity and bloody strife
> Should reign among professors of one faith
>
> (V. i. 11–14)

– though unimpeachable as a statement of Christian pacifism, sets at nought everything Talbot has stood for. When at the opening of Part 2 Gloucester recapitulates the history of the English effort in France, he makes no mention of Talbot (Pt 2, I.i.77–96). It is as though the great man had never lived.

Talbot is impressive; but he is a hero in a practical world in which he is first destroyed and then forgotten. His arena of action is a war that

Shakespeare on the whole conceives quite realistically. Bedford declares, 'An army have I muster'd in my thoughts, / Wherewith already France is overrun' (I.i.101–2), but armies of the imagination are no more use here than they are in *Richard II*. (In *Henry V*, as we shall see, the imagination is a more powerful weapon.) The messenger who brings the first news of loss in France fixes the blame on 'want of men and money' (I.i.69) and goes on to a brutally frank description of the dithering at home that is leading to disaster abroad (I.i.70–7). Salisbury, 'mirror of all martial men' (I.iv.73), is killed by a sniper – a painfully unheroic death. The French look even less dignified when at the siege of Orleans they '*leap over the walls in their shirts*' (II.i.38SD). The fortunes of war are unpredictable. The dead march that opens the play is contrasted with '*Sound a flourish*' (I.ii.SD) for the first French scene, exemplifying what looks like the historical inevitability of English defeat and French victory. But while the tide of history may be flowing in that direction we are mostly aware of cross-currents. The Dauphin's opening words are 'Mars his true moving, even as in the heavens / So in the earth, to this day is not known' (I.ii.1–2), and in fact the first battle we see is an unexpected English victory.

The English indignation at having to cope with a French sorceress – 'Heavens, can you suffer hell so to prevail?' (I.v.9) – is paired with the other side's view of Talbot: 'The French exclaim'd the devil was in arms' (I.i.125). At first the two sides seem equally matched, each with its hero, though the heroes are differently inspired. That is the impression of the battle for Orleans; but in the battle for Rouen there is a more carefully developed contrast between the chivalric English and the pragmatic French. Talbot recalls that in this city 'Great Coeur-de-lion's heart was buried' (III.ii.83), and Bedford defends his decision to appear on the battlefield despite his sickness by citing the example of Uther Pendragon (III.ii.94–6). (We have just had our first sight of the new king, Henry VI, and this seems to reawaken the English consciousness of their royal tradition.) Talbot deplores the unsporting attitude of the French, who, having possession of the town, will not come out and fight for it like gentlemen (III.ii.61–70).[11] After a setback at Orleans, the French squabbled and bickered; they greet a setback at Rouen more calmly, urging Joan to think of 'secret policies' (III.iii.12) to restore their fortunes, and confident of her ability to do so. She fulfils their expectations by winning Burgundy back to the French side. The English think in terms of tradition and principle; the French are more pragmatic and better prepared for the long haul.

Joan la Pucelle might seem an exception to this realism, not just because of the supernatural agencies she uses, but because of the stylized way in which she is caricatured as the converse and parody of the English hero Talbot.[12] (Identified in her first scene as prophet and shepherdess, she also sullies two roles that will later be associated with Henry VI.) The gap between legend and reality, subtly treated in the case of Talbot, is cruder in Joan. Having declared, 'I must not yield to any rites of love, / For my profession's sacred from above' (I. ii. 113–14), she sleeps with the Dauphin (II. i. ii). Where Talbot's death scene is a model of courage and piety, Joan twists and lies in a desperate attempt to save her life. She refuses to acknowledge her father, whose response is not exactly sentimental: 'O, burn her, burn her: hanging is too good' (V. iv. 33). She claims virginity, then pregnancy, and keeps changing the identity of the father; when all else fails, she curses. The black comedy of the scene is an obvious contrast to the stylized dignity of Talbot's death, yet Joan's brazenness becomes admirable in its own way; she is so refreshingly shameless. So far, she seems a caricature; but her approach to the war is realistic. Supernaturally aided or not, she is no more invincible than Talbot, and seems indignant when the Dauphin expects she should be:

> At all times will you have my power alike?
> Sleeping or waking, must I still prevail,
> Or will you blame and lay the fault on me?
> Improvident soldiers! had your watch been good
> This sudden mischief never could have fallen.
>
> (II. i. 55–9)

She slangs the other side, as we might expect. But her cynical, levelling voice can also be applied to her own achievements. She chose her sword, she declares, 'Out of a great deal of old iron' (I.ii.101), and she greets Burgundy's return to the French cause with a line guaranteed to get a laugh from the English audience: 'Done like a Frenchman! [*Aside*.] – turn and turn again' (III. iii. 85).

Her practical spirit gives her an affinity with Talbot; as Tillyard points out, 'both have a touch of breeziness, or hearty coarseness with which Shakespeare liked to furnish his most successfully practical characters'.[13] Certainly no saint, she seems not so much a witch as a tough, cynical girl whose manner is not as far as we might have expected from that of Shaw's modern heroine. But the realism in Shakespeare's treatment of Joan goes deeper than that. She and Talbot are so carefully established as antagonists that we expect a final showdown between them of the sort that occurs between Hal and Hotspur. Yet Shakespeare avoids it; for once he passes up a chance for artistic shaping and lets us feel the untidiness of history. He also has another kind of point to make, for the exploration of Talbot's heroism leads from an interest in the individual to an interest in the collective, from the greatness of a man to the unity and disunity of a group. The *scène à faire* of Part 1 pits Talbot not against Joan but against York and Somerset; in its own way it is as stylized and explicit as the Auvergne scene, as Talbot is ringed with French enemies and Lucy trudges back and forth in mounting frustration between York and Somerset. Conversely the English defeat Joan by ganging up on her; their temporary unity produces what the trilogy shows as their last success in France.

The disunity that kills Talbot can be traced back to the opening scene. While the French wars are dramatized in an open, realistic manner, the civil disputes in England have from the beginning a simple, stylized quality. But it is not the stylization that embodies heroism – the reverse, in fact. Over the corpse of Henry V, Gloucester and Winchester bicker like children, and they go on doing so till halfway through the next play, when Gloucester is murdered and Winchester takes to his bed and dies, still haunted by his old enemy. Though Gloucester is generally the more sympathetic figure, both are equally belligerent. There is some principle of self-destruction at work in the state. Talbot, fighting for England, is denied soldiers; York, plotting civil war, is given an army for his Irish expedition and can hardly believe his luck: ''Twas men I lack'd, and you will give them me' (Pt 2, III. i. 345). The cast shows a tendency to divide into teams, 'Blue coats to tawny' (Pt 1, I. iii. 47) and red roses to white. This tendency is exemplified in the Temple Garden scene in which, in the ironic setting of a garden near a law school, a group of young nobles, tired of debating a problem, put it to a vote, plucking red and white roses off a bush.[14] The fundamental, chilling irony of the scene is that we never know what the quarrel is about – it is the tendency to quarrel and choose sides that matters – yet this seemingly trivial dispute will expand until it sends 'A thousand souls to death and deadly night' (Pt 1, II. iv. 127). The rights and wrongs of the cause are replaced by appeals for allies couched in challenges to pride: 'Let him that is a true-born gentleman ...'; 'Let him that is no coward nor no flatterer ...' (II. iv. 27, 31); and the debate, if there ever was one, degenerates into schoolboy taunts:

> *Plan.* Hath not thy rose a canker, Somerset?
> *Som.* Hath not thy rose a thorn, Plantagenet? (II. iv. 68–9)

As the trilogy develops, the conflict expands in scale but not always in dignity:

*Car.* Ambitious Warwick, let thy betters speak.
*War.* The Cardinal's not my better in the field.
*Buck.* All in this presence are thy betters, Warwick.
*War.* Warwick may live to be the best of all.     (Pt 2, I. iii. 109–12)

By the opening of Part 3 the crown itself is the subject of this edifying exchange:

*K. Hen.* . . . I am thy sovereign.
*York.*                    I am thine.              (Pt 3, I. i. 76)

In much of Part 1 there is a close focus on a single character, Talbot. Whatever ironies surround him, there is plenty of room left for concern and admiration. This full view of Talbot, which includes his own self-awareness, is replaced by a thin and reductive depiction of the nobles, whose style, far from balancing the heroic and the practical, seeks 'the fullest self-assertion at every moment' and whose '*modus loquendi*' becomes the '*modus agendi*' of their society.[15] With monotonous self-assertion everyone tries to climb to the top of the anthill; and what we see is not a collection of great individuals but a swarm of ants. They are the victims of an increasingly ironic dramaturgy, in which the telling juxtaposition of scenes creates a larger picture than any of the characters is aware of. Just as Talbot's meeting with the Countess is succeeded by the Temple Garden scene, so the scene in which Henry dons a red rose and lifts the conflict to a new level is followed by the sequence of Talbot's entrapment and death. The irony in this case works both against Talbot and for him, revealing the forces that will destroy him and showing them up by comparison with his own selfless dedication. Elsewhere the irony is more one-sided in its effect. As Humphrey of Gloucester enjoys his easy and not altogether attractive triumph over the pathetic impostor Simpcox, news is brought that his wife has been arrested for treason, and his own fall begins. Sir John Hume, who has acted as *agent provocateur* to bring about the Duchess's exposure, congratulates himself on playing a clever double game (Pt 2, I. ii. 87–107) but is arrested and sentenced to death with her other accomplices (II. iii. 8). Gloucester's fall is succeeded almost at once by the deaths of his principal enemies Winchester and Suffolk. This is a play for an ensemble, as though Shakespeare is writing in conscious opposition to Marlovian drama with its star parts for overweening heroes. He lets us feel, in Christopher Morris's phrase, 'the invisible atmospheric cobweb men make between them';[16] he also shows that none of them can keep either the political initiative or the theatrical focus for very long.

Our detachment is aided by the economy of the theatre itself, which by speeding and simplifying actions begins to make them look absurd. '*Richard and George whisper*' (Pt 3, V. i. 82SD)[17] is all the explanation we have for George's return to the Yorkist cause; we may compare the much fuller treatment of Joan's persuasion of Burgundy. Warwick, like Peter Quince handing out parts, offers to distribute the power of England: 'Be Duke of Lancaster: let him be King' (Pt 3, I.i.86). Theatrical images contribute to this detachment. The Duchess of Gloucester wants to 'play my part in Fortune's pageant' (Pt 2, I. ii. 67), not remembering how Fortune's pageants usually end. Gloucester sees his own fate as only the first move in a tragedy that will embrace thousands: 'mine is made the prologue to their play' (Pt 2, III. i. 151). Such lines trigger a recognition that all these great events are 'play'd in jest by counterfeiting actors' (Pt 3, II. iii. 28) – both the professionals who are acting *Henry VI* and the dedicated amateurs in history's pageant they are portraying. The most telling of these moments is King Henry's greeting to Richard of Gloucester, who has come to kill him: 'What scene of death hath Roscius now to act?' (Pt 3, V. vi. 10). The King achieves a wry detachment from his killer, and from his own fate. There is also a note of sour comedy here, a note heard increasingly through Part 3. Henry has just signed away his son's inheritance to the house of York:

> *Exe.* Here comes the Queen, whose looks bewray her anger:
>  I'll steal away.
> *K. Hen.*                Exeter, so will I.                (Pt 3, I. i. 218–19)

It is comedy based on the predictable behaviour of characters we are by now familiar with. It also distances us from the seriousness of events. The characters themselves start to acquire a similar comic distance; we may instance not only Henry's greeting to Richard but Edward's remark when he hears his brother is off to London to kill the King: 'He's sudden if a thing come in his head' (Pt 3, V.v.84).

Edward's line seems particularly offhand when we consider what a momentous act it is to kill a king, and when we consider further that with this one stroke Richard will effectively end the Wars of the Roses. But it is part of the special ironic dramaturgy of *Henry VI* that there is no such thing as an effective ending. Part 1 ends, like *1 Tamburlaine* and *Henry V*, with peace and the prospect of marriage. But the peace is an anticlimax for the English – 'Is all our travail turn'd to this effect?' (Pt 1, V.iv.102) – and a temporary expedient for the French: Alençon advises the Dauphin, 'take this compact of a truce, / Although you break it when your pleasure serves' (V.iv.163–4). The marriage is the disastrous linking of Henry and Margaret. By the end of the play Henry has not even met her but is simply dazzled by Suffolk's description. Suffolk, acting as go-between, is playing his own game – not to mention interfering with a better marriage arrangement that was part of the peace agreement. Part 2 ends with York asserting his claim and then (in a passage I want to examine later) frittering away his advantage. This time there is not even a truce, but the beginning of an action that is completed only in the next play. Part 3 ends with the Yorkist victory that was held off in Part 2, but Gloucester is already plotting against Clarence, initiating the action of *Richard III*, and he punctuates Edward's triumph in the final scene with mocking asides. Open-endedness is characteristic of history plays generally, since historical actions are never quite as complete as comic and tragic ones are. But Shakespeare takes unusual care in *Henry VI* to baffle and mock any expectation of completeness.

The technique of the play reflects its content, for this is a world breaking down. Ambition drives the characters, and early in Part 2 there are some telling images of that ambition. One is the falcons of II.i, whose soaring flight Henry takes as a sign of 'how God in all his creatures works! / Yea, men and birds are fain of climbing high' (II. i. 7–8). In the same scene the impostor Simpcox provides a more comic image of ambition:

*Glou.* How long hast thou been blind?
*Simp.* O! born so, master.
*Glou.* What! and would'st climb a tree?
*Simp.* But that in all my life, when I was a youth.
*Wife.* Too true; and bought his climbing very dear.
*Glou.* 'Mass, thou lov'd'st plums well, that would'st venture so.
*Simp.* Alas! good master, my wife desir'd some damsons,
　　　And made me climb with danger of my life.
(Pt 2, II. i. 97–103)

Besides the danger of ambition, and its blindness, there is an ironic parallel with the relations of Gloucester and his own troublesome wife.[18] We have already heard Eleanor urge her husband to set his sights high, but the language she uses is very odd:

　　　Why are thine eyes fix'd to the sullen earth,
　　　Gazing on that which seems to dim thy sight?
　　　What seest thou there? King Henry's diadem,
　　　Enchas'd with all the honours of the world?
　　　If so, gaze on, and grovel on thy face,
　　　Until thy head be circled with the same.
(Pt 2, I. ii. 5–10)

11

There is no Marlovian glamour in this ambition; nor is Eleanor even credited with ironic self-awareness. She betrays quite unconsciously the meanness of the force that drives her.

Yet that force, when spread over a variety of characters, is enough to wreck the fabric of society. Law is one of the first victims. In the Temple Garden, Suffolk declares:

> Faith, I have been a truant in the law
> And never yet could frame my will to it;
> And therefore frame the law unto my will.
>
> (Pt 1, II. iv. 7–9)

The first scene with King Henry – who is in theory the final source of law – begins with Winchester snatching and tearing a document Gloucester has prepared; his scorn for 'deep-premeditated lines' (Pt 1, III. i. 1) and his preference for improvised accusation imply a contempt for due process. In Part 2, as his enemies circle him round, Gloucester first declares his faith in the law – 'I must offend before I be attainted' (Pt 2, II. iv. 59) – only to realize that England is not like that any more: 'A staff is quickly found to beat a dog!' (Pt 2, III. i. 171). Initially, household loyalties count:

> *York.* This is my servant: hear him, noble Prince.
> *Som.* And this is mine: sweet Henry, favour him.
>
> (Pt 1, IV. i. 80–1)

So, particularly in Part 3, do family loyalties. Oxford supports the Lancastrians because Edward killed his brother (Pt 3, III. iii. 101–3); Warwick, exhausted in battle, is driven to fresh effort by the news of his brother's death (II. iii.1–32); and in his own death scene his last thoughts are of his brother Montague (V. ii. 33–49). But these family loyalties mean only that the larger conflict breaks down into a series of private revenge actions, the spirit of which is summed up in Clifford's words to the innocent Rutland: 'Thy father slew my father; therefore die' (I. iii. 46). The futility of revenge is exemplified when the Yorkists in their final act against Clifford 'are reduced to taunting a corpse'.[19] In the end we come down to the individual will: Winchester, Suffolk, and York, left alone on stage at the ends of scenes, reveal the finally private motives that keep the action going. The technically unusual ending of Part 1, with a single figure on the stage, shows the individual, not the group, as the final determining factor. Talbot's sense of the importance of communal effort is gone. Yet no individual, as we have seen, can keep the initiative for long.

The irony with which Shakespeare views his characters and the

ultimate futility he attributes to them can be seen in his dramatization
of the Yorkist cause. On the whole the Yorkists take the initiative and
the Lancastrians react; but from the beginning the Yorkist cause is
shadowed with irony. York's career as pretender begins when Mortimer
passes the torch to him. But Mortimer, imprisoned and dying, 'a
wither'd vine / That droops his sapless branches to the ground' (Pt 1, II.
v. 11–12), is no more auspicious as an image of ambition than the blind
and henpecked Simpcox. (A parallel is suggested by the fact that
Mortimer too is blind (II. v. 8–9, 34–40).) The cause initially goes
underground, 'with advice and silent secrecy' (Pt 2, II. ii. 67), producing
suspense and the promise of action to come. Plotting alone, York
projects an air of excitement:

> Faster than spring-time showers comes thought on thought,
> And not a thought but thinks on dignity.
> My brain, more busy than the labouring spider,
> Weaves tedious snares to trap mine enemies.
>
> (Pt 2, III. i. 337–40)

That unexpected 'tedious' skews the effect. And as York waits and
plots, the prize shrinks with the loss of French territory. In an image
that reduces his dignity, York describes himself as a 'silly owner' (Pt 2, I.
i. 226) robbed of his goods and unable to help himself. Yet York's
frustration also suggests a contained energy that ought to burst forth
excitingly; his soliloquy at the end of the opening scene of Part 2 shows
a view of the whole action, present and future, that no other character
can match. At first these expectations are fulfilled. His return from
Ireland is, for a few lines, tremendous – but for a few lines only:

> From Ireland thus comes York to claim his right,
> And pluck the crown from feeble Henry's head:
> Ring, bells, aloud; burn, bonfires, clear and bright,
> To entertain great England's lawful king.
> Ah! sancta majestas, who'd not buy thee dear?
> Let them obey that knows not how to rule;
> This hand was made to handle nought but gold:
> I cannot give due action to my words,
> Except a sword or sceptre balance it.
> A sceptre shall it have, have I a sword,
> On which I'll toss the fleur-de-luce of France.
>
> *Enter* BUCKINGHAM.
>
> Whom have we here? Buckingham, to disturb me?
> The King hath sent him, sure: I must dissemble.
>
> (Pt 2, V. i. 1–13)

The failure to complete the expected rhyme at l. 4 is one danger signal; the image of an actor who cannot function without his props is another; but the collapse from the heroic to the devious is still surprising, and turns the rest of the speech in retrospect from a great declaration of purpose to a fantasy.

York simultaneously loses the political initiative and the theatrical focus; the one is a signal of the other. 'I must make fair weather yet awhile, / Till Henry be more weak, and I more strong' (Pt 2, V. i. 30–1) – the action, which seemed to be moving in one clear direction, starts to twist. York claims that he has returned only to remove Somerset, and when told that Somerset is in the Tower he dismisses his soldiers and offers loyalty to Henry. When Somerset appears free he reasserts his claim. Legally, that claim is strong enough to dismay Henry – 'I know not what to say: my title's weak' (Pt 3, I. i. 138) – and to win the acceptance of Exeter, who has supported the Lancastrians. But York shifts the basis of his claim from the legal point, where he is strong, to the more open and debatable grounds of power and style:

> That head of thine doth not become a crown;
> Thy hand is made to grasp a palmer's staff,
> And not to grace an awful princely sceptre.
> That gold must round engirt these brows of mine,
> Whose smile and frown, like to Achilles' spear,
> Is able with the change to kill and cure.
>
> (Pt 2, V. i. 96–101)

It was on grounds like these that Tamburlaine built his career, and there is a superficial theatrical appeal in York's contrast of himself and Henry. But York, as we have seen, does not have Tamburlaine's ability to make his boasts good, and in shifting his claim from the legal to what we might call the theatrical – he *looks* more kingly than Henry – he has actually weakened his position. He loses the strong theatrical focus of his earlier soliloquies as his campaign becomes blurred by side-issues. For most of the last scene of Part 2, the question is not how the Yorkist cause is faring in the battle but what has become of Warwick's father Salisbury ('That winter lion' (V.iii.2) – the phrase brings him vividly before us). Even York talks as though Salisbury's fate is the main question:

> This happy day
> Is not itself, nor have we won one foot,
> If Salisbury be lost.                           (Pt 2, V. iii. 5–7)

At the opening of Part 3, having won a decisive battle, filled the parliament house with soldiers, and seated himself on the throne, York settles for a compromise. Whatever sense this may have made in history, the compression and economy of the theatre make it a strange anticlimax, and reveal in York a fatal weakness of grip. This is a case where the theatrical medium – to which York has implicitly appealed – imposes its own judgement.

In Part 3 his son Edward fares little better, politically or theatrically. In II.i, where the Yorkist claim passes to Edward with the death of his father, Richard is at least as prominent in the first part of the scene, and Warwick is the clear centre of attention in the second. Edward's first entrance as king is not spectacular but low-key and domestic: he comes on with his two brothers and Elizabeth Woodville.[20] His first act as king is to do precisely what Henry did: make a disastrous marriage, ignoring the politically superior one that is being negotiated for him. The tone of his courtship, reinforced by the mocking asides of his brothers, is light and flippant: 'Brothers, you muse what chat we two have had' (Pt 3, III. ii. 109). If light comedy is inappropriate to the political seriousness of Edward's mistake, that is just the point: he fails to grasp the significance of what he is doing, and as its implications become clear his self-defence seldom rises above petulance: 'They are but Lewis and Warwick: I am Edward, / Your King and Warwick's, and must have my will' (Pt 3, IV. i. 15–16). If he seems particularly nettled about Warwick, he has some reason. Warwick shows an increasing tendency to treat the Yorkist cause as simply a way of demonstrating his own power.[21] This appears when he first joins it in Part 2:

> *War.* My heart assures me that the Earl of Warwick
>     Shall one day make the Duke of York a king.
> *York.* And, Nevil, this I do assure myself:
>     Richard shall live to make the Earl of Warwick
>     The greatest man in England but the king.     (II. ii. 77–81)

Beneath the exchange of courtesies, York seems properly wary of his new ally. Warwick shows his power particularly after Edward's marriage. 'No more my king, for he dishonours me' (Pt 3, III. iii. 184) is a threat he makes good in short order. In the end he suffers defeat and death, and is forced to conclude, 'what is pomp, rule, reign, but earth and dust?' (Pt 3, V. ii. 27); but for a while he made the Yorkist cause his personal plaything.

What Warwick does is symptomatic of what happens in the trilogy as a whole. As the nobles shout at each other and engage in personal

15

vendettas, we tend to forget – or, rather, we watch *them* forget – that what is at stake is the crown of England. The concern with legitimacy fades as the real issue becomes a test of power. York's retreat from the legal claim to the theatrical is a symptom of this. But the dramatic interest that a pure power struggle can generate is limited, and through Part 3 in particular 'runs the bleary, enervating sense of déjà vu'.[22] Even the concluding couplets begin to sound tired: 'Come on, brave soldiers: doubt not of the day, / And, that once gotten, doubt not of large pay' (IV. vii. 87–8). We may question whether Shakespeare is deliberately showing a tired world, or is simply becoming exhausted as a writer. Probably both; and in either case there is a danger that the audience too will become exhausted. A more controlled effect is the ironic narrowing of the characters' perspective to private will and personal revenge. One would never think that England itself was at stake, or had any existence except as a series of place-names to mark the sites of battles. But England is still there, and there are people in it. The most astonishing demonstration of this comes in the Cade rebellion.

In a number of ways Shakespeare signals his intention of using Cade as an ironic commentary on the main action. His rebellion is placed just before the outbreak of the Wars of the Roses, as a grotesque antimasque. Though he takes off on his own, he is initially the agent of York, and there are indications that he represents a dark comic underside of the great man. York's words, 'This devil here shall be my substitute' (Pt 2, III. i. 371), have a larger range of suggestion than he intends. He admires Cade's capacity for secrecy (III. i. 367–70, 376–8), as we have up to this point admired his, and the appearance of Iden with Cade's severed head during the outbreak of York's own rebellion gives the analogy a final sinister, prophetic twist. When Cade himself appears, the range of parodic associations widens. Cade imitates the self-assertiveness of the nobles by knighting himself (IV. ii. 113–15); the abandonment of law we see elsewhere finds more direct expression in the cheerful cry, 'The first thing we do, let's kill all the lawyers' (IV. ii. 73) and in Cade's declaration, 'my mouth shall be the parliament of England' (IV. vii. 13–14). The shadow of Henry V suddenly returns, and with it echoes of the earlier action:

> *Cade.* ... Go to, sirrah, tell the King from me, that for his father's sake, Henry the Fifth, in whose time boys went to span-counter for French crowns, I am content he shall reign; but I'll be Protector over him.
> *Butcher.* And furthermore, we'll have the Lord Say's head for selling the dukedom of Maine. (IV. ii. 149–54)

Gloucester's role as Protector, and York's indignation over the surrender of Anjou and Maine, find distorted echoes here; York's compromise with Henry is anticipated. It is the ghost of Henry V which undoes Cade. Clifford wins the rabble over by appealing to the glamour of conquest: 'Will he conduct you through the heart of France, / And make the meanest of you earls and dukes?' (IV.viii.36–7). We may be tempted to ask: will you? But Cade's followers are too dazzled by the vision to see how it is being used. The fear of the French bogeyman – who will, Clifford threatens, invade England if it suffers civil war (IV. viii. 41–50) – wins them over, and Cade, who had earlier appealed to the same kind of patriotism by ordering Lord Say killed because he could speak French, exclaims in chagrin, 'Was ever feather so lightly blown to and fro as this multitude? The name of Henry the Fifth hales them to an hundred mischiefs, and makes them leave me desolate' (IV. viii. 55–8). Clifford appeals to the patriotism that means not love of one's country but fear and hatred of the foreigner, and he does so for Bolingbroke's reason: busy giddy minds with foreign quarrels. Once the rebellion has been quashed, no more is heard of the reconquest of France. These are the sour dregs of the cause for which Talbot died.

Cade himself is a paradoxical figure. York's description of him stuck full of weapons suggests a grotesque Morris dancer:

> I have seen
> Him caper upright like a wild Morisco,
> Shaking the bloody darts as he his bells.
>
> (III. i. 364–6)

This demented carnival spirit runs through the rebellion: 'There shall be in England seven half-penny loaves sold for a penny; the three-hoop'd pot shall have ten hoops; and I will make it felony to drink small beer' (IV. ii. 62–5). (When we last see him, Cade is starving to death, and trying to eat grass like Nebuchadnezzar.) A certain manic exuberance even creeps into the stage directions: '*Enter . . . with infinite numbers*' (IV. ii. 30SD); '*Alarums.* MATTHEW GOFFE *is slain, and all the rest*' (IV. vii. SD). But, as that last direction indicates, what we see is mostly the anarchy that is the dark side of carnival. The energy becomes threatening, and the first London audiences must have felt the threat more sharply as it crept towards familiar places: 'But first, go and set London bridge afire, and, if you can, burn down the Tower too' (IV. vi. 12–14). Cade, like the titled rebels, is finally out for himself: 'all shall eat and drink on my score, and I will apparel them all in one livery, that they may agree like brothers, and worship me their lord' (IV. ii. 70–2). Nor is he content with worship: 'The proudest peer in the realm shall not wear

17

a head on his shoulders, unless he pay me tribute; there shall not a maid be married, but she shall pay to me her maidenhead, ere they have it' (IV. vii. 114–17). He goes in one sentence from exploiting the rich to exploiting anyone who has something he wants. He bestows titles on himself, going from Sir John Mortimer to Lord Mortimer; a messenger who fails to use the new title is killed before our eyes (IV. vi. 4–10).

But I think we miss Shakespeare's full purpose in these scenes if we taken them simply as an illustrated lecture on the evils of rebellion. Even before Cade appears, his followers Bevis and Holland have a conversation that makes us sit up and think:

> *Hol.* . . . Well, I say it was never merry world in England since gentlemen came up.
> *Bevis.* O miserable age! Virtue is not regarded in handicraftsmen.
> *Hol.* The nobility think scorn to go in leather aprons.
> *Bevis.* Nay, more; the King's Council are no good workmen.
> (IV. ii. 7–14)

The naïve levelling may produce smug laughter at first, but the King's Council are indeed no good workmen; we've seen the work they do. Cade has his reasons, too, for wanting to do away with reading and writing: 'I did but seal once to a thing, and I was never mine own man since' (IV. ii. 78–9). In his attack on Lord Say, we are just starting to enjoy the comedy when we are once again caught by surprise:

> Thou hast most traitorously corrupted the youth of the realm in erecting a grammar-school; and whereas, before, our forefathers had no other books but the score and the tally, thou hast caus'd printing to be us'd; and contrary to the King his crown, and dignity, thou hast built a paper-mill. It will be prov'd to thy face that thou hast men about thee that usually talk of a noun, and a verb, and such abominable words as no Christian ear can endure to hear. Thou hast appointed justices of the peace, to call poor men before them about matters they were not able to answer. Moreover, thou hast put them in prison; and because they could not read, thou hast hang'd them; when, indeed, only for that cause they have been most worthy to live.
> (IV. vii. 30–44)

Cade is attacking culture and civilization; but in the process he reminds us how those things can look to those who are excluded from the circle of privilege they create. Nor, under Elizabethan law, is it just a joke to say that a man could be hanged for not being able to read.

At moments like this Cade is one of the most articulate social critics in Shakespeare; but when he turns from criticism to action we see that his vision, though penetrating, is narrow. He can achieve his social ends only by treating human life as cheap; it is not by accident that one of his most voluble supporters is a butcher. 'Let's kill all the lawyers' is an easy line to laugh at; but it is not so easy to laugh when the Clerk of Chatham is dragged off before our eyes, or when Cade has the severed heads of Lord Say and his son-in-law kiss each other, 'for they loved well when they were alive' (IV. vii. 125). Even in this respect, however, Cade is raising larger questions than who is King of England, or which noble is on top this time. His rebellion widens the play's issues to include society and human relations seen in depth. Coming between the fall of Gloucester and the outbreak of the Wars of the Roses, the Cade rebellion shows up the relative narrowness of both those actions. It is characteristic that he goads Lord Say into defending not just himself but a whole set of civilized values; characteristic, too, that Say's defence, though it rouses our sympathy (even Cade is moved in spite of himself – IV. vii. 100–2), also leads him to involuntary self-betrayal:

> Justice with favour have I always done;
> Prayers and tears have mov'd me, gifts could never.
> When have I aught exacted at your hands,
> But to maintain the King, the realm, and you?
> Large gifts have I bestow'd on learned clerks,
> Because my book preferr'd me to the King,
> And seeing ignorance is the curse of God,
> Knowledge the wing wherewith we fly to heaven,
> Unless you be possess'd with devilish spirits,
> You cannot but forbear to murder me:
> This tongue hath parley'd unto foreign kings
> For your behoof, –
> *Cade.* Tut, when struck'st thou one blow in the field?
> *Say.* Great men have reaching hands: oft have I struck
> Those that I never saw, and struck them dead.
> *Geo.* O monstrous coward! What, to come behind folks!
>
> (IV. ii. 64–79)

In Say's career there is both culture and unmanly craft; but he reminds us, as Humphrey of Gloucester has occasionally done, that there should be more to life in the state than a game of power with the crown as football. Shakespeare never managed the fusion of social, political, and cultural issues that Jonson achieved in *Sejanus*; but here at least we glimpse a wider range of concern than the play normally shows. In an important reservation to a generally unsympathetic reading, M. M.

Reese credits Cade with recognizing 'that politics have to do with human happiness'.[23]

Cade's dying boast, 'Tell Kent from me, she hath lost her best man' (IV. x. 70–1), is not altogether empty: when he dies, something goes out of the play. These scenes contain the sharpest and most expressive writing in the trilogy, and the fullest view of the common people. It is a grim reflection that they get the sustained attention of the great, and of the audience, only when whipped up to a frenzy of destruction. Elsewhere, they are glimpsed going about their business. Sometimes that business has to do with the affairs of history: 'Chief master-gunner am I of this town; / Something I must do to procure me grace' (Pt 1, I. iv. 6–7). Sometimes there are glimpses of another world, as when the Mayor wonders at the behaviour of Gloucester and Winchester: 'Good God, these nobles should such stomachs bear! / I myself fight not once in forty year' (Pt 1, I. iii. 89–90). This is the world they return to when their role in the brawls of the mighty is over:

> *3 Serv.* Content; I'll to the surgeon's.
> *1 Serv.* And so will I.
> *2 Serv.* And I will see what physic the tavern affords.
>
> (Pt 1, III. i. 146–8)

A note of complaint creeps in, deepening from the relatively mild –

> Thus are poor servitors,
> When others sleep upon their quiet beds,
> Constrain'd to watch in darkness, rain, and cold.
>
> (Pt 1, II. i. 5–7)

– to the serious charges of exploitation in the petitions intercepted by Suffolk (Pt 2, I. iii. 16–22). In one of these the apprentice Peter accuses his master Horner of treason. Thinking he is simply doing the part of a loyal subject, Peter finds himself embroiled in a trial by combat with a dangerous adversary, and Gloucester, so beloved of the commons, is in this case not much help:

> *Pet.* . . . Lord, have mercy upon me! I shall never be able to fight a blow. O Lord, my heart!
> *Glou.* Sirrah, or you must fight or else be hang'd.
>
> (Pt 2, I. iii. 215–17)

The impostor Simpcox and his wife provide an amusing interlude; but as they are bustled out Mistress Simpcox cries, 'Alas! sir, we did it for pure need' (II. i. 150). No one seems to notice.

As part of the general narrowing of focus, the commons are much less prominent in Part 3. But there is one notable exception. King Henry has withdrawn from the Battle of Towton to dream of leading the life of a common man:

> And to conclude, the shepherd's homely curds,
> His cold thin drink out of his leather bottle,
> His wonted sleep under a fresh tree's shade,
> All which secure and sweetly he enjoys,
> Is far beyond a prince's delicates –
> His viands sparkling in a golden cup,
> His body couched in a curious bed,
> When Care, Mistrust, and Treason waits on
>      him.
>
> *Alarum. Enter a Son that hath kill'd his Father,*
>      *with the body in his arms.*
>
> (Pt 3, II. v. 47–54SD)

He is joined by a Father who has killed his Son. The contrast between Henry's dream and the reality is shocking enough;[24] the shorthand image of the horror of civil war is unforgettable. But there is a more insidious horror in the dramatic idiom itself. Horner, Peter, Simpcox, Cade, Bevis, Holland – they had names and lives of their own. These characters have been crushed to single roles: a Son who has killed his Father and a Father who has killed his Son. With a dreadful parody of a love-poetry conceit, Henry shows how the lives of the commons have been branded by the actions of the nobility: 'The red rose and the white are on his face, / The fatal colours of our striving houses' (II. v. 97–8). In a play not generally allegorical, the decision to use allegory makes a point of its own, a point made more naturalistically when the Son declares:

> From London by the King was I press'd forth;
> My father, being the Earl of Warwick's man,
> Came on the part of York, press'd by his master.
>
> (II. v. 64–6)

We may think back to another set piece of fathers and sons, Talbot and John; it would be possible to use the same actors. There, two characters fulfilled a destiny they had chosen for themselves; here, four are crushed by a destiny imposed by others.

The Cade and Towton scenes are radically different in dramatic idiom, but each idiom makes its own statement. The explosive anarchy of Cade, threatening to blow the play apart, actually enlarges its vision so that we are made to think of lives beyond those of the nobles, and of questions that never enter the minds of characters like York and Warwick. The narrowness of the great is shown up by contrast. In the Towton scene the narrowness is just the point: lives that should have been full are reduced to a single note of pain. The formal, stylized manner the early Shakespeare has always at hand is used here to suggest a society reduced to a ritual of blood. Earlier, he had used a formal idiom to show society working properly: in the Auvergne scene, where Talbot's greatness is explained and celebrated; and later in Part 1, when Talbot lays his sword at Henry's feet and Henry creates him Earl of Shrewsbury (III. iv. 1–27). Here, the proper, traditional relations of king and subject are formally set before us.[25] The standards of chivalry are confirmed when Talbot removes the Garter from the cowardly Falstaff, and gives a short lecture on the principles of the Order (Pt 1, IV. i. 13–47). But even this sequence is disrupted by the squabbling of Vernon and Basset (Pt 1, III. iv. 28–45, IV. i. 78–80). The trappings of order sit insecurely on a naturally disordered world. And another set piece, the killing of Cade by the comfortable householder Iden, is not so firm an image of good order as it may look. Iden's values – 'This small inheritance my father left me / Contenteth me, and worth a monarchy' (Pt 2, IV. x. 18–19) – make him allegorically correct as an opponent for Cade. He is also bigger and stronger: 'Set limb to limb, and thou art far the lesser; / Thy hand is but a finger to my fist' (Pt 2, IV. x. 46–7). If the scene were pure allegory, we might take this as a sign of the superiority of Iden's values; but it has also the effect – not just accidental, I think – of casting Cade as David to Iden's Goliath, and of winning sympathy for the rebel when he puts up a fight.[26] Moreover, given Iden's delight in his withdrawn, comfortable life, it is disturbing when he is rewarded not just with a title and money but with a position in the royal household, a dubious honour at best (V. i. 78–80).[27] We never see Iden again, and so the disturbance produced by his fate flickers only for a moment; but it is there.

A more conspicuous case of a symbolic moment that goes awry is Henry's gesture of donning a red rose (Pt 1, IV.i.152–4). He means to show the indifference of the sign; what he actually does is give national scale to what had been a private conflict.[28] And it is typical of the trilogy as a whole for the formal, symbolic moments to embody not order but violence and breakdown: the messengers interrupting Henry's funeral; Winchester snatching and tearing Gloucester's bill; the Yorkists filling the parliament house with soldiers as York, not wearing a crown, sits on the throne; and, of course, the Towton scene, whose picture of a fragmented society includes the fact that while Henry addresses the two men they notice neither him nor each other. Early in Part 3 killing becomes a game, like a contest in a folk-tale:

> *Edw.* Lord Stafford's father, Duke of Buckingham,
>     Is either slain or wounded dangerous;
>     I cleft his beaver with a downright blow:
>     That this is true, father, behold his blood.
> *Falc.* And, brother, here's the Earl of Wiltshire's blood,
>     Whom I encounter'd as the battles join'd.
> *Rich.* Speak thou for me, and tell them what I did.
>                     [*Throwing down the Duke of Somerset's head.*]
> *York.* Richard hath best deserv'd all of my sons.
>
>                                    (Pt 3, I. i. 10–17)

The death of York himself is an improvised ritual slaughter in which the paper crown and bloody napkin suggest a parody of the Crucifixion.[29] Even scenes of disorder that are not overtly violent tend to be stylized; a notable example is the opening scene of Part 2, in which, as different groups of characters leave the stage and others stay behind to comment, layer beneath layer of conspiracy is uncovered, ending with York alone. The formality of such scenes indicates that, while the order represented by Henry and Talbot is a fragile and temporary achievement, disorder is a fundamental principle. What we see in the trilogy as a whole is a society that has lost the forms and myths of order and is evolving new ones to embody violence. It does this at first unconsciously, though the playwright's formal shaping of his material makes the audience aware of what is happening. But by the opening of Part 3 the killings have become consciously ritualized, York's being the conspicuous example, and this last play of the trilogy is full of set pieces of conflict and defiance.

In the process the King, who should be the centre of order, becomes essentially a passive victim; the future belongs to the character who wins the killing game at the opening of Part 3, Richard of Gloucester. Through these opposing figures Shakespeare moves towards a final shaping of his vision of this long period of disorder. Unlike Talbot and Joan, they are brought together for a final confrontation; and there are earlier hints of a relationship between them. Henry imagines the Towton battle as a conflict of elements – cloud and light, wind and tide – and then pictures two figures, 'the shepherd, blowing of his nails' (II. v. 3), and himself, the King, sitting on a molehill. He later wishes that he *were* the shepherd; but at first the connection between the figures is

that they are both observers, tiny isolated figures against a seascape
that is also a vast battle picture. Richard also imagines himself as a
figure in a seascape, but for him the contrast between the vast setting
and the small human figure is a challenge:

> Why then I do but dream on sovereignty;
> Like one that stands upon a promontory
> And spies a far-off shore where he would tread,
> Wishing his foot were equal with his eye;
> And chides the sea, that sunders him from thence,
> Saying he'll lade it dry to have his way.
>
> (Pt 3, III. ii. 134–9)

Later in the same soliloquy the setting closes in on him. He becomes, as
his father was at first, frustrated and imprisoned; but his determination
is all the stronger:

> And I, – like one lost in a thorny wood,
> That rents the thorns and is rent with the thorns,
> Seeking a way, and straying from the way;
> Not knowing how to find the open air,
> But toiling desperately to find it out –
> Torment myself to catch the English crown:
> And from that torment I will free myself,
> Or hew my way out with a bloody axe.
>
> (Pt 3, III. ii. 174–81)

The thorny wood may suggest the ruin of England, or Richard's
frustration at imprisonment in his deformed body, or both; the power
of the image is that it cannot be pinned down exactly. It is the occasion
for Richard to show himself as determinedly active as Henry is
determinedly passive.

In neither case, however, is the character absolutely fixed. As we see
forms and myths being constructed in the trilogy as a whole, so we see
these characters adopting formal roles, with some effort. At first Henry
is an open character, unpredictable in himself and subject to contrary
judgements. He wavers between philosophical indifference to political
life and pained involvement with it.[30] He gets caught briefly in the cycle
of violence, goading Clifford on in his course of private revenge (Pt 3, I.
i. 54–6) and greeting his vow of service 'be thy title right or wrong' with
'O Clifford, how thy words revive my heart!' (Pt 3, I. i. 163, 167).
Banished to Scotland, he returns compulsively to England and is
arrested. He tells the keepers who arrest him, 'my crown is call'd
content' (Pt 3, III. i. 64), but in the same scene he laments the loss of his

titles and honours (15–21) and rebukes the keepers for their disloyalty (74–92). The crown of content sits uneasily; cast by history as the Lancastrian king, Henry can never quite shed the role. But he plays it badly. The authority the office requires is not in his nature as a man, and his passiveness can be not just irritating but culpable. The juxtaposition of his pastoral reverie and the suffering of the Father and Son is damning. The dying Clifford accuses him:

> And, Henry, hadst thou sway'd as kings should do, ...
> I, and ten thousand in this luckless realm
> Had left no mourning widows for our death.
>
> (Pt 3, II. vi. 14, 18–19)

Failing to save Gloucester though he knows he is wrongly accused, Henry constructs an elaborate allegorical picture of himself as a cow unable to save its calf from the slaughter-house (Pt 2, III. i. 202–20); the speech is not just a way of analysing what is happening but a way of fixing himself in the role of helpless onlooker, as though he had no choice in the matter. It is in a curious way a speech of self-justification, and, in the lines that follow, Gloucester's enemies pick up the method, constructing a series of miniature allegories to justify the killing.

Occasionally Henry does some good by making his subjects feel sorry for him. Gloucester ends one of his quarrels with Winchester by saying, 'Compassion on the King commands me stoop' (Pt 1, III. i. 119). Edward claims that if Henry's followers had not been so troublesome the Yorkists would have let their claim sleep 'in pity of the gentle King' (Pt 3, II. ii. 161). There is enough here to suggest a centre of goodness on which a better society could have drawn. And there are times when Henry shows a kind of wisdom. His first contribution is sixty-four lines of silence as Gloucester and Winchester storm around him (Pt 1, III. i. 1–64). He looks ineffective, to be sure, but as we weary of the noise we may begin to see a value in the silence.[31] His contribution to the debate over the regency of France, 'Or Somerset or York, all's one to me' (Pt 2, I. iii. 102), may be irresponsibility or an understandable refusal to be drawn into a fight between Tweedledum and Tweedledee. For him as for Lear in his prison, winning and losing are things indifferent. He greets the final loss of France in a single line, 'Cold news, Lord Somerset: but God's will be done!' (Pt 2, III. i. 86), and the casual way in which the news is dramatized seems to support his attitude. He cries out at Towton, 'Wither one rose, and let the other flourish!' (Pt 3, II. v. 101), and the rest of the scene compels us to agree that an end to the carnage – any end – is more important than victory for one side or the other. In Margaret's words, 'What are you made of? You'll nor fight nor fly' (Pt 2, V. ii. 74), there may be wonder as well as irritation. Henry speaks for that part of the audience's response that remains detached from the partisan struggles, seeing only their cruelty and absurdity. Though we see him briefly caught up by Clifford's revenge code, it is more characteristic when he rebukes Clifford, 'didst thou never hear / That things evil got had ever bad success?' (Pt 3, II. ii. 45–6), and knights his son with the words 'learn this lesson: Draw thy sword in right' (Pt 3, II. ii. 62). We had almost forgotten such values existed, and Edward's reply, 'I'll draw it as apparent to the crown' (64), is not encouraging. Just before he is dragged off to his final imprisonment, Henry defends his kingship by defending his relations with the people, evoking the civil life of which the Cade scenes reminded us, the life which has so often disappeared behind the mayhem of battle:

> I have not stopp'd mine ears to their demands,
> Nor posted off their suits with slow delays;
> My pity hath been balm to heal their wounds,
> My mildness hath allay'd their swelling griefs,
> My mercy dried their water-flowing tears;
> I have not been desirous of their wealth,
> Nor much oppress'd them with great subsidies,
> Nor forward of revenge, though they much err'd.
>
> (Pt 3, IV. viii. 39–46)

The play has shown little of this, apart from Henry's forgiveness of the Cade rebels (Pt 2, IV. ix. 20–2), but that in itself gives an edge of surprise to the speech, making Henry the spokesman for values that the rest of his world has virtually forgotten.

Placed where it is, the speech gives Henry a certain authority. Other characters in their last moments see in themselves only images of mortality (Warwick is a notable example); Henry, like Talbot, stands for something. He is also on two occasions given the formal role of prophet. For this to work, there has to be a supernatural frame of reference, however loosely defined, that he can appeal to. At first we may wonder. This seems a world where miracles have ceased, to be replaced by mockeries like the impostures of Simpcox and the pregnancy of the holy maid Joan. A trial by combat is supposed to show the judgement of God, but when Peter defeats Horner it is mainly because Horner is drunk. York tells the victor, 'Fellow, thank God, and the good wine in thy master's way' (Pt 2, II. iii. 92–3). Yet there is a supernatural dimension all the same. Joan's devils appear only to display their impotence; but they do appear. The spirit summoned by the conjurer Bolingbroke utters prophecies that depend – trivially, it may seem – on word-play and riddles (Pt 2, I. iv. 23–36); but the prophecies work; and the tradition of equivocation they belong to is an ancient one. It will be used again in *Macbeth*. Though the war in Part 1 is realistically dramatized on the whole, there is something more than realism when as the French attack Orleans thunder breaks out and the dying Salisbury raises himself and groans. As York dies and the claim passes to his children, three suns appear in the sky. All these details buttress a moment that would have no place in a realistic history play, when the young Earl of Richmond is presented to Henry:

> Come hither, England's hope.
> *Lays his hand on his head.*
> If secret powers
> Suggest but truth to my divining thoughts,
> This pretty lad will prove our country's bliss.
> His looks are full of peaceful majesty;
> His head by nature fram'd to wear a crown,
> His hand to wield a sceptre; and himself
> Likely in time to bless a regal throne.
> Make much of him, my lords, for this is he
> Must help you more than you are hurt by me.
> (Pt 3, IV. vi. 68–76)

When York rested his claim on strength and style, we felt he was shifting to the wrong ground; but here, just as the dynastic wars are getting tedious, we move to a deeper level, as Henry declares Richmond's claim to be a natural one, part of a national destiny that goes beyond the struggles of York and Lancaster. Richmond's kingly appearance is not, like York's, superficial, for this prophecy will be fulfilled. As the Countess of Auvergne discovers, in the real world appearances do not always count. But in the world of myth they do. It cannot really be shown that the Tudor Myth pervades the cycle as a whole; what Shakespeare does with it is, I think, more interesting and powerful. He allows a tantalizing glimpse of it, as a world of peace and right beyond the normal conditions of history,[32] a glimpse that is registered and then withdrawn. Buttressed by the moral authority he shows elsewhere, Henry is the prophet of that vision.

He also acts in his last scene as a prophet for Richard. He does not know as we do that the two characters he treats in this way will eventually come together; to that extent his vision is limited. But, as he takes us briefly out of history in the scene with Richmond, so he lifts Richard to a new level of significance. To see this we have to remember that Richard was not always the splendid, sharply realized monster we are most familiar with. In his early appearances his characterization, like Henry's, wavers and he speaks with different voices. As early as Part 2 we hear the acid tones we will come to know so well: 'Fie! charity for shame! Speak not in spite, / For you shall sup with Jesu Christ to-night' (V. i. 214–15); but we also hear Marlovian lyricism:

> father, do but think
> How sweet a thing it is to wear a crown,
> Within whose circuit is Elysium
> And all that poets feign of bliss and joy.
>
> (Pt 3, I. ii. 28–31)

He can describe the beauty of the morning in a speech that out of context we would never guess was his (Pt 3, II. i. 21–4). His contempt for humanity is something that develops, not something inherent from the beginning. His first substantial speech is a tribute to Warwick, whom he continues to admire (Pt 2, V. i. 151–6); and he says of York, 'Methinks 'tis prize enough to be his son' (Pt 3, II.i.20). The death of York is for him a psychological turning point.[33] While the softer Edward asks to be spared the details, Richard commands, 'Say how he died, for I will hear it all' (Pt 3, II. i. 49). It is the voice of a man who wants to feel the iron entering his soul.

His great soliloquy in Part 3 is an example of what Stephen Greenblatt has called 'self-fashioning'.[34] His mission to gain the crown has a psychological basis in a reaction against his deformity:

> Then, since this earth affords no joy to me
> But to command, to check, to o'erbear such
> As are of better person than myself,
> I'll make my heaven to dream upon the crown.
>
> (Pt 3, III. ii. 165–8)

But Richard creates a higher view of himself than that. He alternates psychology with allegory:

> Why, Love forswore me in my mother's womb:
> And, for I should not deal in her soft laws,
> She did corrupt frail Nature with some bribe,
> To shrink mine arm up like a wither'd shrub;
> To make an envious mountain on my back,
> Where sits Deformity to mock my body.
>
> (III. ii. 153–8)

Though there are obvious differences between this and the Towton allegory, both involve a radical reduction of humanity. Richard imagines an action that, like many of the stylized actions of the play proper, shows the destruction of normal human order. He is the victim of that action: the role of monster has been stamped on him as the red rose and the white were stamped on the victims of Towton. But for Richard to see himself in this way is also to give himself the scale and dimensions of myth. He operates on that scale when he responds to the conspiracy of Nature and Love by fashioning a role of his own, using familiar figures and promising to outdo them:

> I'll drown more sailors than the Mermaid shall;
> I'll slay more gazers than the basilisk;
> I'll play the orator as well as Nestor,
> Deceive more slyly than Ulysses could,
> And, like a Sinon, take another Troy.
> I can add colours to the chameleon,
> Change shapes with Proteus for advantages,
> And set the murderous Machiavel to school.
>
> (III. ii. 186–93)

The human character we have glimpsed in earlier scenes is turning himself into a formula. He needs to. Early in the soliloquy he expresses human doubts about himself: 'My eye's too quick, my heart o'erweens too much, / Unless my hand and strength could equal them' (III. ii. 144–5). He must shed these doubts by making himself inhuman. By the end he has talked himself into complete confidence, but some sense of effort lingers. In his attempt to place himself beyond normal humanity there is something artificial, and his awareness that he is finally like the rest of us will return to haunt him at the end of *Richard III.*

This soliloquy takes Richard part of the way into myth; Henry does the rest. When Richard comes to kill the King, shreds of the old character, the York loyalist, cling to him: 'O, may such purple tears be always shed / From those that wish the downfall of our house!' (V. vi. 64–5). It is Henry who in his tirade against Richard lifts him to a new level:

> And thus I prophesy: that many a thousand
> Which now mistrust no parcel of my fear,
> And many an old man's sigh, and many a widow's,
> And many an orphan's water-standing eye –
> Men for their sons', wives for their husbands',
> Orphans for their parents' timeless death –
> Shall rue the hour that ever thou wast born.

29

The owl shriek'd at thy birth – an evil sign;
The night-crow cried, aboding luckless time;
Dogs howl'd, and hideous tempests shook down trees.

(V. vi. 37–46)

– and so on in the same vein. The myth-making of Richard's soliloquy was private and subjective, and had about it a quality of fantasy. We could see Richard there as a recognizable man coping with feelings of inferiority by constructing grand images of himself, and renouncing love out of a very human frustration at his inability to win it. He had a particular aim – to get the crown – and to do that he would kill the people he needed to kill. Henry's prophecy gives Richard a new, apocalyptic scale. He says nothing of the crown; such things matter little to Henry. Instead of a particular ambition Henry imagines a generalized evil, a pure principle of destruction. Richard, he declares, came not just to gain the crown but 'to bite the world' (54). And, by reporting the omens that surrounded Richard's birth, Henry gives objective confirmation to what might have looked like Richard's private fantasy. The result is a picture of universal carnage, the Towton allegory writ large, that goes beyond the role Richard had imagined for himself.

At the moment when Richard kills Henry there is agreement between them:

*Rich.* I'll hear no more: die, prophet, in thy speech.     *Stabs him.*
    For this, amongst the rest, was I ordain'd.
*K. Hen.* Ay, and for much more slaughter after this.
    O God, forgive my sins and pardon thee!     *Dies.*

(V. vi. 57–60)

In his last words Henry dies as a Christian, touching on a vision far deeper than the play's cycle of destruction.[35] But in the two central lines killer and victim agree that this one act is part of a larger design. Richard goes on to build on Henry's view of him. He replaces the imagined allegory of the earlier soliloquy with real omens like the ones Henry reported, as though the old King has just reminded him of stories he had forgotten: 'Indeed, 'tis true that Henry told me of' (V. vi. 69). He goes beyond the formula comparisons with Sinon and Machiavel to a more radical dehumanizing of himself, caught in language that is suddenly bare of ornament:

The midwife wonder'd, and the women cried
'O Jesu bless us, he is born with teeth!'
And so I was, which plainly signified

30

That I should snarl, and bite, and play the dog.
Then, since the heavens have shap'd my body so,
Let hell make crook'd my mind to answer it.
I have no brother, I am like no brother;
And this word 'love', which greybeards call divine,
Be resident in men like one another,
And not in me: I am myself alone.          (V. vi. 74–83)[36]

We have seen self-assertion before in the trilogy, but no one has taken it as far as this. There is sinister excitement in watching Richard go this far, an excitement that will be carried over into the next play. And we note that Richard's appearance – like Richmond's and unlike York's or Talbot's – is a key to his true nature. We are back in the world of myth.

*Henry VI* begins with a legendary hero lying dead before us. His legend is only talked of, and is rapidly retreating into the past. The play then goes on to show by practical demonstration the place of heroism in a realistically conceived world, its value and its frailty. But gradually, as order breaks down in England, the realistic manner of the French war scenes is replaced by a thinner, more stylized mode, flattening history and drawing patterns out of it as though expressing the imagination's need to understand disorder. The process involves levelling, distorting, and a pervasive irony. But as the lines of history flatten into a few simple patterns of rise and fall a new myth emerges. Ironic understanding is not enough. As the Towton scene reawakens our almost deadened capacity for pity, so Richard reawakens our capacity for excitement. If Henry speaks for that part of us that sees, wearily, the absurdity of the game of power, Richard embodies our recognition of its dangerous attraction. There is something of that attraction in Cade; but while Cade challenges the body politic Richard's challenge goes even deeper; his renunciation of love strikes at the root of all human relations and takes the breakdown that was initially social and political as far as it can go. Other characters see themselves as out on their own, but Richard's sense of his own life as blighted from the womb gives the idea of isolation a new and frightening depth. At first encounter *Henry VI* looks like a lumbering, shapeless chronicle; but it may begin to make sense if we can see it as framed by the death of a hero and the birth of a monster.

# 2

# *Richard III*

AT THE end of *3 Henry VI* the Yorkist victory looks complete, but there is a shadow over it. Richard of Gloucester makes it clear in asides to the audience that he does not consider himself part of Edward's celebration and that he is about to start on his own private agenda. This device not only reminds us of Richard's ambition but (like his deformity) splits him off from the other characters. Yet he is not completely isolated, for he has a special relationship with the audience, which continues into the next play. We are allowed to hear his thoughts, as no one on stage is; and we are aware of the ironic blindness of his victims. In *Henry VI*, particularly in the scenes with the Duke of York, theatrical authority and political authority went together. The same is true in the early scenes of *Richard III*: Richard's capacity for long-range planning and his mastery of the political situation go along with an extraordinary theatrical control. To this Shakespeare adds a new element: the audience's conscious awareness of its own reactions as an important part of the drama. Sharing knowledge and insight with Richard, even sympathizing with him against our better judgement, we are not just detached spectators: Richard enlists us as his partisans, as no character in *Henry VI* did. I said this is a new element. It is also a revival of something old. To make the audience consciously aware of its own reactions is part of Shakespeare's legacy from the morality play in *Richard III*: direct appeals ranging from jokes to sermons were part of the stock-in-trade of those earlier dramas.[1] Richard, like the Vice, presents himself as a friend to the audience, and as the play develops we discover that this friend is not to be trusted.

*Richard III* is the only play of Shakespeare's to begin with a soliloquy by one of its characters. We may think at first that the effect can be paralleled in Marlowe. But neither Faustus nor Barabas actually begins his play; each is introduced by a chorus, establishing a certain critical distance. Richard is not just hero but chorus and presenter as well. As

other characters come on stage, we depend on Richard to tell us who
they are: 'Dive, thoughts, down to my soul: here Clarence comes' (I. i.
41); 'But who comes here? The new-deliver'd Hastings?' (I. i. 121).[2] The
introduction of Clarence is particularly interesting: the thoughts that
Richard will hide from his brother he has just shared with us. At
another point he shares with us a joke against his own mother:

> *Duch.* God bless thee, and put meekness in thy breast;
>      Love, charity, obedience, and true duty.
> *Rich.* Amen; [*Rises: aside*] and make me die a good old man –
>      That is the butt-end of a mother's blessing:
>      I marvel that her Grace did leave it out.          (II. ii. 107–11)

The mockery includes not only his mother but the decent conventional
values she speaks for. Natural ties are always important for
Shakespeare – hence the shock of the Towton battle scene – and here
we see Richard flouting the most basic of them and establishing new
ties, not with anyone on stage, but with the audience. The brusque,
domestic tone of his language – 'But yet I run before my horse to
market' (I. i. 160) – has an ingratiating quality, as Ralph Berry has noted;
Richard is saying, in effect, 'I am really one of you, you know.'[3] Having
established this relationship, Richard can play on it with jokes that slip
by everyone onstage, but not by us:

> *King.* Is Clarence dead? The order was revers'd.
> *Rich.* But he, poor man, by your first order died,
>      And that a winged Mercury did bear;
>      Some tardy cripple bore the countermand,
>      That came too lag to see him buried.          (II. i. 87–91)

There is no need for an aside or even a wink to the audience here.
Richard is complimenting our intelligence by delivering the joke
absolutely deadpan, for us alone.

One of his favourite ways of playing with his victims is to jest with
them and then pretend to be serious:

>           O, belike his Majesty hath some intent
>           That you should be new-christen'd in the Tower.
>           But what's the matter, Clarence, may I know?
>                                     (I. i. 49–51)[4]

We know that the insensitive joke represents Richard's true feelings,
and the expression of serious concern is a trick. A similar moment in the
scene with Anne – 'To leave this keen encounter of our wits, / And fall
something into a slower method' (I. ii. 119–20) – is the signal that

Richard is about to become really dangerous. When he taunts Brackenbury for not letting him speak with his brother, he seems to be sharing the jokes with Clarence and making Brackenbury the victim (I. i. 88–102); but we know that the ultimate joke will be on Clarence. It is, in fact, dangerous to feel secure with Richard. The council debate over the date of the coronation opens with a somewhat anxious discussion on the question 'Who knows the Lord Protector's mind herein?' (III. iv. 7). The one character who claims he can read Richard easily is Hastings, who is dead by nightfall. Part of his hold over Anne, like Iago's over Othello, lies in creating confusion about his motives. She begins their scene confidently denouncing him; by the end she is saying, 'I would I knew thy heart' (I. ii. 196). He tests and confirms his hold by asking her to trust him: 'For divers unknown reasons, I beseech you / Grant me this boon' (I. ii. 221–2). At this point she capitulates and falls into Hastings's error of assuming she understands Richard: 'With all my heart, and much it joys me too, / To see you are become so penitent' (I. ii. 223–4). We hear in that line the relief of surrender.

The illusion of complicity with Richard that Clarence, Anne, and Hastings have in their different ways may reinforce our sense of superiority over them, but it should also be a warning. The wooing of Anne is a case in point. Here we seem to be Richard's accomplices: he tells us what he will do, and at the end shares with us his delight at having done it. One of his most impudent jokes, when he says that King Henry should be grateful to him for sending him to heaven (I. ii. 108–10), is a joke he has already tried out on us, at Clarence's expense: 'I do love thee so / That I will shortly send thy soul to Heaven' (I. i. 118–19). Part of the excitement of the scene lies in watching the risks Richard takes in telling Anne the truth: that he feels no pity, that he killed King Henry, that he killed Anne's husband Edward (I. ii. 72, 103, 183, 185). He twists the significance of the last fact in particular by claiming he did it for her love, but his openness with her is still extraordinary. In the end he forces her to make a choice, a commitment: kill him on the spot, or marry him: 'Take up the sword again, or take up me' (I. ii. 187). With her alternatives thus reduced, and finding herself unable to kill in cold blood, Anne surrenders. Safe in the auditorium, we cannot be presented with this kind of challenge; but our alternatives too have been reduced. The cast of the early scenes falls into two categories – Richard and his dupes. Faced with this choice, we naturally go with Richard, especially since he is so frank with us. But it seems to Richard's victims that he is being frank with them – as he really is, up to a point, with Anne. Clarence is made to feel, as we are, that Richard is siding with him against the world. The parallel is unsettling; and Richard's prediction about Anne, 'I'll have her, but I will not keep her long' (I. ii.234), also predicts what will happen between Richard and the audience.

This is not just because we turn against him when he becomes exhausted at the end. Our feeling of rapport was always to some degree an illusion. In the very opening lines Richard pretends for a while to be an impersonal chorus – or at least a loyal member of the house of York:

> Now is the winter of our discontent
> Made glorious summer by this son of York;
> And all the clouds that lour'd upon our House
> In the deep bosom of the ocean buried.  (I. i. 1–14)

'Us', not 'them'. He pretends for a moment that the detachment from Edward's victory we saw at the end of the last play has disappeared. His very first joke is on us. Even when in the later part of the soliloquy he seems to be letting us into his mind, there is one curious omission: he never says in so many words that he wants the crown.[5] Perhaps, remembering his great soliloquy in the last play, we do not need to be told. But there is nothing here to suggest that Richard is greeting old friends; he seems, on the contrary, to be starting from scratch. And his odd reticence about his practical ambition may suggest a reluctance to put into words, even when he is alone with the audience, the thing he dreams of – because to put it into words is to share it, and Richard is too much of a loner for that. 'I am myself alone' (*3 Henry VI*, V. vi. 83) is one of his key statements of self-definition. He seems for a while to be not just alone, but alone with us. But as we move more fully into the play we realize how deceptive this appearance is.

The warning signs come early. In the middle of one of his breezy, information-packed soliloquies, there is a small touch of darkness:

> What though I kill'd her husband and her father?
> The readiest way to make the wench amends
> Is to become her husband, and her father:
> The which will I, not all so much for love
> As for another secret close intent,
> By marrying her which I must reach unto.  (I. i. 154–9)

What is that 'secret close intent'? Is it some political advantage, otherwise unrevealed? A need to degrade in Anne's bed the sexual love he professes to despise? We may speculate, but we never know. When at the end of his scene with Anne he has the corpse of Henry VI rerouted from Chertsey to Blackfriars, we wonder what he is up to, and we may entertain dark suspicions. But, again, we never know. From hiding motives he goes to hiding actions. The seduction of Anne is not only the first onstage demonstration of his power; it is also the last. After this he goes underground. When we compare him with other great intriguers like Barabas, Volpone, and Vindice, we are struck by how little of his plotting he actually reveals to us. In I.iii he includes Buckingham among the 'many simple gulls' (328) whom he deceives about his feelings towards Clarence. Then at the end of II. ii Buckingham appears, suddenly and without preparation, as Richard's ally. When Richard claims to be following Buckingham's direction with childlike simplicity we sense a joke that Buckingham does not get. All the same, we have been presented with a *fait accompli* ; Richard is acquiring new allies and shutting us out. The effect is repeated, as one by one Catesby, Ratcliffe, and Lovel appear as Richard's men. Again there is no preparation: they are simply, suddenly, there. Richard likes to strike by surprise, as in the arrest of Rivers, Vaughan, and Grey, and the sudden attack on Hastings; and he is starting to surprise not only the other characters but the audience as well. Even his jokes become odd and private: the rotten armour,[6] the strawberries, the exchange with Buckingham over the jack of the clock. Arguably his most important action as king is the murder of the princes. He gives his final instructions for this onstage, but in a whisper to Tyrrel that the audience cannot hear. The death of Anne is likewise hidden. Though the soliloquies and asides continue, they become more brusque and businesslike, rather like the briefings we can imagine Octavius Caesar giving to Lepidus. The old sharing of enjoyment is gone; not only is Richard getting tired, he no longer seems to care for our company as he once did.

As he approaches the achievement of his ambition, Richard slips out of focus for a while. The sequence leading up to his coronation belongs to Buckingham, who does much of the managing and a surprising amount of the talking. Just when we might expect the spotlight to be more firmly on Richard than ever, it starts to wander. Like the dissipation of the attention on York just as he asserts his claim, this augurs ill for Richard's kingship. Behind the theatrical point there is political thinking. It is appropriate for an intriguer to be a solitary, but a king, whatever final privacy he maintains, must be the centre of a whole network of social and political relationships, and Richard simply cannot function in that way. Ironically, the role he has sought so long is the one role he cannot effectively play.[7] Richard must be king not just of a territory but of a people, and the first sign of grit in the wheels of his plot comes when Buckingham argues his claim before the citizens:

And when mine oratory drew to an end,
I bid them that did love their country's good
Cry, 'God save Richard, England's royal King!'
*Rich.* And did they so?
*Buck.* No, so God help me: they spake not a word,
But like dumb statues or breathing stones
Star'd on each other, and look'd deadly pale.     (III. vii. 20–6)

We may see the citizens as mulish, stupid, or frightened. But we should, I think, distinguish between their silence, which conveys tacit dissent, and the silence of acquiescence we meet elsewhere in the play: when Brackenbury delivers Clarence to his killers with the words 'I will not reason what is meant hereby, / Because I will be guiltless from the meaning' (I. iv. 93–4); when Cardinal Bourchier, Archbishop of Canterbury, agrees 'for once' to break sanctuary (III. i. 57); when the Scrivener says of Hastings's indictment:

Who is so gross
That cannot see this palpable device?
Yet who's so bold but says he sees it not?

(III. vi. 10–12)

The Recorder who repeats Buckingham's arguments with the formula, ' "Thus saith the Duke; thus hath the Duke inferr'd" – / But nothing spake in warrant from himself' (III. vii. 32–3), ensures, perhaps quite deliberately, that Buckingham's oratory will fall painfully flat. The only cheers come from Buckingham's followers planted in the crowd, and his claim to be acting by the 'vehement instigation' of the citizens (III. vii. 138) only underlines his failure. In the end the citizens are herded onstage to watch Richard's impersonation of a saintly king (like the one he killed), but while the stupid Lord Mayor is impressed the general cheer never comes.[8]

The Elizabethans liked to imagine the monarch as having an easy rapport with the common people,[9] and Richard has sought popular approval as the final seal on his claim. But he does so through an intermediary – when the Recorder speaks there are *two* intermediaries – and the results are dubious, to say the least. Richard's first words as king are 'Stand all apart' (IV. ii. 1).[10] His first action is to grasp, a little too quickly and anxiously, at Buckingham's loyalty, and then fling it irritably away. Though he continues to work with assistants, and Catesby in particular is with him to the end, he has had a special rapport with Buckingham, sharing jokes and insights as with no one else onstage; and his rejection of his old henchman signals a retreat into himself:

I will converse with iron-witted fools
And unrespective boys; none are for me
That look into me with considerate eyes.

(IV. ii. 28–30)

He then asks a page to find him a malcontent to do the job Buckingham balked at. Though he claims to 'partly know' Tyrrel (IV. ii. 41), when the man appears he has to ask his name. His fear of Buckingham's 'considerate eyes' is a fear of shared insight, a fear of being understood; he would rather work with children, fools, and strangers. In the end, when Richmond announces, 'this foul swine / Is now even in the centre of this isle' (V. ii. 10–11), it is as though Richard has retreated to the middle of the thorny wood he tried to break out of in *3 Henry VI.*

Along with his fear of shared knowledge goes a fear of language. When he cuts off Henry VI with the words 'I'll hear no more: die, prophet, in thy speech' (*3 Henry VI,* V. vi. 57), the moment is itself prophetic. So is his reason for wanting to kill Margaret after the Battle of Tewkesbury: 'Why should she live to fill the world with words?' (V. v. 43). In *Richard III* he warns Clarence's murderers, 'do not hear him plead' (I. iii. 347), and his misgivings are justified, for Clarence pleads to such effect that the Second Murderer relents, even to the point of refusing the fee. When in IV. iv the women intercept his expedition to exclaim against him, Richard commands drums and trumpets to drown them out with sheer noise, no longer trusting his own capacity to meet words with words as he did with Anne. This fear too is justified, for in the ensuing scene Elizabeth's words are more than a match for his. Finally, when Buckingham asks, 'Will not King Richard let me speak with him?', the answer is predictable: 'No, my good lord' (V. i. 1–2). It is partly because by the end of the play others can out-talk him: as his mother declares, 'in the breath of bitter words let's smother / My damned son' (IV. iv. 133–4). More important, language, if not corrupted – and politicians of Richard's stamp must always try to corrupt it – embodies the shared conventional values Richard is defying. Even before Clarence goes to work on him, the Second Murderer is tripped up by his own language: 'The urging of that word, "Judgement", hath bred a kind of remorse in me' (I. iv. 104–5). The word 'murder' proves too much for both men:

> *Cla.*               Wherefore do you come?
> *Both.*  To – to – to –
> *Cla.*               To murder me?
> *Both.*                               Ay, ay.
> *Cla.* You scarcely have the hearts to tell me so,

38

And therefore cannot have the hearts to do it.    (IV. iv. 162–5)

Language, finally, will not co-operate with Richard, and he begins to lose control over it. In his early scenes he is nimble with words: he can make them dance, juggle, and deceive. But when Buckingham balks at murdering children and Richard complains, 'thy kindness freezes' (IV. ii. 22), it is not so clear that he is in control of the irony or even aware of it. He excuses himself brilliantly to Anne for killing her husband; when he excuses himself to Elizabeth for having killed her children, the comic lameness of 'Men shall deal unadvisedly sometimes' (IV. iv. 292) sounds more like moral stupidity than deliberate irony.

He began the play superior to us, pretending to be an impersonal chorus and then revealing he was no such thing. We end the play superior to him. His last line, 'My kingdom for a horse!' (V. iv. 13), is a joke against himself, of whose irony he seems quite unaware. Our fullest realization of our superiority comes in the soliloquy after the ghost scene. He thinks at first he is in the battle; we know he is dreaming: 'Give me another horse! Bind up my wounds! / Have mercy, Jesu!' (V. iii. 178–9). At 'Soft, I did but dream' he catches up with us. But this time we do not have the sense that he is addressing us. On the contrary, he is quite literally talking to himself, in anxious questions and answers whose circling movement shuts us out:

> What do I fear? Myself? There's none else by;
> Richard loves Richard, that is, I and I.
> Is there a murderer here? No. Yes, I am!
> Then fly. What, from myself?                    (V. iii. 183–6)

'There's none else by' suggests he does not know, as he seemed to do in his earlier scenes, that we are watching him. His earlier rapport with us set him apart from the rest of the cast, giving him a different order of theatrical reality.[11] Now he is a character in the drama, like the others. He accepts conventional values and the language that goes with them: words like 'murder' now shock him as they shocked Clarence's murderers. Having announced blandly in his first soliloquy, 'I am determined to prove a villain' (I. i. 30), he now comes to the role as a terrible discovery, one he would evade if he could: 'I am a villain – yet I lie, I am not! / Fool, of thyself speak well! Fool, do not flatter' (V. iii. 192–3). We might expect a villain touched for the first time by conscience to win new sympathy from the audience. But Richard has won sympathy, as Falstaff will do, by taking us on a moral holiday, appealing to our 'unofficial selves'.[12] And now that he is discovering conscience as something new and disturbing we may say, a bit wryly,

'Tis new to thee.' The Second Murderer, in his wonderful description of conscience as a daily domestic nuisance (I. iv. 128–38), has been there before him. Clarence and Edward in their last scenes have also been haunted by remorse – giving the lie, incidentally, to Richard's claim, 'I am like no brother' (*3 Henry VI*, V. vi. 80).[13] His defiance of conscience in his oration to his soldiers (V. iii. 309–12) may be a flash of the old Richard, but it contradicts what we have seen of his private feelings and leaves us not quite convinced. Richard had seemed to stand outside the world of the play, setting against the onstage community a different community consisting of himself and the audience. But at the end the onstage community seals over, with Richard simply a part of it, accepting its values. We realize that the sort of bond Richard had with us, founded as it was on an agreement to mock love and treat humanity with contempt, could never have lasted.

Shakespeare has brought us to this realization, and the view of the self-seeking individual it implies, through a conscious use of one of the conditions of theatre itself, the special relationship between actor and audience. To have the comic villain's subversive rapport with the audience contained and controlled by a work that publicly affirms conventional values is another debt to the morality play. By using this strategy in *Richard III* Shakespeare gives the action, as he did in Henry VI's prophecy, a significance deeper than that of politics narrowly conceived. What is at stake is nothing less than the 'great bond' Macbeth will violate and Cordelia will embody, the human relations that begin in natural family ties and express themselves in the mutual love and respect that lie at the root of a good society. The levelling wit that makes Richard temporarily attractive has as its price a final rejection of this bond. When he says of King Edward, 'He cannot live, I hope, and must not die / Till George be pack'd with post-horse up to Heaven' (I. i. 145–6), Richard is joking with the lives of his brothers. The heartlessness of the wit is temporarily liberating, finally chilling. This critique of comedy, even of comedy we find genuinely amusing, will return in *Henry IV*.

But the play has other and more disturbing business than to place Richard against a decent human community. Richard is not the sole criminal in a good world. If Clarence and Edward are torn by remorse they have reason, and we may wonder what hidden desire to be corrupted Richard is touching in his amazing victory over Anne.[14] (In so far as he attracts us, he may also make us wonder about ourselves.) In *Henry VI* Richard seemed to be the final and most dramatic embodiment of an egotistic drive for power that affected a wide range of characters. So in *Richard III*, Murray Krieger has argued, 'there are no innocents; . . . evil stems not from Richard but from a history he shares with the others'.[15] If this is going too far – what are the young princes guilty of, other than being Edward IV's sons? – it seems, with *Henry VI* behind us, to be going in the right direction. In particular, we are constantly reminded of the guilt other characters incurred in the killings of York and Prince Edward. Even more important than the guilt itself is the presence of the past. Simply by making *Richard III* the last in a series of four plays, Shakespeare has created an action too large for any one character to control or be responsible for. Richard's machinations are only partly his own; they share the momentum of a longer action carried over from the earlier plays, an action that (as we saw) Shakespeare conceived in a spirit of irony. As Richard is placed in moral terms by the conventional values he accepts at the end, so he is placed in plot terms as an instrument of this larger action. The prophecy 'which says that "G" / Of Edward's heirs the murderer shall be' (I. i. 39–40) he uses as a trick against George of Clarence; but as Richard of Gloucester he fulfils it. When we see the action in its broadest perspective we realize that he is not just its creator but its instrument.

He is also its victim. In his later scenes he no longer attempts to manipulate prophecies; he is simply frightened by them (IV. ii. 94–9, 101–5). Besides his solitude, the start of his kingship is shadowed by other ironies. Richard's accession is first signalled in a slip of the tongue by Brackenbury, as though this most public event were a state secret (IV. i. 17–18); but the first open announcement comes from Stanley, whose possible treachery will worry Richard for the rest of the play and whose desertion will be an important factor in the Battle of Bosworth. Shakespeare could not have picked a more ironic herald for the new king. Anne's disgust at the thought of being Richard's queen turns the coronation itself into death by torture:

> O would to God that the inclusive verge
> Of golden metal that must round my brow
> Were red-hot steel, to sear me to the brains.
> Anointed let me be with deadly venom,
> And die ere men can say 'God save the Queen'.
>
> (IV. i. 58–62)

Literally she is wishing for death, and will get it soon enough; but the images are haunting enough to escape from their literal function and to make us in the next scene look at the crowned and anointed Richard with new eyes. It is here too that Anne tells us for the first time of Richard's 'timorous dreams' (IV. i. 84), and the word 'timorous' for so brazen a villain is sharply revealing. At what should have been his moment of victory, the great manipulator suddenly looks like a creature driven, cursed, and haunted.

This sense of a larger action affects the dramatic idiom. On the surface the play is full of trivial political detail, by turns fussy and amusing. We are treated to complaints about the petticoat government of the Queen and Jane Shore, grumbling about upstart courtiers, Rivers's bland description of himself as the Vicar of Bray – 'We follow'd then our lord, our sovereign king: / So should we you, if you should be our king' (I. iii. 147–8) – and little calculations about the behaviour of little people:

> *Buck.* What think'st thou then of Stanley? Will not he?
> *Cat.* He will do all in all as Hastings doth. (III. i. 167–8)

(This is evidently true: it is clear in a later scene that though he senses danger Stanley will not flee unless Hastings does – III. ii. 14–17). These are the minutiae of political gossip. But like the gargoyles on a cathedral they only emphasize by contrast the larger scale of the whole work. And this capacity for realistic observation is put to different use in the fall of Hastings. The sequence is full of circumstantial detail, the result of Shakespeare's following his sources more closely than usual.[16] On the last morning of his life Hastings scorns Stanley's fears and gloats over the execution of his old enemies. Less relevantly, it appears, he chats with a pursuivant (who in the Quarto text bears his name and therefore functions as a *Doppelgänger*) and a priest. We seem to be watching a man go through a day. But, as Hastings himself realizes once the trap has sprung, every detail is significant:

> O, now I need the priest that spake to me;
> I now repent I told the pursuivant,
> As too triumphing, how mine enemies
> Today at Pomfret bloodily were butcher'd,
> And I myself secure in grace and favour.
>
> (III. iv. 87–91)

With artificial clarity the details fall into place as part of a simple picture of over-confident pride riding for a fall. Having thought he was the master of his fate, Hastings now realizes he is its victim, repeating in little the larger story of Richard.

Hastings adds, 'O Margaret, Margaret, now thy heavy curse / Is lighted on poor Hastings' wretched head' (III. iv. 92–3). We seldom touch on the larger action without touching on Margaret. The literal incredibility of her presence – Richard asks in some annoyance, 'Wert thou not banished on pain of death?' (I. iii. 167) – puts her, like Richard himself, on a plane of reality different from that of the other characters.[17] She is there, in defiance of both history and probability, to do a job for the playwright. The last survivor of the cast of *1 Henry VI*, she embodies the long historical action of which Richard's career is only the final episode. In I.iii she presents the first serious challenge to Richard's domination of the play,[18] using his technique of punctuating scenes with asides, relating everything to herself and her sufferings. She then imposes her own will openly in a comprehensive series of curses that make Richard simply part of the grand pattern of wrath fulfilled: 'Live, each of you, the subjects to his hate, / And he to yours, and all of you to God's' (I. iii. 302–3). Richard tries to regain control, turning her curse on him against herself by substituting her name for his; but the trick is forced and ineffective, stopping Margaret's flow only for a moment. When he is alone with the audience again Richard seems anxious to assure us that this is still his play: 'I do the wrong, and first begin to brawl' (I. iii. 324). Margaret opens her last scene with a soliloquy that counters and parodies Richard's opening of the play: 'So now prosperity begins to mellow, / And drop into the rotten mouth of death' (IV.iv.1–2). Her theatrical language suggests that a counter-play, no longer dominated by Richard, is beginning:

> A dire induction am I witness to,
> And will to France, hoping the consequence
> Will prove as bitter, black, and tragical.     (IV. iv. 5–7)

She will not attempt to manipulate the action of this play in Richard's fashion, for she is confident it will find its own natural end.

The frank artifice involved in Shakespeare's use of Margaret links her to the outbreaks of stylized, patterned writing, which are more disturbing here than they were in *Henry VI*. In the Towton allegory the repetitions shaped the characters into a generalized pattern without destroying the pathos:

> *Son.* How will my mother for a father's death
>       Take on with me and ne'er be satisfied!
> *Fath.* How will my wife for slaughter of my son
>       Shed seas of tears and ne'er be satisfied!
>                          (*3 Henry VI*, II. v. 103–6)

What is ritual lament, and still moving, in the earlier play becomes a shrill, nagging competition of grief in *Richard III*:

> *Eliz.* . . . Ah, for my husband, for my dear lord Edward!
> *Children.* Ah, for our father, for our dear lord Clarence!
> *Duch.* Alas for both, both mine Edward and Clarence!
> *Eliz.* What stay had I but Edward, and he's gone.
> *Children.* What stay had we but Clarence, and he's gone.
> *Duch.* What stays had I but they, and they are gone.
> *Eliz.* Was never widow had so dear a loss.
> *Children.* Were never orphans had so dear a loss.
> *Duch.* Was never mother had so dear a loss.          (II. ii. 71–9)

The pattern of repetition suggests this time a mounting mutual irritation as the characters try to top each other. Repetition also lends itself naturally to the language of curse and retribution: 'O God! which this blood mad'st, revenge his death; / O earth! which this blood drink'st, revenge his death' (I. ii. 62–3). This is Anne over the body of Henry VI, and if we remember Henry's own forgiveness of his murderer we may be struck by the contrast. In *Richard III* mourning and cursing naturally go together. Both ideas are summed up in the figure of Margaret; but they are also pervasive. The action carried over from *Henry VI* is seen now as a cycle of crime and punishment, and there seems no sign of an end to it. Suspecting his father's death, Clarence's son declares, 'God will revenge it, whom I will importune / With earnest prayers, all to that effect' (II. ii. 14–15). Edward predicts that the punishment for Clarence's death will embrace not only himself but everyone in the room: 'O God, I fear Thy justice will take hold / On me, and you, and mine and yours for this' (II. i. 132–3). The Third Citizen sees a curse on the whole land: 'All may be well; but if God sort it so / 'Tis more than we deserve, or I expect' (II. iii. 36–7). The values of charity and reconciliation appear only to be mocked, in Edward's futile attempt to reconcile the court factions at his deathbed[19] (an attempt which is overshadowed by the murder of Clarence) and Richard's ironic misuse of Christian values in his appeal to Anne: 'Lady, you know no rules of charity, / Which renders good for bad, blessings for curses' (I. ii. 68–9). The irony deepens as characters with relatively clean records curse themselves – Anne pronouncing a malediction on Richard's future wife, Buckingham asking to be betrayed by his closest friend. Even Richard in his scene with Elizabeth is driven to the extremity of 'Day, yield me not thy light, nor, night, thy rest!' (IV. iv. 401). We already know that his nights are shaken with dreams, and the sun refuses to rise for him at Bosworth.

This cycle of cursing involves keeping the past alive; again, Margaret embodies most vividly a process that goes on all through the play. What happens in Clarence's dream –

> thence we look'd toward England,
> And cited up a thousand heavy times,
> During the wars of York and Lancaster,
> That had befall'n us. (I. iv. 13–16)

– happens throughout. The deaths of Rutland and York are recalled in detail, including not just the striking points, the paper crown and bloody napkin, but the smaller ones: 'Northumberland, then present, wept to see it' (I. iii. 187). The ghosts who appear to Richard include Henry VI and his son Edward, ensuring that our sense of Richard's guilt reaches back to the previous play. Rivers, dying in Pomfret Castle, goes even further back: 'Within the guilty closure of thy walls / Richard the Second here was hack'd to death' (III. iii. 11–12). The opening of I.ii, with the obsequies of a dead king shockingly interrupted, loosely recalls the opening of *1 Henry VI*, and Henry himself, 'Poor key-cold Figure of a holy king' (I. ii. 5), represents a dead virtue as his father had represented a dead heroism. It may be dangerous to forget: Edward accuses himself of having forgotten Clarence's kindness to him, and Richard crows over Anne's surrender: 'Hath she forgot already that brave prince, / Edward, her lord . . .?' (I. ii. 244–5). But the principal effect of this brooding on the past is a deepening exhaustion. Anne's instructions to her fellow mourners suggest a tired routine: 'And still, as you are weary of the weight, / Rest you, while I lament King Henry's corse' (I. ii. 31–2). At the end of *3 Henry VI* there was a reduction to mere statistics as Edward counted up the casualties of the Wars of the Roses: 'Three Dukes of Somerset . . . Two Cliffords . . . And two Northumberlands' (V. vii. 5–8). This deepens in *Richard III* as the old Duchess of York generalizes the past to something like Lear's packs and sects of great ones, all seen through a haze of exhaustion:

> Accursed and unquiet wrangling days,
> How many of you have mine eyes beheld!
> My husband lost his life to get the crown,
> And often up and down my sons were toss'd
> For me to joy and weep their gain and loss;
> And being seated, and domestic broils
> Clean over-blown, themselves, the conquerors,
> Make war upon themselves, brother to brother,
> Blood to blood, self against self. O preposterous

And frantic outrage, end thy damned spleen,
Or let me die, to look on earth no more.

(II. iv. 55–65)

Shakespeare plays on our own sense of how much we have seen in the tetralogy as a whole, and how memory tends to blur it. Even Richard does not stand out as an individual here.

He does emerge, however, at the end of an even more striking passage of brooding in IV.iv:

> *Marg.* . . . I had an Edward, till a Richard kill'd him;
> I had a husband, till a Richard kill'd him:
> Thou hadst an Edward, till a Richard kill'd him;
> Thou hadst a Richard, till a Richard kill'd him.
> *Duch.* I had a Richard too, and thou didst kill him.
> I had a Rutland too: thou holp'st to kill him.
> *Marg.* Thou hadst a Clarence too, and Richard kill'd him.
> From forth the kennel of thy womb hath crept
> A hell-hound that doth hunt us all to death. (IV. iv. 40–8)

The names return, but the identities they stand for vanish in a blur of sound.[20] We feel surrounded by the dead. (It is no coincidence that Buckingham, Richard's last victim, dies on All Souls' Day.[21]) Ultimately the rhythm of the passage seems to generate a vision of Richard as the final monstrous horror that will end it all. But there is no glimmer of light beyond the horror. It is wasteful, inhuman, and finally absurd. Margaret herself catches something of this when Richard tells her she is under a curse for the deaths of York and Rutland:

> Did York's dread curse prevail so much with heaven
> That Henry's death, my lovely Edward's death,
> Their kingdom's loss, my woeful banishment,
> Should all but answer for that peevish brat?
> Can curses pierce the clouds and enter heaven?
> Why then, give way, dull clouds, to my quick curses.

(I. iii. 191–6)

She recognizes a crazy disproportion between crime and punishment, but her response to this horror is to exploit it: over the next few lines she curses Edward, his son, Elizabeth, Rivers, Dorset, and Hastings. With one exception (to which I shall return) these curses go off like time-bombs through the rest of the play, many of them coinciding with Richard's approach to the throne, as though that released them. We cannot blame Clarence and Rivers for praying in their last hours that divine vengeance should spread no further (I. iv. 69–72; III. iii. 19–23).

46

Whatever force is at work here, whether it is an angry God or an unrelenting pattern in history itself, it is not exactly economical.

There is finally no satisfaction in this cycle of nemesis. As in her first scene Margaret glimpsed the absurdity of wholesale revenge, so in her last, her own curses spent and satisfied, she tells the other women how she did it and admits something worked-up and artificial in the whole process:

> Forbear to sleep the nights, and fast the days;
> Compare dead happiness with living woe;
> Think that thy babes were sweeter than they were,
> And he that slew them fouler than he is:
> Bettering thy loss makes the bad-causer worse.
> Revolving this will teach thee how to curse.
>
> (IV. iv. 118–23)

A few lines earlier she called the whole action 'this frantic play' (IV. iv. 68). Like Henry VI in his last scene, she seems to have achieved a weary ironic detachment. Her own career, which has spanned four plays, comes full circle and she goes back home: 'Farewell, York's wife, and Queen of sad mischance; / These English woes shall make me smile in France' (IV. iv. 114–15). Nothing in history, we may think, ends this neatly – but then Margaret is no longer a figure from history. And her early exit means that she cannot finally be seen as the presiding genius of the play.

Margaret returns to France; there is still England to deal with. Contemplating its fate, we see it, and ourselves, caught between upper and nether millstones. Richard's wit and energy spend themselves as it becomes clear that because of the inhumanity that goes with them he can achieve nothing positive. But the larger action, seen as a cycle of nemesis, is equally inhuman, and here again Shakespeare uses theatrical means, the blatant artificiality of the scenes of mourning and cursing, to make the point. The grinding repetitions, quite simply, get on our nerves. This is a long play, and directors usually cut it heavily to make it tolerable in the theatre. But perhaps it should be a little *in*tolerable. By the end Richard is getting tired – 'What, is my beaver easier than it was . . .?', 'Look that my staves be sound, and not too heavy' (V. iii. 51, 66) – and so are we. This is where Richmond comes in. Dorset escapes both Richard's machinations and Margaret's curse by fleeing to him; and his escape foreshadows the rescue of England. That rescue was foretold in Henry VI's prophecy; but in *Richard III* itself

Richmond is held back for a long time, so that when he appears there is a freshness, a sense of relief. His mother is referred to briefly in I.iii, but only to establish her dislike of the Queen's family as part of the general tension and backbiting of the court. The timing of the first references to Richmond himself suggests that it is Richard who has in some way activated the prophecy by becoming king. Richmond is first named, as a refuge for Dorset, within a few lines of Stanley's announcement of Richard's accession (IV. i. 1–2). The news of Dorset's flight coincides with Richard's decision to get rid of Buckingham (IV.ii. 42–9). It is as though Richard, by becoming king, has sealed his own doom – not just by taking on a role for which he is unfitted, but by provoking his destroyer into action. And this is a nemesis of which, we might note, Margaret shows no awareness at all.[22] Richmond is something new, something from outside the play's system as we have seen it so far.[23]

Yet not altogether so, for in a deeper sense Richard has generated Richmond. The coincidence of the timing suggests this, as does the coincidence of the names. These are clues to something more fundamental; again, the dramatic idiom itself is what matters. We saw how in *Henry VI* Richard conferred on himself the status of myth. Other characters confirm this: Anne calls him a devil and tries to keep him away from the corpse of King Henry: 'Thou hadst but power over his mortal body: / His soul thou canst not have' (I. ii. 47–8). Margaret warns Buckingham, 'Sin, death, and hell have set their marks on him, / And all their ministers attend on him' (I. iii. 293–4). Richard's own myth-making language was classical and secular – Sinon, Ulysses, Machiavel. The language of the women is Christian. It is the language not of craft and power but of good and evil. It also allows a mounting sense of apocalypse as Richard approaches his end: 'Earth gapes, hell burns, fiends roar, saints pray' (IV. iv. 75). Literally and historically, nothing is happening that would justify such language: there is a power struggle in Westminister and a few royal and noble personages are executed. As we shall see again in *Antony and Cleopatra*, there is an action taking place at the level of the characters' imaginations – and ours, if we respond – that cannot be traced in maps and history books. The result seems to some critics 'less a history than a melodramatic fantasy',[24] operating in 'the world of myth'.[25]

Richard's scene with Elizabeth is important here. As his seduction of Anne is the first demonstration of his power, this is his first really striking failure. He thinks at the end that he has won her consent to marry her daughter – 'Relenting fool, and shallow, changing woman!' (IV. iv. 431) – but in the next scene we learn that Elizabeth has bestowed the girl on Richmond. Has she changed her mind, or was she stalling

Richard at the end of the scene by agreeing to pass on his proposal?
Elizabeth has become, as Richard was earlier, a bit hidden. This itself
suggests she is a match for him; and if we think back to the first time we
saw her, in *3 Henry VI*, we remember that she got the better of Edward
in a scene of courtship, and we may conclude that she has done the
same to Richard. More important for the present purpose, her
technique of countering every one of Richard's protestations with a
stern reminder of his evil establishes the scale of the corruption he has
caused. This goes from his office –

> *K. Rich.* Now by my George, my Garter, and my crown –
> *Eliz.* Profan'd, dishonour'd, and the third usurp'd.     (IV.iv. 366–7)

– to the family, the land, the spiritual universe, time past, and time
future:

> *K. Rich.* Now, by the world –
> *Eliz.*                         'Tis full of thy foul wrongs.
> *K. Rich.* My father's death –
> *Eliz.*                         Thy life hath it dishonour'd.
> *K. Rich.* Then by my self –
> *Eliz.*                         Thy self is self-misus'd.
> *K. Rich.* Why then, by God –
> *Eliz.*                         God's wrong is most of all.
>                     . . .
> *K. Rich.*                   The time to come!
> *Eliz.* That thou hast wronged in the time o'erpast.
>                                      (IV. iv. 374–7, 387–8)

This is the grand scale to which Henry's prophecy lifted Richard; and
in the movement of the dialogue we see that Richard, far from
controlling his myth, is now trapped by it as he tries unsuccessfully to
talk like a normal man and Elizabeth will not let him. He has reason for
wanting to escape, for this lifting of the whole action to the level of myth
allows the conception of Richmond as an idealized good to match
Richard's idealized evil. The dry and cunning Henry VII of history (we
see him in Ford's *Perkin Warbeck*) would not do, and Shakespeare
allows us to forget him. He also allows us to forget the devious route of
inheritance on which the Tudor claim was based. Richmond is a
saviour of a simple kind; his claim to the crown is based on the fact that
he comes from over the sea to kill the demon king.[26] This way of seeing
Richmond draws on a general tendency to idealize that has been
established in earlier scenes. Anne's husband Edward did not appear, in
*Henry VI*, to be notably virtuous. But Anne now calls him, by contrast

with Richard, 'my other angel-husband' (IV.i.68), and Richard himself declares:

> A sweeter and a lovelier gentleman,
> Fram'd in the prodigality of Nature,
> Young, valiant, wise, and no doubt right royal,
> The spacious world cannot again afford.
>
> (I. ii. 247–50)

If Edward is simplified for the sake of a contrast with Richard, this helps to anticipate the similar contrast of dark and light when Richmond comes on the scene. The young Duke of York is as chatty and irritating as only a boy of a certain age can be, but his brother Edward V greets his new responsibilities with a sense of history and heroic destiny, in his praise of Julius Caesar (III. i. 84–8) and his ambition to 'win our ancient right in France again' (III. i. 92). Once again this shrunken England is briefly visited by the giant ghost of Henry V. In death the two princes, 'girdling one another / Within their alabaster innocent arms' (IV. iii. 10–11), become a simple picture of slaughtered innocence, moving even their murderers to tears. Shakespeare could be a little mischievous about the tendency to idealize, as when the Third Citizen laments the golden reign of Henry VI when 'this land was famously enrich'd / With politic grave counsel' (II. iii. 19–20), but, on the whole, idealization is made possible by Richard himself: if we can imagine such complete evil, we can also imagine a complete good to counter it. Moreover, Richmond's late appearance and the sparing use of images of good in the earlier scenes ensure that our capacity to make the effort is still fresh when he arrives.

He takes the play from Richard more decisively than Margaret did, and once again the language of the theatre makes the point, this time in the split staging: two tents, two sets of addresses by the ghosts, two battle orations, a prayer for Richmond and a guilt-stricken soliloquy for Richard, the fussiness and forced *bonhomie* in Richard's camp, the calm unity of purpose in Richmond's. This time the repetitions in the dialogue, notably in the ghost scene, are used not for mourning, brooding, or cursing but for balancing good against evil. It may be objected that Richard is still more vital and interesting than his adversary: Richmond's oration is stately and patterned, full of end-stopped lines, while Richard's has speed, freedom, and racy vernacular energy.[27] But this only confirms that Richard is one half of a contrasted pair, no longer a single, dominant figure. Richard's violation of the human bond has made his sexual language particularly corrupt:

*Anne.* And thou unfit for any place but hell.
*Rich.* Yes, one place else, if you will hear me name it.
*Anne.* Some dungeon?
*Rich.* Your bed-chamber.                                    (I. ii. 111–14)

In Richard's implied equation of the three places we are close to Lear's
discovery of hell, darkness, and the sulphurous pit in the female body.
But his promise to Elizabeth is worse:

*Eliz.* Yet thou didst kill my children.
*K. Rich.* But in your daughter's womb I'll bury them,
    Where, in that nest of spicery, they will breed
    Selves of themselves, to your recomforture.    (IV. iv. 422–5)

At this point she brings the interview to an end – unable, I think, to listen
any more. Rousing his troops, Richard appeals to their patriotism with
images that simply show how his own imagination works: 'Shall these
enjoy our lands? Lie with our wives? / Ravish our daughters?' (V. iii.
337–8). Richmond brings clean and natural values back to England. He
will marry Elizabeth, without the complication of being her uncle and
the killer of her brothers. The murdered princes tell him, 'Live, and
beget a happy race of kings' (V. iii. 158), taking away the taste of
Richard's monstrous notion of burying the corpses in Elizabeth's body.

As Margaret imagines saints praying for Richard's death while hell
splits open, Richmond declares, 'The prayers of holy saints and
wronged souls, / Like high-rear'd bulwarks, stand before our faces'
(V. iii. 242–3). His address to his soldiers embodies 'deeply felt
commonplace[s]'[28] whose value the play has made us feel by showing
their violation:

    If you do sweat to put a tyrant down,
    You sleep in peace, the tyrant being slain;
    If you do fight against your country's foes,
    Your country's fat shall pay your pains the hire;
    If you do fight in safeguard of your wives,
    Your wives shall welcome home the conquerors;
    If you do free your children from the sword,
    Your children's children quits it in your age.

                                                    (V. iii. 256–63)

Proper relations between husbands and wives, parents and children;
the reward of due service, even untroubled sleep – all of these
Richmond promises, in a restoration of the human bond Richard has
violated.[29] Elizabeth sums up the case against Richard in language that
recalls Towton:

> The children live whose fathers thou hast slaughter'd:
> Ungovern'd youth, to wail it in their age;
> The parents live whose children thou hast butcher'd:
> Old barren plants, to wail it with their age.
>
> (IV. iv. 391–4)

As in *Henry VI* Englishmen killed each other, so as the myth has developed Richard is killing everybody. The corruption has gathered into one place, and one stroke will finish it.

Richard has taken England out of history into myth; and on those terms Richmond can rescue it. This makes possible in *Richard III* a full and satisfying resolution of the sort Shakespeare will allow only once more in his treatment of history, in *Henry VIII.* It may be objected, of both plays, that the myth is not a way of sharpening our perception of reality, but a mere retreat into fantasy. *Henry VIII* I shall consider later; in *Richard III* Shakespeare is, I think, well aware of the problem, and his way of dealing with it is to link the myth with a concern for the normal conditions of life, the ordinary decencies of family, state, even sexual relations, that Richmond promises to restore. These values, not Margaret's grinding wheels of nemesis, are what finally control the play. And these values concern us all. Stylized though it is by the simultaneous staging, the sequence leading up to the battle is full of small, realistic details. One of these is Richmond's apology for sleeping in on the morning of Bosworth: 'Cry mercy, lords and watchful gentlemen, / That you have ta'en a tardy sluggard here' (V. iii. 225–6). This not only humanizes Richmond but reminds us what a dreadful night Richard has had. The reference to something as normal as sleep on the brink of England's rescue shows Shakespeare's characteristic habit of locating wonder in the familiar and natural. And a concern with the natural runs through the play, in small domestic touches like the jokes – so painful in the circumstances – about how fast the young Duke of York is growing (II. iv. 4–30).

In another and more political way, the myth is linked to the lives of the audience. While uniting the red rose and the white (V. v. 19) and promising that fathers and sons will no longer kill each other (V. v. 23–6), Richmond extends his ordering vision from the past of the tetralogy to the present life of England:

> O now let Richmond and Elizabeth,
> The true succeeders of each royal House,
> By God's fair ordinance conjoin together,
> And let their heirs, God, if Thy will be so,
> Enrich the time to come with smooth-fac'd peace,

With smiling plenty, and fair prosperous days.
Abate the edge of traitors, gracious Lord,
That would reduce these bloody days again,
And make poor England weep in streams of blood.
Let them not live to taste this land's increase,
That would with treason wound this fair land's peace.
Now civil wounds are stopp'd, peace lives again.
That she may long live here, God say Amen.

(V. v. 29–41)

He speaks to the theatre audience, but not quite as Richard did. Richard proclaimed a reign of peace, but with hidden irony; Richmond is open and serious in both the promise and the warning. He speaks of himself in the third person, acting as the impersonal chorus Richard only pretended to be. As Richard made us accomplices in his crimes, Richmond makes us fellow members of the community of England; there may even be a direct challenge in 'What traitor hears me and says not Amen?' (V. v. 22).[30] Our involvement this time includes our responsibility to interpret his words and apply them to the present dangers of the state, whatever they may be. 'Tudor England', M. M. Reese has reminded us, 'lived on its nerves',[31] and Richmond's golden vision is bordered and made more precious by the audience's awareness of its own troubles. If *Richard III* takes us out of history into myth, it may in its last moments take us back to history again.

# 3

# *Richard II*

The idealized England we glimpse at the end of *Richard III*, though a relief and a reassurance, is also somewhat abstract. It is a construction of ideas – reconciliation, family peace – and Richmond's language for it is comparatively bare. In *Richard II* the dying John of Gaunt gives us his vision of the ideal England in language that is anything but bare. The opening of his famous speech, 'Methinks I am a prophet new inspir'd' (II. i. 31), links him with Henry VI. The gift of prophecy he claims means initially that he can foretell the King's future:

> His rash fierce blaze of riot cannot last.
> For violent fires soon burn out themselves;
> Small showers last long, but sudden storms are short.
>
> (II. i. 33–5)

He continues for a few lines in this vein, predicting the ruin of the King's vanity. The lines are end-stopped, and all they do is repeat a single idea, through proverbial illustrations that lie side by side rather than building on each other. Gaunt's mind is stuck, and he seems short of breath. Then suddenly the speech takes off, and we hear the voice of a prophecy that is more than mere prediction:

> This royal throne of kings, this scept'red isle,
> This earth of majesty, this seat of Mars,
> This other Eden, demi-paradise,
> This fortress built by Nature for herself
> Against infection and the hand of war,
> This happy breed of men, this little world,
> This precious stone set in the silver sea,
> Which serves it in the office of a wall,
> Or as a moat defensive to a house,
> Against the envy of less happier lands;

54

This blessed plot, this earth, this realm, this England,
This nurse, this teeming womb of royal kings,
Fear'd by their breed, and famous by their birth,
Renowned for their deeds as far from home,
For Christian service and true chivalry,
As is the sepulchre in stubborn Jewry
Of the world's ransom, blessed Mary's son;
This land of such dear souls, this dear dear land,
Dear for her reputation through the world,
Is now leas'd out – I die pronouncing it –
Like to a tenement or pelting farm.                    (II. i. 40–60)

Against the temporary man who happens to be king this England stands in majestic permanence. It is also full of life: images tumble over each other, thoughts expand through line after line. This England is a bundle of paradoxes – small, enclosed, protected, yet sending heroes out to conquest; a fertile garden plot, a manor house, a fortress. It is a place that breeds kings, but the kings are simply a sign of its greatness; England itself comes first. At the line, 'This blessed plot, this earth, this realm, this England', Gaunt seems to try out different epithets, finding none of them quite right; only when he finds the word 'England' is the thought complete and the line ended.

This England has been ruined by Richard, who reduces it to a single image, a farm leased out for his own convenience. (A garden is symbolic; a farm is merely practical.) Yet in the grammar of the speech the ideas are not related quite as we might have expected. Gaunt does not say, England was a royal throne of kings but is now leased out like a tenement; he says, this royal throne of kings is now leased out. A few lines later, he will contrast past and present: 'That England, that was wont to conquer others, / Hath made a shameful conquest of itself' (II. i. 65–6). Here the past achievement is a verifiable fact. But in the speech as a whole there are no verbs attached to the ideal England. It exists not in the past, not in history, not in time at all, but in a timeless realm of the imagination. In a way this protects it from scepticism: it cannot be checked against (say) the reign of Edward III in the way in which the Third Citizen's nostalgic view of the reign of Henry VI (*Richard III*, II. iii. 19–21) can be checked against the reality. This is not nostalgia but vision: a true, inner England, always elusive in fact, always available to the imagination. It is a standard against which the characters in the play can be measured. Gaunt uses it here as a way of attacking Richard. When Richard himself later greets the earth of England by caressing it sentimentally and urging it to generate spiders, toads, and adders to attack his enemies (III. ii. 6–22), his sense of owning the land is very different from Gaunt's view of the land as magic in itself, giving birth to kings but not dependent on them.[1] Bolingbroke thinks as his father does, calling England 'My mother and my nurse' (I. iii. 307). The idea of England as a crusading nation is fulfilled not by Richard, who is preoccupied with secular wars, but by Mowbray, who dies in the service of the old ideal (IV. i. 92–100). When we set Mowbray's heroic end against Henry IV's futile attempt to revive the crusade for his own purpose, we see one of the many similiarities between Richard and his successor: both abuse ideals proclaimed by John of Gaunt.

But these contacts between Gaunt's vision and the rest of the play are sporadic. The price for having an ideal detached from history is that it cannot always inform the necessary actions of the present. The heroic Mowbray is remote, offstage, hard to relate to the character we actually saw in the early scenes. The crusading kings are even more remote. Gaunt speaks of a warlike nation. *Richard II* is unique among Shakespeare's earlier history plays in having no battle scene. Bolingbroke's armies march and Richard's armies desert; that is what the military action comes to. If Gaunt's vision seems far from the immediate business of the play, it is not because it is vague or abstract – far from it – but because England under Richard has departed so far from this ideal that it belongs to a different order of existence altogether. Earlier, we saw Gaunt caught in the dilemmas of the real world – wronged by the King and unable to strike back, implicated in the banishment of his own son: 'You urg'd me as a judge, but I had rather / You would have bid me argue like a father' (I. iii. 237–8). Now that he is dying he can allow himself to express a clear, straightforward judgement on the erring King, and we feel the relief as he unburdens himself; but we also feel that this vision of a dying man is not quite of this world.

Gaunt's tendency to idealize, however, is picked up by other characters and applied to the England they have to live in. Richmond's England was threatened only by the abstract possibility of treason; the England of *Richard II* is threatened by the King himself. The Duke of York does what Gaunt has not done: he idealizes the immediate past, and uses it as a standard by which to rebuke the present King, comparing him with his father, Edward the Black Prince:

> In war was never lion rag'd more fierce,
> In peace was never gentle lamb more mild,
> Than was that young and princely gentleman.
> His face thou hast, for even so look'd he,

> Accomplish'd with the number of thy hours;
> But when he frown'd it was against the French,
> And not against his friends; his noble hand
> Did win what he did spend, and spent not that
> Which his triumphant father's hand had won;
> His hands were guilty of no kindred blood,
> But bloody with the enemies of his kin.
>
> (II. i. 173–83)

Here the contrasts are direct and pointed: York's picture of a dead ideal does not float free of the present, but is shaped around specific offences committed by the King. If he is simplifying the past, it is for functional reasons. The speech is less poetic and more practical than Gaunt's. It may even suggest a psychological basis for Richard's difficulty: he is the disappointing son of a brilliant father.

It is also part of a general sense of ruin that pervades the play. The murder of Gloucester has left not only an angry widow but 'empty lodgings and unfurnish'd walls, / Unpeopled offices, untrodden stones' (I. ii. 68–9). More spectacular portents accompany Richard's fall: 'The bay-trees in our country are all wither'd, / And meteors fright the fixed stars of heaven' (II. iv. 8–9). Finally the Bishop of Carlisle takes up Gaunt's role of prophet and imagines a future in which the crusading nation will turn on itself and Eden will become Golgotha, a garden fertilized with blood:

> And if you crown him, let me prophesy –
> The blood of English shall manure the ground,
> And future ages groan for this foul act,
> Peace shall go sleep with Turks and infidels,
> And, in this seat of peace, tumultuous wars
> Shall kin with kin, and kind with kind, confound.
> Disorder, horror, fear, and mutiny,
> Shall here inhabit, and this land be call'd
> The field of Golgotha and dead men's skulls –
>
> (IV. i. 136–44)

This is recognizably Gaunt's England reversed; the future, like the realm of the imagination, is a place where facts cannot be checked. But this time the audience can bring its own knowledge to bear, and the reference to kin confounding kin may stir a memory of the Towton battle scene. Allowing for the concentration of the prophetic vision, Carlisle is telling us what we know will really happen. This time the horror is not (as in *Richard III*) a human figure turned into a monster.

The land itself has become a living, suffering thing.

Carlisle projects the immediate troubles of England on to a universal scale. But, ringing and confident though his voice is, the lessons of this play are not as easy as the lessons of *Richard III*, where we learn in the end that reconciliation is a good thing and that killing people is wrong. Instead we hear different voices trying to understand the world in different ways, and the overall effect is speculative. For the Duchess of Gloucester the order of the world is fixed and static, and Richard has broken it by violence:

> Edward's seven sons, whereof thyself art one,
> Were as seven vials of his sacred blood,
> Or seven fair branches springing from one root.
> Some of those seven are dried by nature's course,
> Some of those branches by the Destinies cut;
> But Thomas, my dear lord, my life, my Gloucester,
> One vial full of Edward's sacred blood,
> One flourishing branch of his most royal root,
> Is crack'd, and all the precious liquor spilt,
> Is hack'd down, and his summer leaves all faded,
> By envy's hand, and murder's bloody axe.
>
> (I. ii. 11–21)

The overt patterning of the speech recalls the repetitive laments of *Richard III* and the Towton allegory: a moment of violence is frozen for our contemplation, giving the violence itself a ritual quality. A rigid order is broken; and the mind of the speaker tries to understand and control the outrage by fixing it in a neat pattern.

More important for our purposes here, the Duchess's world is inherently stable and it takes violence to break it. For the Gardener, on the other hand, the world is inherently unstable and it take violence to control it. The opening of the garden scene might have come from one of Shakespeare's comedies: the Queen has time on her hands, and speculates playfully on how to drive away melancholy: 'What sport shall we devise here in this garden, / To drive away the heavy thought of care?' (III. iv. 1–2); every sport suggested is the occasion for a witty pun about her grief. There is playful artificiality, too, in her assumption that the gardeners are going to be thematically important: 'My wretchedness unto a row of pins, / They'll talk of state' (III. iv. 26–7). And of course they do; as in the Towton scene, though less terribly, the commons are not allowed independent lives but are pressed into the service of an allegorical commentary on the crisis of the state. There is nothing playful, however, in the lesson the Gardener draws from his analogy between ruling and gardening, and the scene's initial lightness only sets off the grimness of its message (it is worth recalling at this point that Elizabethan gardens were severely geometrical):

> Go thou, and like an executioner
> Cut off the heads of too fast growing sprays,
> That look too lofty in our commonwealth.
>
> (III. iv. 33–5)

Richard has been, not too brutal, but not brutal enough:

> We at time of year
> Do wound the bark, the skin of our fruit-trees,
> Lest, being over-proud in sap and blood,
> With too much riches it confound itself;
> Had he done so to great and growing men,
> They might have liv'd to bear, and he to taste
> Their fruits of duty. Superfluous branches
> We lop away, that bearing boughs may live;
> Had he done so, himself had borne the crown,
> Which waste of idle hours hath quite thrown down.
>
> (III. iv. 57–66)

As Wilbur Sanders has pointed out, Richard might fairly object that he has followed this advice, lopping Gloucester as a 'superfluous branch' (the Duchess's image, used with very different import) and relieving his subjects of 'too much riches' by severe taxation – and that having done this he has had 'nothing but trouble for his pains'.[2] It could be objected in turn that Richard has struck the wrong people. The art lies in knowing *when* to be severe. But how does one know that? Clear and practical though it sounds, the Gardener's advice is problematic in the long run.

An ordered world, broken by violence; a disordered world that needs violence to control it; a world, finally, in which answers do not come easily. In Gaunt's description of England as 'This other Eden, demi-paradise' there may be unconscious ambiguity. 'Other' in what sense – duplicating the condition of Eden or differing from it? Eden before or after the Fall? The Queen's attack on the Gardener is confused and unfair, but it reminds the audience what happened to that first garden:

> Thou, old Adam's likeness set to dress this garden,
> How dares thy harsh rude tongue sound this unpleasing news?
> What Eve, what serpent, hath suggested thee
> To make a second fall of cursed man?          (III. iv. 73–6)

If gardens now need constant work to keep them ordered, it is because the first gardener betrayed his trust. This leads to the question of the King's responsibility for the fall of England. Concerned to defend Richard, the Queen associates him with Adam seen as the victim of temptation. She is not alone; friends like York and foes like Northumberland agree that 'The king is not himself, but basely led / By flatterers' (II. i. 241–2). But for all we hear of this we never see it: Richard always takes his own initiatives.[3] To be under a guilty king puts loyal subjects in a dilemma, and those who palliate Richard's faults in this way may be trying not only to preserve sympathy for him but to lighten their own problem. The play itself, however, keeps insisting on the King's guilt. Outrage at this guilt fires the excitement of Gaunt's vision. Yet the solution is not to get rid of him, for, as Carlisle points out, that will only produce a more terrible ruin. More than in the earlier history plays, England itself is emerging as a presence, shifting its image as it passes through different minds, an object of concern for everyone. Its fate, however, cannot be separated from the fate of its king, any more than Eden can be imagined without Adam.

In the first tetralogy, kingship was essentially the prize in a game of power. As we saw how Henry, Edward, and Richard failed at it in their different ways we may have thought about the demands of the office, but the characters themselves were more concerned to get or keep the crown than to understand what it meant. Moments like Henry's defence of his conduct in office (*3 Henry VI*, IV. viii. 39–46) stand out as exceptional. In *Richard II* this changes. In no other play of Shakespeare's is the office of kingship subjected to such intense scrutiny, from such a wide variety of angles. We see its ritual, quasi-religious significance, its practical underpinnings, and above all the importance of the man who holds it. Richard himself is one of Shakespeare's sharpest studies of a personality. Intensifying his scrutiny of the office, he was bound, it seems, to intensify his scrutiny of the man, and to test man and office against each other. One reason why Gaunt's England seems remote from the England of the play is that its kings come and go so quickly, and are so faceless. It seems we can feel confident about the office only if we do not look too closely. Gaunt talks of his kings; Shakespeare shows his, slowly and in detail, not in a remote world of legend but in the sometimes pitiless daylight of a public theatre.

In this arena the myth of kingship as a divine office and the stylized forms that go with it are tested against the realities of politics and personality. Bolingbroke's stylized, exaggerated confrontation with

Mowbray that opens the play may recall the scenes of ritual defiance in *Henry VI*, but here the forms of law are respected. The characters are not just asserting their own wills but working through a larger order which they implicitly accept. The elaborately technical preparations for the lists at Coventry confirm this effect. The ritual builds, the symmetry intensifies – to a startling anticlimax:

> *1 Herald.* Harry of Herford, Lancaster and Derby,
>    Stands here, for God, his sovereign, and himself,
>    On pain to be found false and recreant,
>    To prove the Duke of Norfolk, Thomas Mowbray,
>    A traitor to his God, his king, and him,
>    And dares him to set forward to the fight.
> *2 Herald.* Here standeth Thomas Mowbray, Duke of Norfolk,
>    On pain to be found false and recreant,
>    Both to defend himself, and to approve
>    Henry of Herford, Lancaster and Derby,
>    To God, his sovereign, and to him disloyal,
>    Courageously, and with a free desire,
>    Attending but the signal to begin.
> *Mar.* Sound trumpets, and set forward, combatants.
>                                            *A charge sounded.*
>    Stay, the king hath thrown his warder down.     (I. iii. 104–18)

As the ritual is at once decorous and a bit tedious, its violation is at once a shock and a relief. The gesture itself is part of the language of the occasion, but its timing makes it theatrical. It is splendid theatre, but it is theatre at the cost of ceremony (a point to which I shall return), and what is most disturbing is that the violation has come right from the centre. The King, the custodian of order, has himself broken the order of a formal occasion. The structure is not smashed from without, like the vials and branches of the Duchess's speech; the shock that destroys it comes from its very centre, and it collapses inwards.

The moment is a striking image of Richard's responsibility for the disorder of his kingdom and the later collapse – so sudden and complete – of his own rule. The murder of Gloucester remains in some respects murky; the question is never fully brought out and resolved, and Richard never admits his own guilt. But on two occasions – once to Richard's face – Gaunt makes it clear that Richard is ultimately responsible (I. ii. 37–9, II. i. 124–31). The opening lines, with their contrast of time-honoured Lancaster and bold Herford (I.i.1–3) may have led us to expect a conservative order violated by a rebellious young subject. But it is the King himself who rebels, and it is the older generation who first think the unthinkable in return. In the very second scene the old Duchess of Gloucester proposes that Gaunt kill the King in order to protect himself (I. ii. 33–6). She puts it less bluntly than that, for the idea, if not unthinkable, is still unspeakable (even Bolingbroke will not give a direct order); but this is clearly what she means. Even York is provoked by the seizure of the Hereford estate to 'those thoughts / Which honour and allegiance cannot think' (II. i. 207–8). Not 'should not' – 'cannot'. The inference is that Richard is not just qualifying York's allegiance but destroying it. York points to a more fundamental danger: in seizing the estate, Richard is striking at his own kingship:

> Take Herford's rights away, and take from time
> His charters, and his customary rights;
> Let not to-morrow then ensue to-day:
> Be not thyself. For how art thou a king
> But by fair sequence and succession?          (II. i. 195–9)

It is a fundamental violation, like stopping time itself; and its ultimate effect is self-destructive.

For all Richard's reputation as the great spokesman for the mystique of kingship, his problem in the early scenes is that he is too pragmatic. Gaunt's accusation, 'Landlord of England art thou now, not king' (II. i. 113), shows he has violated his office by his exclusive concern with revenue.[4] A king does indeed have to be concerned with such things, but a king who is simply a tax-gatherer will get funds only by losing allegiance:

> The commons hath he pill'd with grievous taxes,
> And quite lost their hearts. The nobles hath he fin'd
> For ancient quarrels and quite lost their hearts.
>                                               (II. i. 246–8)

This is an unfortunate kind of national unity. Bagot puts it differently, saying of the commons,

>                         their love
> Lies in their purses, and whoso empties them,
> By so much fills their hearts with deadly hate.
>                                               (II. ii. 128–30)

His bitter tone suggests that the people ought to be able to look beyond material things and keep their loyalty while the King empties their purses. But if they are reduced to money-grubbers it is the King who made the first move. As with York and the Duchess, the commons' rebellious thoughts are a reaction to the King's own abuse of his office.

Richard as administrator is not so much inept as insensitive. Cheerfully admitting that his court has been too lavish, he comes up with ingenious ways of raising money – farming the realm, issuing blank charters – but what really counts is the casualness with which he talks of these things (I. iv. 42–52). In the anonymous *Woodstock*, in many ways a companion piece to Shakespeare's play, these and other abuses are dramatized at great length. Shakespeare's Richard only speaks of them briefly, but his airy manner is in itself a devastating criticism of him. The author of *Woodstock* is concerned with what is happening in England; Shakespeare by comparison is more concerned with the state of the King's mind. The flippant manner we glimpse in the first scene – 'Forget, forgive, conclude and be agreed: / Our doctors say this is no month to bleed' (I. i. 156–7) – deepens into shocking callousness at the impending death of Gaunt:

> Now put it, God, in the physician's mind
> To help him to his grave immediately!
> The lining of his coffers shall make coats
> To deck our soldiers for these Irish wars.
> Come, gentlemen, let's all go visit him,
> Pray God we may make haste and come too late!
>
> (I. iv. 59–64)

The initial joke is in the manner of Richard III. But, while that Richard's inhumanity was the result of a conscious philosophy and a controlled strategy, this one's seems flippant and unthinking. The speed with which he seizes the estate as soon as he hears of Gaunt's death is tactless to the point of stupidity (II. i. 153–62), and he greets York's eloquent (and perfectly lucid) protest with 'Why, uncle, what's the matter?' (II. i. 186).

But is Richard always as stupid as he looks? His misunderstanding of Gaunt's word-play (II. i. 89–93) may be obtuseness, or it may be a deliberate refusal to let Gaunt make his point. His appointing York Governor during his absence in Ireland is in some respects a clever move: Richard is co-opting an eloquent critic, and exploiting his fundamental loyalty. He does not anticipate (and neither do we) York's administrative incompetence and failure of will – though we might add that, while the first is York's own, the second has been made possible by the intense strain Richard has placed on the old man's loyalty. Whatever we may think of his administrative decisions, Richard is capable of shrewd and sometimes ironic insights. When the combatants of I.i greet him with fulsome (and, of course, symmetrical) compliments, he takes malicious pleasure in pointing out the absurdity:

> We thank you both, yet one but flatters us,
> As well appeareth by the cause you come,
> Namely, to appeal each other of high treason.
>
> (I. i. 25–7)

One reason why Richard is unreliable on occasions requiring tact and dignity is that there is something in him of the little boy who points out that the emperor isn't wearing any clothes. (This is complicated by the fact that he is also the emperor.) He senses the reason for Bolingbroke's courtship of the common people: 'As were our England in reversion his, / And he our subjects' next degree in hope' (I. iv. 35–6). Like Cassius, he is a great observer and looks quite through the deeds of men.

He is also, as criticism has endlessly pointed out, something of an actor. He savours the performances of Bolingbroke and Mowbray – 'How high a pitch his resolution soars!' (I. i. 109) – but this is nothing compared to the relish with which he enjoys his own. Through the opening scenes the two lords compete for dominance, and when Richard fails to control them he is reduced to weak, petulant anger. But he upstages them nicely at Coventry. According to Allan Bloom, when Richard stops the trial by combat he unwittingly brings the age of chivalry to an end.[5] I have already suggested that he is replacing ceremony with theatre. A ceremony, properly conducted, enacts and affirms the shared values of a community. It is therefore predictable, and meant to be predictable. (Only in periods of liturgical renewal do congregations at a Communion service wonder what is coming next.) Richard's intervention is a surprise, and it directs attention from the occasion to Richard himself and his own will. Even the timing is stagy. The reasons Richard gives for stopping the fight could have been invoked at any time; he intervenes when he does for maximum theatrical effect. This is not only self-indulgent; it is bound to sharpen the irritation of the combatants. It is good theatre but bad politics, and it is a direct violation of the principles of ritual.

When, as his fall begins, Richard tries to evoke the divinity of his office, he has already shown himself insensitive to the ceremonial way of thinking that ought to be one of his principal supports. We might expect to see a divinely appointed king at the centre of a ceremony; we do – and we see him violate it. So, when he tries to invoke the mystique of kingship, all he can do is give a performance:

Not all the water in the rough rude sea
Can wash the balm off from an anointed king;
The breath of wordly men cannot depose
The deputy elected by the Lord;
For every man that Bolingbroke hath press'd
To lift shrewd steel against our golden crown,
God for his Richard hath in heavenly pay
A glorious angel: then, if angels fight,
Weak men must fall, for heaven still guards the right.

*Enter* SALISBURY

Welcome, my lord: how far off lies your power?
(III. ii. 54–63)

The language is brilliant. Richard calls on divine protection in driving, vivid words matched only by Gaunt's evocation of his ideal England. We find ourselves believing it, or wanting to believe it. But any chance we may have of doing so is blocked when we realize that Richard does not finally believe it himself. He wants to hear how many soldiers he has. Richard's kingship, like Talbot's heroism, is helpless without the support of 'that article'. Ideal and reality collide within his mind, and the final appeal is to reality. His later assertions of his power have the dry irony we have heard him apply to others:

Is not the king's name twenty thousand names?
Arm, arm, my name! a puny subject strikes
At thy great glory.                    (III. ii. 85–7)

Richard III also claimed 'the King's name is a tower of strength / Which they upon the adverse faction want' (V. iii. 12–13). But Richard II's phrasing suggests a sharper awareness of the futility of the claim.

Richard is left with his actor's ability to call attention to himself, even if it means calling attention only to his own disaster. As at Coventry when he threw down his warder, he knows how to fix all eyes on himself. 'For God's sake let us sit upon the ground / And tell sad stories of the death of kings' (III. ii. 155–6) suggests that Richard himself sits at this point, but no one else does. The only seated figure, and that figure a king – it is a striking effect. He ensures that he will live in memory: 'Tell thou the lamentable tale of me, / And send the hearers weeping to their beds' (V. i. 44–5). According to one theory of the mystery of kingship, he is entitled to some identification with Christ,[6] but when he sees himself as a Christ-figure it is not to assert his office but to dramatize his sufferings – with the blasphemous addition that they are greater than

65

Christ's: 'he, in twelve, / Found truth in all but one; I, in twelve
thousand, none' (IV. i. 170–1). Carlisle voices a natural exasperation:
'My lord, wise men ne'er sit and wail their woes, / But presently prevent
the ways to wail' (III. ii. 178–9) – and insists that God helps those who
help themselves (III. ii. 29–32). But Richard has posed extreme
alternatives for himself: 'Either the rebellion will be overturned by
sheer force of his majesty without additional help; or he will despair.'[7] It
is easier to despair. It is also satisfying, even exciting. As though trying
to keep control even of his ruin, Richard falls faster than anyone can
push him. He anticipates moves against him before they have been
made:

> What must the king do now? Must he submit?
> The king shall do it. Must he be depos'd?
> The king shall be contented. Must he lose
> The name of king? a God's name, let it go.          (III. iii. 143–6)

He goes from resignation – 'Say, is my kingdom lost? why, 'twas my
care' (III.ii.95) – to a flaming excitement at the sheer scale of his ruin:

> Down, down I come like glist'ring Phaeton,
> Wanting the manage of unruly jades.
> In the base court? Base court, where kings grow base,
> To come at traitors' calls, and do them grace!
> In the base court? Come down? Down, court! down, king!
> For night-owls shriek where mounting larks should sing.
>                                                       (III. iii. 178–83)

Besides its obvious self-dramatization, Richard's hunger for his own
ruin has a subtler political effect. Bolingbroke is trying to be guarded
and careful, and to move slowly. Richard forces the pace and flushes
out Bolingbroke's hidden motives. For a while Bolingbroke maintains
his posture of aggrieved but loyal subject under persistent needling
from Richard; but he finally cracks:

> Set on towards London, cousin, is it so?
> *Bol.* Yea, my good lord.
> *Rich.*                            Then I must not say no.     (III. iii. 208–9)

Their going to London can have nothing to do with the Hereford
estate; they are going to the centre of power, so that power can change
hands.[8] The play's bluntest statement of *Realpolitik* comes not from
Bolingbroke or even from Northumberland, but from Richard himself:
'Well you deserve. They well deserve to have / That know the strong'st
and surest way to get' (III. iii. 200–1). Richard's prediction that

Northumberland will turn against his master is deadly accurate (V. i. 55–65). But his most devastating criticism is embodied in the way in which he dramatizes his deposition. Here his acting skill and his limited but acute political insight come into their own and work together. In other plays of the period, kings were overthrown and murdered, and nothing (or not much) was said by the licensing authorities. But when *Richard II* was first published the whole deposition sequence was cut. It shows not just the suffering of a king but the violation of his office; and its manner of doing so is slow, gruelling, and merciless; this time the authorities must have caught the smell of gunpowder. The unthinkable is happening before our eyes, and Richard ensures that the audience (onstage and off) knows it is unthinkable.[9] Bolingbroke imagines that a public transfer of the kingship will ease men's minds:

> Fetch hither Richard, that in common view
> He may surrender; so we shall proceed
> Without suspicion.                              (IV. i. 155–7)

Richard ensures that the effect is just the opposite. When he asks, 'To do what service am I sent for hither?' (IV. i. 176), he creates unexpected doubt about his intentions, thereby startling his hearers and fixing attention on himself; Bolingbroke complains, in some exasperation, 'I thought you had been willing to resign' (IV. i. 190). More important, he calls attention to the absurdity of what is happening: a king summoned to do service. The transfer of the crown is more strikingly absurd: 'Here, cousin, seize the crown' (IV. i. 181). Richard uses his old flippant manner to show how the crown is degraded by being passed from hand to hand,[10] and Bolingbroke evidently takes the point and hesitates, for Richard has to repeat his invitation. When he poses Bolingbroke and himself, each with a hand on the crown and neither wearing it, Richard creates an unforgettable and disturbing stage picture. The rule is: one king at a time. Here we see two kings – which is impossible. Or do we see no king at all? Both men are bareheaded, and the crown is empty.

Richard then, in effect, formally reverses the ceremony of the coronation:[11]

> Now, mark me how I will undo myself.
> I give this heavy weight from off my head,
> And this unwieldy sceptre from my hand,
> The pride of kingly sway from out my heart;
> With mine own tears I wash away my balm,
> With mine own hands I give away my crown,
> With mine own tongue deny my sacred state,

With mine own breath release all duteous oaths;
All pomp and majesty I do forswear;
My manors, rents, revenues, I forgo;
My acts, decrees, and statutes I deny.
God pardon all oaths that are broke to me,
God keep all vows unbroke are made to thee!

(IV. i. 203–15)

Richard shows a full if belated sense of what the office means, of what the symbols stand for. The ceremonies that create a king make him the centre of a whole structure of oath and obligation, property and law, radiating outwards from the crown and informing all society. Now we see that structure being undone, step by step and deliberately, from the centre. Richard speaks here in a stately, formal manner quite unlike his earlier flippancy. He does more than violate ceremony; he perverts it, even parodies it. As Margaret Loftus Ranald has shown, there were established ceremonies for removing a man from chivalric, military, or ecclesiastical office; but there was no such ceremony for deposing a king, and for good reason: to have a set way of doing it was to admit that the thing could be done, and that was inadmissible.[12] Richard has to invent a ceremony, and it can be argued that such an invention is not a true ritual but a theatrical imitation of one. Certainly Richard is, as so often, thinking theatrically: his refusal to read the list of crimes presented by Northumberland is a refusal to play by another man's script (IV. i. 222–44). The way in which he fixes attention on himself, demonstrating as he does the absurdity of the deposition, is strikingly theatrical. And at one point Richard deliberately initiates a ceremonial exchange he knows will not be completed: 'God save the king! Will no man say amen? / Am I both priest and clerk? well then, amen' (IV. i. 172–3). He turns a ceremony into a theatrical trick to make his audience feel uncomfortable, and so dramatizes their complicity. At Flint Castle, York sums up the strength and weakness of Richard's appeal when he laments 'That any harm should stain so fair a show' (III. iii. 71); after the deposition the Abbot of Westminister declares, 'A woeful pageant have we here beheld' (IV. i. 321). If 'show' is an elusive word, 'pageant' exactly indicates a middle state: a pageant is not quite a ceremony, not quite a play. What Richard has staged is a perverted ceremony, using theatrical means, to dramatize the outrage of his fall.

If kingship and the ceremony that goes with it are to be degraded, the theatre is the place to do it: there, kings are played by ordinary men; and we should remember that, for all the historical affinities between drama and religious ritual, the theatres of Shakespeare's day doubled not as churches but as sporting arenas for cockfighting and bearbaiting. Unable to function in his divine office, Richard is reduced to competing for attention. He does it brilliantly; but it could be said that, in making the assertion of his kingship a matter of practical skill rather than sanctity, Richard is playing by Bolingbroke's rules and giving away more than his crown. What, we may ask, does Richard gain by doing this, other than the private satisfaction of scoring his points? He seems to be using 'the weapon of the powerless: the seizure of *symbolic* initiative'.[13] He 'manages to embarrass Bolingbroke, but in no way diverts him from his advance to power'.[14] Bolingbroke does indeed get the power; but in a real sense Richard manages to deny him the kingship. In a coronation the king receives his crown from a representative of the church; but Richard uncrowns himself, and removes by his own act all the other attributes of his royalty. This is not just a violation but a paradox: I, the King, declare I am not the King; and only I can do this because I am the King. It is as though the Pope in his last infallible pronouncement were to declare himself fallible. For the rest of the play Richard is (like the hero of Beaumont and Fletcher's tragicomedy) a king and no king. And so, by logical inference, is Bolingbroke. There is a persistent difficulty about what to call Richard once he is uncrowned: 'I was a poor groom of thy stable, king, / When thou wert king' (V. v. 72–3). Even his murderer calls him 'the king at Pomfret' (V. iv. 10). Richard himself, with deliberate impudence, narrowly avoids calling himself King Richard: 'God save King Henry, unking'd Richard says' (IV. i. 220). We see the long-range effect of this when York declares 'To Bolingbroke are we sworn subjects now, / Whose state and honour I for aye allow' (V. ii. 39–40) and we notice he does not call him 'King Henry'. Even the early texts reflect the problem: the new king is King Henry in the Quarto, 'Bullingbrooke' in the Folio.

The difficulty about naming is crucial, and its ramifications are more than political. C. L. Barber has described the Renaissance as 'a moment when educated men were modifying a ceremonial conception of human life to create a historical conception', adding that in the ceremonial conception 'names and meanings are fixed and final'.[15] So, when the ceremonial role of kingship is violated, names become unfixed. Richard's paradoxical strategy is to make his kingship seem unremovable, even in the act of removing it; one implication of this is that, if he is no king, he is nothing:[16]

> I have no name, no title;
> No, not that name was given me at the font,

But 'tis usurp'd. Alack the heavy day,
That I have worn so many winters out,
And know not now what name to call myself!

(IV. i. 255–9)

In giving away his crown he is giving away his very identity. He
dramatizes this too, again emphasizing the wrongness and absurdity of
what he is doing. This time his prop (befitting an actor) is a mirror, and,
like Talbot and the Countess of Auvergne, he plays with shadow and
substance. With characteristic irony he claims that the face in the
mirror is, as a reflection of his sufferings, disappointing: 'No deeper
wrinkles yet?' (IV. i. 277). As in the decoronation, Richard has to make
the significant gesture himself, hurling the mirror to the ground, not
just damaging the face but smashing it utterly. The gesture recalls his
hurling down his warder at Coventry; there, he violated a ceremony;
here, he violates his own identity. Like all Richard's self-destructive
gestures, this has a whiff of real danger; directors usually find a way of
keeping the mess under control, but Shakespeare may have imagined
that from this point on there would be broken glass all over the stage.[17]
At this moment Bolingbroke makes his one serious attempt to
upstage Richard, an attempt that nearly succeeds:

Mark, silent king, the moral of this sport –
How soon my sorrow hath destroy'd my face.
*Bol.* The shadow of your sorrow hath destroy'd
The shadow of your face.
*Rich.*                              Say that again.
The shadow of my sorrow? ha! let's see –
'Tis very true, my grief lies all within.

(IV. i. 290–5)

Richard fumbles a moment before deciding (like Hamlet) to admit that
the gesture is an external show but to insist there is substance beneath
it: 'the unseen grief / That swells with silence in the tortur'd soul' (IV. i.
297–8). He then completes his recovery by thanking Bolingbroke for
helping him lament. The insistence that his grief is the one substantial
thing about him may give us a more sympathetic view of Richard's
emotional self-indulgence: he may not know who he is, but he knows
what he feels, and he clings to grief as the only reality he has: 'You may
my glories and my state depose, / But not my griefs; still am I king of
those' (IV. i. 192–3). Behind this clinging to one certainty is Richard's
ultimate fear, which is also his ultimate desire: 'Ay, no; no, ay; for I must
nothing be' (IV. i. 201). The tricky language enforces close listening; the
way 'ay' and 'no' seem to cancel each other out prepares for a

cancellation of being itself. In his prison soliloquy Richard imagines himself in a variety of different roles, quickly assumed and quickly discarded, none satisfying or authentic. The actor's versatility has become a nightmare, and Richard, in the ultimate expression of his drive to self-destruction, longs to get it over with:

> But whate'er I be,
> Nor I, nor any man that but man is,
> With nothing shall be pleas'd, till he be eas'd
> With being nothing.                    (V. v. 38–41)

Even his last exciting outburst of physical resistance is introduced by the words 'Patience is stale, and I am weary of it' (V.v.103), as though the gallant fighter we see at the end is just one more role assumed to fill in the time. But Richard does not end in silence and nothingness: he ends with an assertion of his own identity and the significance of his death: 'Exton, thy fierce hand / Hath with the king's blood stain'd the king's own land' (V. v. 109–10). Seen in this way, his death is meaningful, not absurd; but its meaning depends on the identity he gave away. Richard is paradoxical to the end.


Richard defends himself by a brilliant, showy, and pointed use of appearances. Bolingbroke is also a politician of appearances, but his strategy is very different. Richard calls him 'silent king'; Brents Stirling sums up a general verdict by declaring, 'Never, in an age of drama marked by discursive self-revelation, has a character disclosed his traits with such economy and understatement.'[18] There is masterly ambiguity in his reasons for repealing his own banishment and returning to England: 'The noble Duke hath sworn his coming is / But for his own' (II. iii. 147–8). When he tries to explain himself more fully, he descends to sophistry: 'As I was banish'd, I was banish'd Herford; / But as I come, I come for Lancaster' (II. iii. 112–13). We see in that moment why he is usually more guarded. Richard cuts through the soft words to see the true significance of Bolingbroke's defiance of his sentence: 'every stride he makes upon my land / Is dangerous treason' (III. iii. 92–3). Bolingbroke demonstrates his political strength and acumen by exterminating the caterpillars while sending gentle words to the Queen (III. i). At the first sign of yielding from York, he presses the old man politely but firmly and makes him part of his entourage (II. iii. 161–70). But these shows of strength are rare. For the most part his strategy is to do nothing, so that his succession will look natural and inevitable (hence Richard's insistence that the deposition is *un*natural, and his strategy of making it as showy as possible). At one point Shakespeare himself creates a significant ambiguity: at the end of II. i, shortly after the death of Gaunt, we hear that Bolingbroke is already on his way back to England. If we take this literally, it turns the public reason for his return into a flagrant lie; but no one on the stage takes it in that way, and we wonder if the timing is to be accepted as an artificial theatrical economy. Bolingbroke presents us here with an acute problem of interpretation – and not for the last time.

Richard and Bolingbroke between them shift the kingship into a theatrical arena where skilled manipulation of appearances is the determining factor. Bolingbroke no less than Richard degrades the sanctity of the office, and not just by usurpation. In his courtship of the common people – 'Off goes his bonnet to an oyster-wench' (I. iv. 31) – he sounds like a man running for president. It is in the realm of appearances, of theatrical effect, that Bolingbroke, like Richard of York and Richard of Gloucester before him, is most subtly devalued. Early in IV. i we are treated to a bizarre replay of the opening quarrel of Bolingbroke and Mowbray as a group of nobles challenge each other on the subject of Gloucester's murder. The repetition this time becomes absurd (at l. 52 Shakespeare seems to run out of names and resorts to '*Another Lord*'), and the floor is littered with gages. It is as though the new reign is beginning with a parody of the play's opening. Bolingbroke tries to bring the proceedings to a sensible conclusion, and resolve the problem with which the play began, by recalling Mowbray to face trial and settle the issue – only to be told that Mowbray is dead. The new king shows executive firmness, but the absurdity of the squabble and the surprise of Mowbray's death compromise his effectiveness. In handling the tricky business of Aumerle's treachery and the conflicting demands of his parents – York clamouring for his son's death, the Duchess for mercy – Bolingbroke hardly puts a foot wrong. He is firm, kindly, and tactful; he shows unexpected humour. But the manner of the sequence, remarkably, in view of the seriousness of the issue, is bustling comedy, with York calling for his boots,[19] the Duchess declaring, 'For ever will I walk upon my knees' (V. iii. 91), and Bolingbroke admitting that the whole tone of the occasion has collapsed: 'Our scene is alt'red from a serious thing' (V. iii. 77). The upshot is that the new king looks like a friendly neighbour settling a family row; his considerable skill is exercised on a scale that is made to look trivial.

Like Richard III and the warring nobles of *Henry VI*, he is also placed against a larger sweep of time and history in which his success is just a temporary episode. Right at the start of his campaign he is offered loyalty by young Henry Hotspur, and promises gratitude in return (II. iii. 41–50).[20] At the opening of V. iii he is worrying about his 'unthrifty son' in whom he sees, none the less, 'some sparks of better hope' (V. iii. 1, 21). One of his less guarded statements during the campaign, 'A while to work, and after holiday' (III. i. 44), predicts an ease and relaxation he will never enjoy; Henry's reign will be full of trouble, and England will have a secure and effective kingship only with his death. His son, meanwhile, will use holiday for political purposes. The brushfire rebellions we hear of in the last scene are easily stamped out, but they are a bad omen; and when Exton presents him with the corpse of King Richard he speaks more truly than he knows in calling it 'Thy buried fear' (V. vi. 31).[21] The new king has a number of ironic affinities with Richard, not the least of which is blood guilt. In the first scene he declared that Gloucester's blood cried for revenge 'like sacrificing Abel's' (I. i. 104); in the last, he tells Exton, 'With Cain go wander thorough shades of night' (V. vi. 43). Each of them discovers mortality – Richard (when he learns of the deaths of his favourites) at great length, and with his usual aesthetic relish: 'Let's talk of graves, of worms, and epitaphs' (III. ii. 145); Bolingbroke, just as typically, by stumbling on it in the course of business. His first executive action is frustrated by Mowbray's death, and the clumsy fulsomeness of his response, 'Sweet peace conduct his sweet soul to the bosom / Of good old Abraham' (IV. i. 103–4), shows him uncharacteristically flustered. It may be that the seed of ambition is first planted in Bolingbroke's mind when Richard's reduction of his banishment shows the King's power over time: 'Four lagging winters and four wanton springs / End in a word: such is the breath of kings' (I. iii. 214–15). But Gaunt insists the King's power over time is limited – 'Shorten my days thou canst with sullen sorrow, / And pluck nights from me, but not lend a morrow' (I. iii. 227–8) – and Richard later makes a more devastating discovery: 'O, call back yesterday, bid time return, / And thou shalt have ten thousand fighting men!' (III. ii. 69–70). Richard finally comes to see time as his nemesis: 'I wasted time, and now doth time waste me' (V. v. 49). If Bolingbroke too realizes he is time's victim, he does not say it in so many words; but when we see him rattled by Mowbray's death, and when we see him looking anxiously into the future as he worries about his son, we may sense that he has in his own way made Richard's discovery. Gaunt's England is beyond time; the England of the two kings is not.

The affinities between Richard and Bolingbroke take us back to the haunting stage picture of the two crownless kings with the hollow crown between them. The effect is different from the symmetrical stage picture of the night sequence in *Richard III*, with hero and villain in their respective tents at opposite sides of the stage. It is different, too, from what we imagine as the opening picture of Mowbray facing Bolingbroke, with Richard in the middle. Now there is not so much an opposition as a dilemma; and the figure of the king has abandoned the centre and split in two. It is not just that the two men have complementary and opposite strengths and weaknesses: each is, as I have tried to argue, a king and no king. The dilemma is England's, dramatized by York's pathetic hesitations when Bolingbroke returns, by the later strife within York's family, and by the split in his own nature when as a loyal subject he has to plead for his son's death. The pain is covered by comedy, and alleviated by Bolingbroke's mercy; but York is prepared to cast himself in the role of the Father who has killed his Son. As human relations suffer, so does language; when Bolingbroke addresses York as 'loyal father of a treacherous son' (V. iii. 58), we may reflect that terms like 'loyal' and 'treacherous' have become relative. Many of the play's key images have a curiously reversible quality: the kings are two buckets in a well (IV. i. 184–9), two pans in a set of balances (III. iv. 84–9). Even Richard's identification of himself with the sun and Bolingbroke with the darkness (III. ii. 36–53) is reversed by Richard himself: 'Discharge my followers; let them hence away, / From Richard's night, to Bolingbroke's fair day' (III. ii. 217–18). York finally describes them as two actors playing for a crowd, and in the process both are degraded. Richard keeps his dignity but is pelted with rubbish. Bolingbroke gets the cheers but debases himself in acknowledging them, 'from one side to the other turning, / Bare-headed, lower than his proud steed's neck' (V. ii. 18–19). This is our sharpest image of what happens when kingship is subjected to what Shakespeare calls elsewhere the 'public manners' of the theatre (Sonnet 111).

The image of the actor, used here overtly, suggests that kingship is a role that can be transferred from one man to another – as in John Barton's 1973 Royal Shakespeare Company production, when two actors alternated the parts of Richard and Bolingbroke, and each performance began with the choice of the actor who was to play the king that night.[22] This is in direct opposition to Richard's insistence on the absolute identification of his office and himself. Yet Richard himself has jeopardized that identification, I have argued, by being an actor-king; and his full realization of what he has done comes only when the loss is irreparable. Nor is Richard the only loser. Kingship is the play's central idea, and when it becomes relative, not absolute, other absolutes fall with it. One of the play's most striking features is its pervasive self-consciousness about language, from Mowbray's complaint that exile will mean 'speechless death' (I. iii. 172) to the Duchess of

York's comic hammering on the word 'pardon' (V. iii. 110–33). In both cases – since the Duchess is pleading for her son – there is an association between language and life itself. In *Richard III* language conveyed moral absolutes; hence Richard's fear of it. Here, however, it tends to be slippery and elusive, requiring feats of interpretation: 'Ay, no; no, ay; for I must nothing be' (IV. i. 201); 'My gracious lord, I come but for mine own' (III. iii. 196). 'Ay' or 'I'? And what is Bolingbroke's 'own'? It all depends on how you look at it. What the Duchess of Gloucester would call damage the Gardener would call pruning. The question of perception is debated by Gaunt and Bolingbroke: 'Think not the king did banish thee, / But thou the king'; 'O, who can hold a fire in his hand / By thinking on the frosty Caucasus?' (I. iii. 279–80, 294–5). This anticipates the debate over Helen in *Troilus and Cressida*: does value inhere in the object itself, or in the mind's decisions about it? Bolingbroke, who takes the former position, may seem to have the better of the debate (though the rest of the play makes us wonder), but the fact that the debate can take place at all, and be a real one, indicates a loosening of certainty.

The Renaissance was fond of perspective tricks in painting. Perhaps the best-known example is Holbein's *Two Ambassadors*, in which a diagonal blur at the base of the painting, when looked at sideways, resolves itself into a skull. This device is the basis for Bushy's attempt to tell the Queen that her sorrows are illusory:

> For sorrow's eye, glazed with blinding tears,
> Divides one thing entire to many objects,
> Like perspectives, which, rightly gaz'd upon,
> Show nothing but confusion; ey'd awry,
> Distinguish form. So your sweet Majesty,
> Looking awry upon your lord's departure,
> Find shapes of grief more than himself to wail,
> Which, look'd on as it is, is nought but shadows
> Of what it is not. (II. ii. 16–24)

The speech is itself a perspective trick, for Bushy insists, contrary to expectation, that the 'right' view is not the one that reveals the hidden image but the one that conceals it. When concepts like right and wrong, true and false become reversible in this way, it is more than just a painter's trick. So, when we contemplate the two crownless kings, we are looking at a trick picture with disturbing implications. Which is the king? Or is it both? Or neither? One man has stolen the crown, the other has violated it. Change places, and which is the justice, which is the thief?

The dilemma can be resolved only by the crime of murder. In the last scene a stylized, repetitive sequence in which loyal subjects bring good news and the King thanks them is broken and parodied when Exton enters with Richard's body, to be greeted with shock and outrage. On the significance of the killing there is firm agreement between Richard and Bolingbroke, signalled by the echoing language of their last speeches. Richard's words, 'Exton, thy fierce hand / Hath with the king's blood stain'd the king's own land' (V. v. 109–10), lead directly into Bolingbroke's:

> Lords, I protest my soul is full of woe
> That blood should sprinkle me to make me grow ...
> I'll make a voyage to the Holy Land,
> To wash this blood off from my guilty hand.
>
> (V. vi. 45–50)

In his last speech King Henry – as he now unequivocally is – has become identified, as Richard was, with his land. Both are soaked in blood. Blood, as Carlisle predicted, has manured the garden and made him grow. It could only have happened in this way; when he tells Exton, 'They love not poison that do poison need' (V. vi. 38), he admits that he did in fact need it. There is only one king now; the ambiguities and perspective tricks are over. But the clarity that has emerged is the clarity of guilt; the only way in which Henry can imagine to relieve that guilt is to revive the old dream of the crusade. And that dream belonged to Gaunt's England, a kingdom that was not of this world.

# 4

# *Henry IV*

When in his last battle Richard III cries, 'I think there be six Richmonds in the field: / Five have I slain today instead of him' (*Richard III*, V. iv. 11–12), the literal explanation may be that Richmond has disguised several followers as himself. But we do not think of that; we think of Richard's own nightmare: his enemy is indestructible. Richmond is the true king and cannot be killed; we touch here on the theory of the king's two bodies, one of which is immortal. At the Battle of Shrewsbury, which forms the climax of *Henry IV*, Part 1, where Henry has many followers 'marching in his coats', the effect is very different. Douglas declares, 'I will kill all his coats; / I'll murder all his wardrobe, piece by piece' (Pt 1, V. iii. 26–7). The focus is on the disguise as disguise, not on some inner mystery. But the effect is more complicated when Douglas encounters the King himself:

> *Doug.* Another king! They grow like Hydra's heads:
> I am the Douglas, fatal to all those
> That wear those colours on them. What art thou
> That counterfeit'st the person of a king?
> *King.* The King himself, who, Douglas, grieves at heart
> So many of his shadows thou hast met,
> And not the very King. I have two boys
> Seek Percy and thyself about the field,
> But seeing thou fall'st on me so luckily
> I will assay thee, and defend thyself.
> *Doug.* I fear thou art another counterfeit,
> And yet, in faith, thou bearest thee like a king.

(Pt 1, V. iv. 24–35)

The word 'counterfeit' has a special edge, given Henry's dubious legitimacy; and the proliferation of kings suggests he is debasing the coinage by overproduction. But, though he makes it clear he has not sought this encounter, Henry faces his challenger with dignity and courage. Douglas admits that whether he is a true king or not he looks like one. Henry asserts his claim by a mastery of appearances. So he did as Bolingbroke in the previous play. So did Richard II when the sanctity of his office failed him (or, rather, he failed it). In *Henry IV*, as Derek Traversi has observed, 'the traditional sanctions of monarchy are no longer immediately valid, [and] the implications of the royal office need to be reconsidered in a new world of uncertainties.'[1] One implication is that kingship now has to be *earned*; and the mastery of appearances is recognized by both Henry and his son as a principal means of earning it. After the débâcle of *Richard II* it may no longer be possible to *be* a king; the best you can do is look like one. The acting skill Richard II called on in moments of crisis is now simply part of the job.

The rebels are concerned with appearances, no less than the King and his son, and this concern replaces the simpler aggressiveness that drove the rebels of *Henry VI*. When Hotspur promises his colleagues,

> yet time serves wherein you may redeem
> Your banish'd honours, and restore yourselves
> Into the good thoughts of the world again.
>
> (Pt 1, I. iii. 178–80)

we catch echoes from the end of the previous scene, Hal's soliloquy announcing his strategy. Hotspur even uses two of Hal's key words, 'redeem' and 'time' (cf. I. ii. 212). The rebels' calculations before Shrewsbury include considerations of reputation: Worcester thinks Northumberland's absence will make the rebellion look bad; Hostpur argues it will make it look better, showing they can carry on without his help. The anxiety behind these calculations shows that the world of appearances demands tricky manoeuvring; Hotspur says he would praise Douglas properly 'If speaking truth / In this fine age were not thought flattery' (IV. i. 1–2). Besides kingship, there are other kinds of coinage that can be debased. Moreover, the characters' attempts to master appearances are complicated by the fact that they are not in a single world where everyone speaks the same language, but in a fragmented one. This is no longer the tight stage community of *Richard II*, in which all eyes could be fixed on one figure; there, no one, down to the meanest gardener or groom, was excluded from the circle of attention centred on Richard. The world of *Henry IV*, on the other hand, is widely dispersed and richly varied. When Sir Walter Blunt appears in the first scene 'Stain'd with the variation of each soil / Betwixt that Holmedon and this seat of ours' (I. i. 64–5), the lines evoke the physical variety of the land, and anticipate the play's treatment of other kinds of variety. No single image can stand, as did the sea-walled garden of the earlier play, for the entire nation. Similarly, when Mortimer complains, 'My wife can speak no English, I no Welsh' (III. i. 187), this is a simple reflection of a general problem; in other ways, as we shall see, characters in *Henry IV* do not speak each other's languages. (Shakespeare is not just making a cheap joke about political marriages here; through the barrier imposed by language we see the affection of a couple who really wish they *could* speak to each other.)

Misinformation is a recurring motif. Part 2 opens under the aegis of the presenter Rumour with a totally garbled version of the ending of the previous play. Characters are always complaining of being mis-understood or misquoted. In the controversy over whether Hotspur denied the King his prisoners, Northumberland claims they 'Were . . . not with such strength deny'd / As is deliver'd to your Majesty' (Pt 1, I. iii. 24–5), while Hotspur flatly declares, 'My liege, I did deny no prisoners' (I.iii.28), only to admit later that he cannot remember what he said (I. iii. 51–2). Hal blames his troubles with his father on 'many tales devis'd . . . By smiling pickthanks, and base newsmongers' (III. ii. 23–5), and having rescued him at Shrewsbury declares, 'O God, they did me too much injury / That ever said I hearken'd for your death' (V. iv. 50–1). Worcester is wary of any accommodation with the King, because 'Look how we can, or sad or merrily, / Interpretation will misquote our looks' (V. ii. 12–13). By the time John of Lancaster assures the rebels at Gaultree, 'My father's purposes have been mistook' (Pt 2, IV. ii. 56), the complaint has become a regular part of political discourse, and they believe it.

This is a world, then, in which appearances matter, and are not to be trusted. At its centre is the counterfeit king who is the only king England has. He is no longer the quietly expert politician of *Richard II.* At the opening of Part 1 he appears surrounded with his nobles, a familiar image of power and authority, but his first words are 'So shaken as we are, so wan with care' (Pt 1, I. i. 1). He goes on to promise domestic peace and harmony:

> No more the thirsty entrance of this soil
> Shall daub her lips with her own children's blood,
> No more shall trenching war channel her fields,
> Nor bruise her flow'rets with the armed hoofs
> Of hostile paces.                                    (Pt 1, I. i. 5–9)

He sounds like Richmond at the end of *Richard III*; but the promises are all negative, and the placing of the speech at the beginning of the play makes it vulnerable. Plays do not *begin* with reconciliation and harmony; the expectations built into the dramatic form itself sabotage Henry's vision. Richard of Gloucester also began his play announcing peace, but his announcement was frankly ironic, and he was in control of the irony as Henry is not. Elsewhere Henry shows executive firmness and strength of will. But the tact he demonstrated in dealing with the York family in *Richard II* has deserted him, or he no longer bothers to exercise it, in dealing with the Percies. He loses his temper with Worcester and orders him out, cutting off Northumberland in mid-sentence as he does so (I. iii. 10–21). When Blunt proposes a reconciliation, Henry will have none of it; he wants, and gets, a confrontation (I. iii. 69–91). This may be sound strategy in the long run, but the initial impression is of a man whose nerves are on edge. He has also a curious capacity for seeing the bad side even of good news. Told that Hotspur has won a victory on his behalf, he reflects gloomily on the contrast between Hotspur and his son (I. i. 77–85). This deepens in Part 2 into a terrible pessimism, a belief that it is better not to be born at all. If one could 'read the book of fate, / And see the revolution of the times' (Pt 2, III. i. 45–6), then

> The happiest youth, viewing his progress through,
> What perils past, what crosses to ensue,
> Would shut the book and sit him down and die.
> (Pt 2, III. i. 54–6)

Yet his torments are different from those of Richard III on the eve of Bosworth. Richard suffered a sharp and specific guilt; Henry, a deep but curiously unfocused *malaise*. Richard is haunted by his victims and tormented by his deeds; Henry is denied, or denies himself, such moral clarity. If he feels guilty he does not at this point say so.[2]

For one thing – and this reflects the more realistic idiom of this play – Henry does not sense around him the supernatural framework that Richard sees so clearly. He recalls Richard II's prophecy that Northumberland would betray him, but seems to accept Warwick's analysis of it. Richard, like Henry VI, has turned out to be a true prophet. But, while Henry's accuracy can be attributed only to supernatural inspiration, Richard's (Warwick argues) was simply an intelligent observation of the principles of political behaviour; anyone who studies the past carefully can make a fair stab at predicting the future (Pt 2, III. i. 80–92). In place of Richard III's flamboyant defiance of his conscience, we hear Henry's quiet 'Are these things then necessities? / Then let us meet them like necessities' (Pt 2, III. i. 92–3). As we would expect, there is nothing supernatural in his view of kingship. It is, for him, an office to be earned; his persistent habit of comparing Hal with Hotspur leads to one of his most characteristic utterances:

> Now by my sceptre, and my soul to boot,
> He hath more worthy interest to the state
> Than thou the shadow of succession.
> For of no right, nor colour like to right,
> He doth fill fields with harness in the realm.
>
> (Pt 1, III. ii. 97–101)

To reinforce this pragmatic view by swearing on his sceptre and his soul is another of Henry's unconscious ironies. In Part 2 we see what the crown means to him: a possession to be laid on his pillow, like a child's favourite toy. As York in *2 Henry VI* described himself as 'the silly owner of the goods' (I. i. 226) and thus destroyed the dignity of his claim, the language of Henry's rebuke to Hal for stealing the crown is that of a middle-class father whose son has broken into the cashbox: 'How quickly nature falls into revolt / When gold becomes her object!' (Pt 2, IV. v. 65–6). Though he predicts that the orderly succession from father to son will settle the dynastic problem, he also warns Hal that he will have to work to keep his position: 'all my friends, which thou must make thy friends, / Have but their stings and teeth newly ta'en out' (Pt 2, IV. v. 204–5). (This is a sad revelation of what the word 'friend' means in politics.)

The audience, however, may see the guilt behind the pragmatism. Henry has not just worked within the social order, like a successful merchant; he has violated that order. If there is petty thievery on the highways of England there has been grand larceny at Westminster. Falstaff makes the connection for us when he tells Hal, 'thou cam'st not of the blood royal, if thou darest not stand for ten shillings' (Pt 1, I. ii. 136–7). Some awareness of this seems to be at the bottom of Henry's mind, but he has trouble admitting it. He wonders, in a general sort of way, if Hal's misbehaviour is God's punishment 'For some displeasing service I have done' (Pt 1, III. ii. 5); he insists of the usurpation, 'necessity so bow'd the state / That I and greatness were compell'd to kiss' (Pt 2, III. i. 73–4). On his deathbed, alone with his son, he gets closer to a direct confession of guilt, but the language is still oddly evasive:

> God knows, my son,
> By what by-paths and indirect crook'd ways
> I met this crown. (Pt 2, IV. v. 183–5)[3]

We remember Falstaff's jibe against Worcester, 'Rebellion lay in his way, and he found it' (Pt 1, V. i. 28). Only at the end of his last long speech does he see himself as a penitent: 'How I came by the crown, O God forgive, / And grant it may with thee in true peace live!' (Pt 2, IV. v. 218–19). He experiences a twofold release at this moment: from the crown itself, which he gives at last to his son, and from the burden of evasion and double-talk that has gone with it.

If Richard III was haunted by his past, Henry is haunted in a more subtle way, by an impossible dream of the future. At the end of *Richard II* he both admitted his guilt and promised to deal with it by going to the Holy Land, picking up the image of the crusade from his father's vision of an ideal, unreal England. In *Henry IV* the guilt is suppressed almost to the end, and the crusade has become a futile obsession. In the opening scene of Part 1 Henry proclaims the crusade as though it were the main item on his agenda, then adds:

> But this our purpose now is twelve month old,
> And bootless 'tis to tell you we will go;
> Therefor we meet not now.              (Pt 1, I. i. 28–30)

This is more subtly deflating than a simple cancellation would have been. The crusade is put in the category of things that are always *going* to happen, and we sense that Henry's announcement of it has become one of the court's routines.

It is also involved with Henry's manipulation of appearances. Henry, like the other characters of the political scenes, is concerned with how he looks. There is a sharp juxtaposition between Hal's account of his plan to deceive the world and Henry's statement that he has appeared too gentle to the Percies and will now reveal his true authority (Pt 1, I. iii. 1–9). Hal seems confident about his use of appearances; Henry thinks he has fumbled. He also gives his son a lecture on the subject, telling him that he won the people's hearts by carefully rationing his appearances so that he was 'Ne'er seen but wonder'd at' (Pt 1, III. ii. 57), while Richard let people get tired of him. This does not square with what we hear in *Richard II* about Bolingbroke's courtship of the common people: 'Off goes his bonnet to an oyster-wench' (I. iv. 31). One might say that we are not meant to remember the earlier play, and so the inconsistency does not matter. But that argument would be easier to sustain if *Henry IV* as a whole were not so full of detailed recollections of *Richard II*. I think we *are* meant to notice the inconsistency, and to be curious about it. Henry – 'this forgetful man' (Pt 1, I. iii. 159), as Hotspur calls him – is indulging in the politician's trick of rewriting history. He may be revising the past in order to say what he thinks his son needs to hear now; he may even have convinced himself that the past was as he describes it. We do not know, and our ignorance is just the point. Henry is, as Puck called Oberon, a king of shadows. He works by appearance, and the reality behind the appearances becomes increasingly elusive. It is a common observation that someone who begins by lying can end by not knowing whether he is lying or not.

This affects our reception of Henry's final revelation about his crusade:

> I cut them off, and had a purpose now
> To lead out many to the Holy Land,
> Lest rest and lying still might make them look
> Too near unto my state. Therefore, my Harry,
> Be it thy course to busy giddy minds
> With foreign quarrels, that action hence borne out
> May waste the memory of the former days.
>
> (Pt 2, IV. v. 209–15)

If this is to be taken at face value, it is damning. There is no sense of guilt here, and certainly no religious dedication; merely a cynical, self-protective strategy. But is it the whole truth? We sense guilt beneath Henry's *malaise*, and we see it more clearly before the scene is over. In his real anguish at the thought of what may happen to England under his son, we see a king whose concerns are larger than the protection of his own position. If we can carry our thinking back to *Richard II*, the first announcement of the crusade seemed a desperate but sincerely meant response to the shock of Richard's death. As the idea of being a king may have been planted when Bolingbroke saw Richard's apparent power over time, the idea of being a crusader may have been planted when he heard of Mowbray's noble death – and, just possibly, envied it. All this is to infer that the lines of cause and effect in Henry's mind are long and deeply buried. But the inference is not impossible, and Henry's withdrawn, enigmatic character encourages us to think about him in this way. Again, the real point is our final ignorance; Henry's last statement of the motive for his crusade leaves us unsatisfied and unconvinced. Like his earlier speech about how he rationed his appearances, it is designed to make a particular point to his son, and it seems too neat and simple, too obviously *useful*, to be the whole truth. It is possible that this explanation occurs to Henry for the first time just as he utters it. It is also possible that as he utters it he believes it.

Seen in this light, Henry's career has been one long deception, nor has the deception been as simple and controlled as in his moments of apparent revelation he likes to claim. But there is something oddly touching, as well as appropriate, about his end. Learning that he was stricken in the Jerusalem Chamber, he cries:

Laud be to God! Even there my life must end.
It hath been prophesied to me, many years,
I should not die but in Jerusalem,
Which vainly I suppos'd the Holy Land.
But bear me to that chamber; there I'll lie;
In that Jerusalem shall Harry die.

(Pt 2, IV. v. 235–40)

This recalls, and parodies, the machinery of prophecy fulfilled we saw in the first tetralogy. But there is more than cynical amusement in the parody. The old actor is giving his last performance, and there is a paradoxical integrity in his acceptance of his end: the counterfeit king-crusader dies in a counterfeit Jerusalem. He has also achieved in his last days something of Richard II's supernatural rapport with his land. His sickness and the land's are connected, and his death, like Richard's fall, is preceded by portents in the natural world (Pt 2, IV. iv. 121–8). From his first days as king his role has been to put down rebellions, and when the last rebel is quashed his final illness begins. He himself comments bitterly on the coincidence, blaming the unfairness of Fortune (Pt 2, IV. iv. 102–8). But it may be Fortune's way of telling him he has done his job. (There was a similar effect in *2 Henry VI*; as soon as Gloucester was murdered, his old enemy Winchester took to his bed and died.) In the end he himself comes to see his death as the best service he can do for England. Like Henry VI before his murder, he achieves detachment expressed in a theatrical image: 'all my reign hath been but as a scene / Acting that argument' (Pt 2, IV. v. 197–8), the argument of disorder. Now the play is over. He expects nothing for himself: his words, 'all the soil of the achievement goes / With me into the earth' (Pt 2, IV. v. 189–90), suggest that he will not be cleansed, but will take his guilt with him into the grave. But by dying he will cleanse England: 'And now my death / Changes the mood' (Pt 2, IV. v. 198–9). Simply and without fuss he accepts the role of scapegoat. Nothing in his kingship becomes him like the leaving it.

As guilt brought a final clarity to Bolingbroke's relations with Richard in the previous play, so it brings a final clarity to his relations with England here. It means that he has, after all, a mysterious connection with the land, a connection made, ironically, not by his legitimacy but by his usurpation. King and kingdom are sick together, and the one by his death can cure the other. Shakespeare places the final emphasis not here, but on the king of shadows, the old deceiver. But there is enough of the other view of Henry to confirm our impression that he is for the time being the true king of England, and not just because he wins battles. The impression is aided by the fact that the rebels exert no effective counter-claim, either politically or theatrically. The rebels of Part 1 sum up their view of England by dividing it in three, even agreeing after some debate to alter the course of one of its great rivers. As with the abuses of Richard II, we are shocked not just by the action but by the casual way in which they talk about it. In theory, Mortimer has the alternative claim to the crown, for Richard named him his heir (Pt 1, I. iii. 143–55). Yet it is Mortimer who says of the land, with evident satisfaction, 'The Archdeacon hath divided it / Into three limits very equally' (Pt 1, III. i. 68–9). Besides his casual acceptance of the loss of two-thirds of his inheritance, Mortimer, in a play full of lively and sharply defined characters, is very close to being a nonentity. He is a particularly clear example of Shakespeare's technique of measuring political and theatrical authority together.

Mortimer is of course overshadowed, as are the other rebels of Part 1, by Hotspur. Arthur Colby Sprague has commented on the double fate of this character, 'so likable in the theatre, so frequently scolded by scholars'.[4] His strong initial appeal is undeniable, but it is bound up with our misgivings. His dedication to honour is couched in language that is exciting but unconsciously self-critical:

> By heaven, methinks it were an easy leap
> To pluck bright honour from the pale-fac'd moon,
> Or dive into the bottom of the deep,
> Where fathom-line could never touch the ground,
> And pluck up drowned honour by the locks,
> So he that doth redeem her thence might wear
> Without corrival all her dignities.
>
> (Pt 1, I. iii. 199–205)

An honour that has to be fetched from the moon or the depths of the sea is an honour that is lost or at least remote, needing extravagant effort for its restoration. Hotspur's insistence that it cannot be shared means, as we shall see, that his loss to Hal is devastating. Hal's tribute to him as the bravest gentleman 'To grace this latter age with noble deeds' (Pt 1, V. i. 92) suggests a picturesque throwback. In the shadow-world of the Bolingbrokes his absoluteness is refreshing, but it is also a little disturbing. He seems to quarrel for the sake of quarrelling, and admits as much when Glendower gives way on the turning of Trent (Pt 1, III. i. 131–4). It is almost impossible to hold a conversation with him,[5] for – comically and maddeningly – he repeats the same points over and over. Worcester, exhausted by the effort of arguing with him, advises him to return his prisoners to the King 'for divers reasons / Which I shall send you written' (Pt 1, I. iii. 258–9). But in II.iii we see that Hotspur can argue even with a letter.[6]

As the battle approaches, he seems excited not by the thought of achievement but by the thought of destruction: 'Doomsday is near; die all, die merrily' (Pt 1, IV. i. 134). King Henry sinks into despair at the course of his life but finds meaning in his death. Hotspur has a clear centre for his life, his ideal of honour; but when he loses it in death he has nothing left, and when he looks over the edge of his own life his bleak vision is more far-reaching than Henry's:

> But thoughts, the slaves of life, and life, time's fool,
> And time, that takes survey of all the world,
> Must have a stop. O, I could prophesy,
> But that the earthy and cold hand of death
> Lies on my tongue: no, Percy, thou art dust,
> And food for – (Pt 1, V. iv. 80–5)

Hal has to finish the sentence for him. Hotspur does in fact prophesy, though not as Henry VI and John of Gaunt did. His vision of time – the time that, as we shall see, Hal tries to master and redeem – is startlingly close to Macbeth's: a meaningless procession of days that will one day stop. Not end, in some kind of fulfilment, but simply stop. Henry can finally see himself as part of a larger action, and so accept his death. Hotspur, wrapped up in himself, cannot. His has been a brilliant solo performance, going nowhere; a flash of light in a great void.

Hotspur's death leaves the rebels of Part 2 exhausted and enervated. Lady Percy, warm and lively in the first play, has shrunk to a bitter woman who, it seems, does not want the new rebels to succeed where her husband failed. Lord Bardolph argues at length for the sort of caution and prudence Hotspur found so irritating in the letter of the nameless lord. Northumberland, having greeted his son's death with a ranting call for universal destruction, repeats his disappearing act from Part 1 and is finally disposed of, so quickly that we hardly notice, by the shrieve of Yorkshire (Pt 2, IV. iv. 97–9). What energy the new rebellion has is fired by the Archbishop of York, who proclaims a holy war 'with the blood / Of fair King Richard, scrap'd from Pomfret stones' (Pt 2, I. i. 204–5), while expressing contempt for the popular revulsion against Bolingbroke that he himself is exploiting:

> Thou, beastly feeder, art so full of him
> That thou provok'st thyself to cast him up.
> So, so, thou common dog, didst thou disgorge

> Thy glutton bosom of the royal Richard;
> And now thou wouldst eat thy dead vomit up,
> And howl'st to find it.                    (Pt 2, I. iii. 95–100)

In Part 1 the dynastic alternative was Mortimer, who did not seem to notice his own importance. In Part 2 it is the memory of the dead Richard, and we are made to reflect again that Henry is the only king England has.

The last rebellion peters out in the humiliation of Gaultree Forest, which leaves us wondering which is more irritating, Prince John's deviousness or his victims' stupidity. Part 1 built to an exciting climax in the Battle of Shrewsbury; the anticlimax of Gaultree seems designed to counter and parody it, and John's summary catches the tone of the occasion: 'Most shallowly did you these arms commence, / Fondly brought here, and foolishly sent hence' (Pt 2, IV. ii. 118–19). The contrast with Hal's honouring the dead Hotspur is striking. Yet even in Part 1 there was an underlying futility in the rebel cause seen as a whole. The theatrical liveliness of the Glendower scene depends on sharp differences of tone and temperament that augur ill for the rebellion. Worcester's canny self-protective strategies – 'What I have done my safety urg'd me to' (Pt 1, V. v. 11) – end in his death, and he seems unaware of the irony. Northumberland's contribution to any major battle is to be somewhere else. Glendower brings a thrill of Celtic mystery to his one scene, but Shakespeare's treatment of him is delicately balanced between fascination and mockery. He really does seem to have spirit-musicians who play at his command – Hotspur says grudgingly, 'Now I perceive the devil understands Welsh' (Pt 1, III. i. 224) – but he delays his contribution to the rebellion, needing time to muster his 'tenants, friends, and neighbouring gentlemen' (Pt 1, III. i. 86). In the end he 'comes not in, o'er-rul'd by prophecies' (Pt 1, IV. iv. 18). The kindest interpretation is that this figure from the Celtic twilight would be out of place in the pragmatic world of the Bolingbrokes.

As in *Richard III*, England and the audience are in a dilemma. There we were caught between an exhausted Machiavel and an inhuman cycle of nemesis until Richmond came at the last hour to effect a rescue. Here England's choice seems to be a king who can do no more than conduct a holding action against rebellion while proclaiming a crusade that will never happen; and an increasingly fragmented party of rebels who provide no alternative order and become increasingly pusillanimous and futile. A theatre audience naturally looks for an action leading to a climax and a resolution. Quite simply, we want something to *happen*. The best the King can do is die; the rebels just peter out. For some sense of purpose and achievement we look to Hal. If Hotspur's satisfactions belong to the passing moment and Henry's to an ever-receding future, Hal seems to have got time under control. And time is the medium of drama. He is also determined, as an actor would be, to master appearances, and appearances (as we have seen) are the key to public life in the England his father has created. Like Richmond, he is working for a late emergence. The difference is that we *see* him at work. Richmond was held back by the playwright, and was kept deliberately generalized and conventional when he appeared. Hal holds himself back from the other characters but allows the audience to see from the beginning the inner machinery of his transformation from wastrel prince to heroic king. We saw King Henry rewriting history. The rebels do this too: there is a Percy family version of Bolingbroke's return to England in which they are simply his innocent, well-meaning dupes (Pt 1, IV. iii. 56–65; V. i. 30–71).[7] But for characters to rewrite the past, when the theatre audience can check its own memories, simply makes them look futile and duplicitous. Hal sets out not to rewrite the past but to write the future.

At the end of his first scene he makes his intentions startlingly clear:

> I know you all, and will awhile uphold
> The unyok'd humour of your idleness.
> Yet herein will I imitate the sun,
> Who doth permit the base contagious clouds
> To smother up his beauty from the world,
> That, when he please again to be himself,
> Being wanted he may be more wonder'd at
> By breaking through the foul and ugly mists
> Of vapours that did seem to strangle him.
> If all the year were playing holidays,
> To sport would be as tedious as to work;
> But when they seldom come, they wish'd-for come,
> And nothing pleaseth but rare accidents:
> So when this loose behaviour I throw off,
> And pay the debt I never promised,
> By how much better than my word I am,
> By so much shall I falsify men's hopes;
> And like bright metal on a sullen ground,
> My reformation, glitt'ring o'er my fault,
> Shall show more goodly, and attract more eyes
> Than that which hath no foil to set it off.

I'll so offend, to make offence a skill.
Redeeming time when men think least I will.

(Pt 1, I. ii. 190–212)

Hal's promise to imitate the sun takes us back to *Richard II*; but while Richard, as rightful king, was naturally identified with the sun, Hal can only promise to *imitate* it – to produce, as his father did, a good performance in the role of king. In that admission there is satisfying honesty, and the rest of the speech has the same clear-eyed quality. Hal has his father's awareness of how quickly the people get tired of a public figure; but instead of expressing, as the Archbishop of York does, revulsion at the idea, he sets out calmly to deal with it. Henry and Hotspur have become helplessly fixed; Hal will change, not surrendering to the natural vicissitudes of time but using and controlling them. His pragmatism is seen in the movement of the images, from nature to society, and from society to craftsmanship.

Throughout *Henry IV* we are aware of time. The play is full of time signals: 'tomorrow morning, by four o'clock early at Gad's Hill' (Pt 1, I. ii. 120–1). Henry sees even Christ's redemption of mankind not as an ever-present grace but as something that happened 'fourteen hundred years ago' (Pt 1, I. i. 26). Timing, the essential art of the actor, the art of knowing when to make one's move, is equally important. Northumberland chides his son, 'Before the game is afoot thou still let'st slip' (Pt 1, I. iii. 272), and Hotspur has to be dissuaded from beginning the Battle of Shrewsbury the previous night (Pt 1, IV. iii). John of Lancaster rebukes Falstaff, on the other hand, for his 'tardy tricks' (Pt 2, IV. iii. 26–9). Hal is not explicit about when he plans to make his self-revelation, and, as we shall see, this becomes a problem. But he knows that for his strategy to work he must move 'when men think least I will', exploiting the element of surprise. Time is also involved in the keeping of promises and the paying of debts, a recurring motif in both parts. The King, says Hotspur bitterly, 'Knows at what time to promise, when to pay' (Pt 1, IV. iii. 53). Falstaff in the end owes Shallow a thousand pounds, the very sum he tried unsuccessfully to borrow from the Lord Chief Justice (Pt 2, I. ii. 224–5). We know Shallow will never see his money again. Hal is in a way guilty of the same bad debt. He jokingly promises Francis a thousand pounds (Pt 1, II. iv. 60), and Falstaff makes a deeper claim on him:

*Host.* . . . [Falstaff] said this other day you ought him a thousand pound.
*Prince.* Sirrah, do I owe you a thousand pound?
*Fal.* A thousand pound, Hal? A million, thy love is worth a million, thou owest me thy love. (Pt 1, III. iii. 132–6)

The recurrence of this sum is one sign of the interconnectedness of *Henry IV*; and Falstaff's insistence that Hal owes him his love takes the image to a deeper level. Hal does the same, challenging Falstaff:

> *Prince.* Why, thou owest God a death.                                   [*Exit*].
> *Fal.* 'Tis not due yet, I would be loath to pay him before his day –
>                                                           (Pt 1, V. i. 126–8)

As Falstaff is reluctant to recognize this debt, Hal will not recognize his debts to Francis and Falstaff; they are, in their different ways, not serious to him. But he introduces himself to Douglas as 'the Prince of Wales ... / Who never promiseth but he means to pay' (Pt 1, V. iv. 41–2), and he ensures that the money from the Gad's Hill robbery will be paid back 'with advantage' (Pt 1, II. iv. 540–1). His strategy of surprise includes being better than his word: not just paying with advantage, but paying a debt he never promised yet chooses to incur. It is part of his comic predictability that Falstaff will take no debt seriously, whether the creditor is Mistress Quickly, Justice Shallow, or God; Hal is more flexible and discriminating.

He is also looking ahead. Like *Richard III, Henry IV* is full of reminiscence, though in a more realistic vein. Falstaff revives John of Gaunt's own joke about his name (Pt 1, II. ii. 64), and we hear in Part 2 that he was page to Thomas Mowbray, Duke of Norfolk (III. ii. 24–5). Part 2 especially is full of memories, Shallow's and ours. There are detailed recollections of Richard II's entry into London (I. iii. 103–5), his prophecy of Northumberland's treachery (III. i. 57–79), and the lists at Coventry (IV. i. 115–29). As in *Richard III*, this weight of the past, together with the general air of age and sickness that hangs over Part 2, suggests a world becoming exhausted. It matters, then, that, as Robert Hapgood has noted, Hal's 'most important speeches are cast in the future tense'.[8]

All this makes Hal's plan look satisfying. He knows the world he is in and has a strategy for controlling his own appearance in it. Yet there is something unsettling in the sheer neatness of the scheme. It reduces Hal's role and that of his audience to simple absolutes; it imagines one clear moment of revelation. In the boldly stylized world of *Richard III* such thinking might fit well enough. But Shakespeare has drawn a more disorderly, varied, and realistic world in *Henry IV*, and against this background Hal's plan may look not just simple but simple-minded. It is also, for some critics, distasteful. John F. Danby describes it as 'a bold attempt to enlist the machiavel in the ranks of virtue', adding: 'But virtue itself wilts when it is made object of a machiavellian strategy. It sinks to reputation, and that to the acclamation of one's dupes.'[9] As Cecily Cardew says to 'Ernest Worthing', 'I hope you have not been leading a double life, pretending to be wicked and being really good all the time. That would be hypocrisy.' It is worth noting that many critics have refused to take this speech as Hal's statement about himself, preferring to see it as Shakespeare's own reasssurance of the character's reform, for which the character himself is a mere choric mouthpiece.[10] Others have preferred their own explanations to Hal's: he is studying his companions to enrich his own nature;[11] he is going through the career of a morality-play prodigal.[12] These theories and others like them require a rejection of Hal's own statement. Dr Johnson, without restoring to the device of seeing Hal as a choric mouthpiece, finds human and natural reasons for rejecting it: it exhibits, he argues, 'a natural picture of a great mind offering excuses to itself, and palliating those follies which it can neither justify nor forsake'.[13] Hal is, as we would say, rationalizing. This is more convincing, for it confronts the soliloquy directly instead of trying to wish it away. Certainly the character's account of himself seems intolerably narrow. In the slanging matches with Falstaff and the easy chats with Poins, Prince Hal shows a real enjoyment of the Eastcheap world that is outside the bounds of his theoretical scheme.

The speech, then, has given widespread dissatisfaction. But there is no need to retreat to the expedient of seeing it as Shakespeare's utterance, not Hal's. The Bolingbrokes, father and son, regularly offer explanations of their conduct that seem too neat and edifying to be altogether convincing: we see the King do it, in conversation with his son; and I think we see Hal do it here. Each is trying, as a second-rate playwright might, to find a formula that explains everything; behind them stands a playright who does not work in that way. Neither man is necessarily insincere; each may really be describing how he sees himself. But it is worth insisting on the reservations in that last statement. The Bolingbrokes are never more opaque than when they explain themselves. Richard of Gloucester's self-fashioning was convincing because he acted out his vision of himself in a world of myth tuned to his self-image. *Henry IV* does not create such a world, and the Bolingbrokes' attempts to present themselves in neat formulae produce an imaginative resistance that sends us looking for other ways of reading them, a search that produces no certain answers.

There is another problem. Hal's strategy involves reducing his companions to a nameless supporting cast, 'you all'. But the scene that this soliloquy ends has been dominated by the vast bulk of Falstaff. Hal speaks of his companions in the plural; Falstaff is nothing if not singular. The strain we feel in trying to take the soliloquy at face value includes our awareness that Falstaff is just not reducible. This, more than anything, alerts us to the artificiality of Hal's thinking. For the rest of Part 1 especially, Falstaff constantly pulls the focus to himself, not just by his size and energy but by the authority of his mind. If Hal is trying to master time, Falstaff is trying to stay out of it altogether. As 'All-hallown summer' (Pt 1, I. ii. 154–5) he suggests a scrambling of youth and age.[14] His account of his own birth, 'about three of the clock in the afternoon, with a white head, and something a round belly' (Pt 2, I. ii. 186–8), combines a precise timing of the event itself with a claim that, once he was born, time could do nothing more to him: he has always looked like this, and he always will. Hal believes in alternating holidays and workdays, keeping life fresh through variety. Falstaff, as Norman Rabkin puts it, is 'playing holiday every day'.[15] He is supremely indifferent to mere facts:

> *Fal.* ... Give me a cup of sack: I'm a rogue if I drunk today.
> *Prince.* O villain! Thy lips are scarce wiped since thou drunk'st last.
> *Fal.* All is one for that. (Pt 1, II. iv. 149–53)

Living for the moment, he cancels the past as he goes along – or, like the politicians, he revises it: 'These nine in buckram that I told thee of' (II. iv. 206–7). In the dispute over the Gad's Hill robbery, Hal tries to insist on the prosaic facts of arithmetic – 'We two saw you four set on four' (II. iv. 249) – but Falstaff prefers his own higher mathematics. Finally, as Hal deals with the sheriff, Falstaff settles behind the arras and goes to sleep as naturally as a child or a cat.

He also has his own fully worked out philosophy to see him through the war:

> Can honour set to a leg? No. Or an arm? No. Or take away the grief of a wound? No. Honour hath no skill in surgery then? No. What is honour? A word. What is in that word honour? What is that honour? Air. A trim reckoning! Who hath it? He that died a-Wednesday. Doth he feel it? No. Doth he hear it? No. 'Tis insensible, then? Yea, to the dead. But will it not live with the living? No. Why? Detraction will not suffer it. Therefore I'll none of it. Honour is a mere scutcheon – and so ends my catechism. (Pt 1, V. i. 131–41)

The speed and decisiveness of the argument are compelling, but they also suggest the drawing of a tight circle. Falstaff is cutting out any consideration but physical survival. In that way his speech is as reductive as Shylock's insistence on common humanity in physical terms – if you prick us, do we not bleed? if you tickle us, do we not laugh? His awareness of living in a world of detraction is like Hal's; but, while Hal plans to cope with the problem, Falstaff plans to walk away from it. All the same, both Hotspur and Sir Walter Blunt, by lying dead on the stage, make Falstaff's principal point for him in a compelling way. Falstaff's epitaph for Sir Walter, 'there's honour for you!' (Pt 1, V. iii. 32–3), is his way of saying 'QED'. And when in Part 2 Morton says that Hotspur was beaten to the ground 'From whence with life he never more sprung up' (I. i. 111) we remember that Falstaff performed just that impossible feat. His comic resurrection, all the more striking in that the audience does not know he is shamming, signifies a victory over time, fact, and mortality itself; it illustrates his ability – in Part 1, for Part 2 is another matter – to live on his own terms. We recognize the limits of those terms, but we respect their authority.

Right from the start, then, Hal's insistence on playing his life his own way meets with stiff competition, with Falstaff setting up an opposite system of values. In the process we become aware of Hal's limitations. And there are problems throughout. In a key scene in Part 1 Hal mocks both Francis and Hotspur for their comic automatism. Francis, who has 'fewer words than a parrot', when asked 'What's o'clock . . .?' replies, 'Anon, anon, sir' (II. iv. 94–7). Hotspur (whose wife calls him a 'paraquito' – II. iii. 86) is imagined by Hal as a fighting machine who 'kills me some six or seven dozen of Scots at a breakfast, washes his hands, and says to his wife, "Fie upon this quiet life, I want work" ' (II. iv. 100–3), and whose automatic reply to questions is not 'Anon, anon, sir' but 'Give my roan horse a drench' (II.iv.104–5). Against these comic human machines Hal proclaims his own versatility: 'I am now of all humours that have showed themselves humours since the old days of goodman Adam to the pupil age of this present twelve o'clock at midnight' (II. iv. 90–3). But the word 'now' is revealing. This is a temporary mood, a flash of high spirits. Hal's strategy requires him to be a chameleon; but – though he is more flexible than Francis or Hotspur – he does not always take to his adopted roles naturally or convincingly, and in the process he reveals not how full his humanity is, but how limited.

In particular, he is never quite of Falstaff's humour. His wit has a moralizing streak, like the sort of rogue literature that ends with repentance and the gallows. This is the turn he gives to Falstaff's fantasy of thieves as Diana's foresters:

the fortune of us that are the moon's men doth ebb and flow like the sea, being governed as the sea is, by the moon – as for proof now, a purse of gold most resolutely snatched on Monday night, and most dissolutely spent on Tuesday morning, got with swearing 'Lay by!',

and spent with crying 'Bring in!', now in as low an ebb as the foot of
the ladder, and by and by in as high a flow as the ridge of the gallows.

(Pt 1, I. ii. 30–8)

When Falstaff asks, 'shall there be gallows standing in England when
thou art king?' (I. ii. 57–8), Hal's offer of the job of hangman means that
the answer is yes.[16] Unlike his counterpart in *The Famous Victories of
Henry the Fifth*, he never takes easily to the criminal life, much as he
enjoys the informal encounters of Eastcheap. He goes on the Gad's Hill
robbery only because he can see it as essentially a practical joke, and
he insists on paying the money back. Even as a practical joker he gives
Poins a certain amount of initial trouble. His objections to the scheme –
'How shall we part with them in setting forth?'; ''tis like that they will
know us'; 'I doubt they will be too hard for us' (I. ii. 163, 169, 176) – if they
are not designed simply to aid the exposition of the scene, show an
unexpected foot-dragging obtuseness. Though he tries for the rapport
with the common people that Richard of Gloucester so signally failed
to achieve, his amused appreciation of the jargon of the drawers is that
of a collector, an amateur anthropologist studying 'an alien tribe'.[17]

He shows a simpler enthusiasm for dealing with Hotspur, for here he
is moving in his own class. His promise to his father begins with
language of heart-stopping beauty:

> I will redeem all this on Percy's head,
> And in the closing of some glorious day
> Be bold to tell you that I am your son.

(Pt 1, III. ii. 132–4)

Chivalry and piety go together in a vision of achievement that has all
the excitement of Hotspur without his desperation or self-centredness.
But the speech continues, picking up the more prosaic connotations of
the word 'redeem':

> Percy is but my factor, good my lord,
> To engross up glorious deeds on my behalf,
> And I will call him to so strict account
> That he shall render every glory up,
> Yea, even the slightest worship of his time,
> Or I will tear the reckoning from his heart.

(III. ii. 147–52)

The thinking is that of a chivalric hero, but the words belong to the
counting-house. Even his tribute to his fallen rival has an element of
calculation: 'If thou wert sensible of courtesy / I should not make so

94

dear a show of zeal' (Pt 1, V. iv. 93–4). (So far Falstaff was right; it will not live with the living.) We may ask what audience Hal is playing for this time, as he is, so he thinks, alone with a dead man. One passage in the speech suggests he is trying to sit well with himself: 'And even in thy behalf I'll thank myself / For doing these fair rites of tenderness' (V. iv. 96–7). Hal does not give himself wholeheartedly to the achievements of the battlefield, any more than to the pleasures of Eastcheap. They are always secondary to his strategy of manipulating appearances, a strategy so ingrained that it operates even when he is alone.

Up to a point, the killing of Hotspur is the fulfilment of that strategy. The mere promise is enough to win his father over; in fact, Hal gets more than he asks for, not just a chance to prove himself but 'charge and sovereign trust herein' (Pt 1, III. ii. 161). What is implicit here will be explicit in the second reconciliation of the two men, after the crown-stealing:

> O my son,
> God put it in thy mind to take it hence,
> That thou mightst win the more thy father's love,
> Pleading so wisely in excuse of it!
>
> (Pt 2, IV. v. 177–80)

In both scenes the old King is really interested in his son's ability to defend himself, to put a good face on his apparent crimes; and in both cases he is satisfied. He understands the strategy from within, for it is a variation on his own. Vernon stands for the public that is simply impressed: 'England did never owe so sweet a hope / So much misconstru'd in his wantonness' (Pt 1, V. ii. 67–8). Even Hotspur accepts Hal's interpretation of his victory. He too sees it as a game of winner-take-all in which Hotspur has been collecting the prizes and Hal takes them away from him, as he took the booty of Gad's Hill from Falstaff: 'I better brook the loss of brittle life / Than those proud titles thou hast won of me' (Pt 1, V. iv. 77–8). From Hotspur's refusal to share honour (Pt 1, I. iii. 204–5) it follows that, like Brutus in *Julius Caesar*, he cannot imagine 'glory by this losing day' (*Julius Caesar*, V. v. 36). It is all or nothing, and on those terms Hal has won.

His victory caps the *scène à faire* of Part 1. In King Henry's persistent comparison of the two men, always to Hal's detriment, and in the coincidence of the names (emphasized when they meet – Pt 1, V. iv. 58–60), there is the built-in expectation of a showdown. To that extent Hal's strategy and the strategy of the play are in harmony, and with Hotspur's death both strategies achieve their ends. The action is complete – the action, that is, of Part 1. But *Henry IV* is 'both one play

95

and two',[18] and so the Battle of Shrewsbury is both an ending and not an ending. It is preceded by a brief glimpse of the Archbishop of York (Pt 1, IV. iv), anticipating the next rebellion; it is followed by a division of the royal party in three and a promise of further action that puts the achievement of peace, like Henry's crusade, into a receding future: 'Rebellion in this land shall lose his sway, / Meeting the check of such another day' (Pt 1, V. v. 41–2). More strikingly, the clear lines of the encounter between Hal and Hotspur are blurred. As the heroes clash, Falstaff is fighting with Douglas in a comic sideshow to the main event. Falstaff goes one stage further, claiming to have killed Hotspur himself. They fought, he says, 'a long hour by Shrewsbury clock' (Pt 1, V. iv. 147), suggesting a fantasy-time of Falstaff's own devising. And Hal, without batting an eyelid, lets him get away with it. This is bewildering, until we understand that Falstaff is solving a problem for Hal, and for the playright. We return to the question of the timing of Hal's revelation; and we realize that he has not really thought it out. If detraction always attacks the living, Hal should reveal his true virtue when he becomes king, and not a minute sooner. Otherwise he will wear out his reputation too soon, and this is precisely what he is trying to avoid. In taking on Hotspur, Hal has met a challenge to prove himself that he could hardly have refused – his father's bitter admiration for the other man must be galling – but he has blown his cover too early. And so we have an ending that is not an ending, a victory that Hal must achieve and then give away. The very fact that *Henry IV* is a two-part play allows it to reflect the problems of manipulating time. What looks like (and to some degree is) an ending is revealed as a pause *en route*. The survivors of any great achievement have to get up the next morning and begin the rest of their lives.

Hal's prediction that he could work towards a single revelation now appears over-simple; time plays a trick on him, and the challenge comes too soon. In one way he solves the problem by giving the credit to Falstaff. But he is not so flexible that he can now return to Eastcheap on the old terms, and he cannot yet take his proper place at Westminister. As a result he is, in the early scenes of Part 2, a character in limbo. II.ii, in particular, shows him as we have never seen him before – tired, out of sorts, irritable with Poins, unable either to suppress or to satisfy his appetite for small beer (II. ii. 5–6). The details of common life, which it amused him to collect in Part 1, have now become otiose:

What a disgrace is it to me to remember thy name! or to know thy face tomorrow! or to take note how many pair of silk stockings thou hast – viz. these, and those that were thy peach-coloured ones! or to bear the inventory of thy shirts – as, one for superfluity, and another for use! (II. ii. 12–18)

He has lost his feeling of mastery over time and his confidence that he can impress an audience: 'Well, thus we play the fools with the time, and the spirits of the wise sit in the clouds and mock us' (II.ii.134–5). As for the earthly audience of public opinion, the necessity of playing to it now leaves him bitter:

> *Prince.* . . . But I tell thee, my heart bleeds inwardly that my father is so sick; and keeping such vile company as thou art hath in reason taken from me all ostentation of sorrow.
> *Poins.* The reason?
> *Prince.* What wouldst thou think of me if I should weep?
> *Poins.* I would think thee a most princely hypocrite.
> *Prince.* It would be every man's thought; and thou art a blessed fellow, to think as every man thinks. (II. ii. 45–53)

His suppression of natural feeling is consistent with the strategy announced in his soliloquy; but we now realize, and so perhaps does Hal, how abstract and theoretical that soliloquy was, and how little it anticipated the actual cost of distorting his own nature.

His dilemma has become brutal. What he needs now is something he does not want: his father's death. As it will free England from disorder, it will free Hal from play-acting. He approaches the deathbed with a tactless joke that is presumably part of his act, 'How now, rain within doors, and none abroad?' (Pt 2, IV. v. 9). What follows is even more tactless. The crown-stealing, like the surrender of Hotspur to Falstaff, is puzzling until we understand that Hal's timing has gone awry. His belief that the old man is dead is a simple and understandable mistake (he made a similar one at Shrewsbury), but his action in seizing the crown is an impropriety that can be most naturally accounted for, I think, as the reaction to a long period of frustration and impatience. Henry calls attention to the mistiming: 'What, canst thou not forbear me half an hour?' (IV. v. 109). It is also improper for a king to crown himself; he is part of a larger structure of order and law, not a tyrant who for good or ill has achieved the position on his own. In his preoccupation with his own strategy, the need to *earn* his place, Hal has forgotten that; he will make good the omission in the scene with the Lord Chief Justice.

The soliloquy that leads to his self-crowning is a curious mixture of insight and blindness:

> Why doth the crown lie there upon his pillow,
> Being so troublesome a bedfellow?

97

O polish'd perturbation! golden care!
That keep'st the ports of slumber open wide
To many a watchful night! Sleep with it now:
Yet not so sound, and half so deeply sweet,
As he whose brow with homely biggen bound
Snores out the watch of night . . .
                       By his gates of breath
There lies a downy feather which stirs not:
Did he suspire, that light and weightless down
Perforce must move. My gracious lord! My father!
This sleep is sound indeed; this is a sleep
That from this golden rigol hath divorc'd
So many English kings. Thy due from me
Is tears and heavy sorrows of the blood,
Which nature, love, and filial tenderness
Shall, O dear father, pay thee plenteously.
My due from thee is this imperial crown,
Which, as immediate from thy place and blood,
Derives itself to me. [*Putting it on his head*] Lo where it sits,
Which God shall guard; and put the world's whole strength
Into one giant arm, it shall not force
This lineal honour from me. This from thee
Will I to mine leave, as 'tis left to me.       (Pt 2, IV. v. 20–46)

He makes here discoveries we see other kings in Shakespeare make: his father's discovery, and Henry VI's, that the king's life may make him envy the life of a peasant; his father's discovery, and Richard II's, that the king has no power over death. (The image of the feather will return in *Lear*, when another king makes the same discovery.) In offering mourning in return for the crown he is giving vent to the natural grief he has had to suppress. Though the phrasing, as in his dealings with Hotspur, suggests a business transaction, he is achieving a balance between public role and private feeling. Other kings discovered the cares of office after they were crowned; Hal approaches his new role with no illusions on that score. But as soon as he puts the crown on his head he becomes, as his father was earlier, the victim of unconscious ironies. He invokes God's protection as Richard II did, and we know what happened to him; he calls the crown 'this lineal honour', though in his case it is hardly that; and when he promises to leave it to his son 'as 'tis left to me' he seems to forget that he has snatched it. When we last saw the crown change hands, in *Richard II*, the effect was deeply disturbing. There is a similar disturbance here, as we watch it being taken from a living king. That shock is muted, however, for the King looks dead and the man who takes it is his natural heir. What Shakespeare emphasizes instead is that donning the crown seems to affect Hal's mind. He begins, as he did more briefly before the dead Hotspur, to pose to himself, claiming a lineal and divinely sanctioned dignity where the audience has seen at best a pragmatic transfer of power.

Henry's satisfaction that his son can excuse 'so wisely' his stealing of the crown shows the Prince proving himself before a private audience, one that matters deeply. He still has to prove himself, now once for all, to the world. His rejection of Falstaff is the final touch in Hal's shaping of his career, the moment that symbolizes his last surrender of his former self. Yet it also brings to a head whatever misgivings we may have about Hal's strategy: many have found the human cost, to Hal as well as to Falstaff, intolerable. Others, with varying degrees of enthusiasm, have called it necessary. But before I enter this critical minefield I want to raise some other questions that will, I hope, prove relevant to a full consideration of the ending. I have so far said little of a fact that is apparent to all readers and audiences of *Henry IV*: that it seems to be only half a history play. The rest of the space is taken up not just by Falstaff but by the likes of Bardolph, Quickly, Tearsheet, Pistol, and Shallow – characters on whom Hall and Holinshed are silent, but who have an enduring place in the annals of English comedy. The low-life characters are not enlisted as choric commentators, like the Father and Son of Towton or the Gardener of *Richard II*; nor do they mount a direct challenge to political authority, as Cade and his followers do. They inhabit their own fully developed, self-sufficient world. Since that world is largely comic, we have through the two parts an interplay of genres, History and Comedy moving side by side, sometimes working together, frequently going their own ways. The concerns of history we have seen: order and rebellion in the state, public achievements on the battlefield and elsewhere, the gaining and losing of reputation, the manipulation of appearances. The end is the orderly exercise of power. The concerns of the comic world are money (in small quantities), drink (in large quantities), food, song, sex, and laughter. There is no particular end. That in itself disturbs our formula a little, for we are used to seeing comedy tell a story, ending in a marriage or the winning of a game of trickery (usually both). But this is comedy seen not as a certain kind of story but as a certain attitude to life – a concentration on the common and material, and a stance that is light-hearted, irresponsible, and self-gratifying. Falstaff stands for all of this, and this is what Hal must reject in order to prove himself the king the world of history needs. One way of looking at the ending is to say that, while the two genres coexist peacefully for much of the play, Comedy finally steps into the path of History and is crushed.

Seen this way, and bearing in mind the reductive contrivance in Hal's plan for his career, we might say that the human and natural, in Hal no less than in Falstaff, have been suppressed so that Hal can create a public image of himself as a good king. But while it is true that throughout both parts Shakespeare emphasizes the artifice and deception of the political world, or so I have tried to argue, the comic world is not simply free and natural. As in the mature comedies that he is writing around the same period, Shakespeare in *Henry IV* both exploits the spirit of comedy and examines it. The examination, I shall argue, goes beyond Falstaff alone; but it naturally centres on him.

Falstaff, no less than Hal, deals in artifice. The extempore play in the Boar's Head Tavern is a key example. Like so much comedy, it is triggered by nervousness; news of the rebellion has reached Eastcheap, and, as Falstaff puts it, 'thy father's beard is turned white with the news; you may buy land now as cheap as stinking mackerel' (Pt 1, II. iv. 354–6). Besides the possible ruin of England there is the knowledge – for Falstaff, more serious – that Hal will be recalled to his public duties: 'Well, thou wilt be horribly chid tomorrow when thou comest to thy father; if thou love me practise an answer' (II. iv. 368–70). The resulting play is for Falstaff an exercise in reassurance and control. Whether he is playing the King or the Prince he creates a fantasy world in which Falstaff is the centre of attention and royal approval smiles on him. Playing the King, Falstaff tries to drive a wedge between Hal and his real father by mocking his paternity: 'That thou art my son I have partly thy mother's word, partly my own opinion, but chiefly a villainous trick of thine eye, and a foolish hanging of thy nether lip, that doth warrant me' (II. iv. 397–400). Playing the Prince, he rises to this climax:

> but for sweet Jack Falstaff, kind Jack Falstaff, true Jack Falstaff, valiant Jack Falstaff, and therefore more valiant, being as he is old Jack Falstaff, banish not him thy Harry's company; banish not him thy Harry's company, banish plump Jack, and banish all the world.

*Prince.* I do, I will.

> [*Enter*] BARDOLPH, *running.*[19]

*Bard.* O my lord, my lord, the sheriff with a most monstrous watch is at the door.

*Fal.* Out, ye rogue! Play out the play! I have much to say in the behalf
of that Falstaff.  (II. iv. 469–79)

Falstaff's fantasy is challenged from two directions – by Hal's sudden
switch to the future tense, which takes us out of the inner play and
predicts how the play proper will end; and by Bardolph's announcement
that the watch has arrived, which means that yesterday's joke at Gad's
Hill could have serious consequences. Falstaff insists on playing out the
play, but it is clear that the play as he sees it will be just more of the same
– a long oration praising Falstaff. Good listening, of course, but not
much of a play. Falstaff's timeless world is finally undramatic, for
nothing in it can change. It is Hal who is manipulating a drama leading
through time to a climax. Falstaff's fantasy, even more than Hal's
strategy, is too simple to be fully tuned to the world he lives in, and we
see it collapse before our eyes.

Not only that, but the parody interview is succeeded by the real one,
and the arrangement gives the real one the stronger authority. The
effect is that Falstaff is not allowed to come along behind the serious
scene and poke fun at it; the joke is got out of the way first, and then
Falstaff is silenced while Hal and his father play the scene properly.
(*Mutatis mutandis*, there is a similar arrangement in *Paradise Lost*,
where Satan spends the first two books parodying ideas and images
that will be put right by God and Messiah in Book III.) One moment in
particular is worth comment. In III. ii, Henry finds himself, to his
surprise and ours, suddenly in tears as he lectures his son:

> Not an eye
> But is a-weary of thy common sight,
> Save mine, which hath desir'd to see thee more,
> Which now doth that I would not have it do,
> Make blind itself with foolish tenderness.
> (Pt 1, III. ii. 87–91)

The Bolingbrokes tend to address each other as though they were
public meetings, and this revelation of loneliness and hurt affection is
more moving for being unexpected and even embarrassing. Falstaff
has already mocked it: 'Give me a cup of sack to make my eyes look red,
that it may be thought I have wept' (Pt 1, II. iv. 379–81). We enjoy the
joke at the time, partly because it plays on our impression of Henry as
coldblooded. Then we see that we were wrong, and the joke in
retrospect (assuming we remember it) becomes heartless.

There is in fact a critique of comedy going on throughout the play.
What Falstaff does to the King, various characters, and not just the

low-life ones, do to each other. They reduce each other to vivid, amusing caricatures that with our larger view we recognize as over-simple. Comedy is, in *Henry IV*, the medium by which characters misunderstand each other. Hotspur thinks of Hal as a lout who can be 'poison'd with a pot of ale' (Pt 1, I. iii. 230) and so never appreciates what he is really up against. Hal's caricature of Hotspur is close on some points but misses his eloquence, and he is wide of the mark with Lady Percy: ' "O my sweet Harry", says she, "how many hast thou killed today?"' (Pt 1, II. iv. 103–4). She says no such thing, and Hal's idea of a play in which Falstaff will play Lady Percy (II. iv. 107–8) seems designed to crush both characters. In the play as a whole the characters are vividly defined and sharply contrasted. But Shakespeare never simplifies them as they simplify each other. Like other critics, I have commented on Falstaff's attempt to live outside time; but his first line is, 'Now, Hal, what time of day is it, lad?' and Hal's retort, 'What a devil hast thou to do with the time of the day?' (Pt 1, I. ii. 1, 6–7), makes him sound like a tidy-minded critic insisting that Falstaff behave in character.

Comedy, then, can be a barrier to understanding. At some level of their difficult relationship, Hotspur and his wife love each other; that is why it is so painful to watch the relationship falling apart. But Lady Percy's need to be assured of that love is frustrated by her husband's defensive joking. To her plea, 'Do you not love me? / Nay, tell me if you speak in jest or no', he replies with a jest:

> Come, wilt thou see me ride?
> And when I am a-horseback I will swear
> I love thee infinitely.
>
> (Pt 1, II. iii. 99–103)

This is close to the comic *non sequitur* Hal puts in his mouth: 'Give my roan horse a drench.' Amusing though it is for the audience, it is not the kind of answer Lady Percy needs. Right from their first scene, the banter of Hal and Falstaff, with Falstaff demanding Hal's favour and Hal refusing it, reveals the relationship that will end in the rejection. Hal's insults allow him to say in jest what he will one day say in earnest. But the joking manner leaves the relations between the two characters unresolved, allowing Hal to hold off the final reckoning and Falstaff to believe it will never come.

There is a time to joke and a time to be serious; when in the thick of battle Falstaff produces a pistol-case of sack, Hal is not amused: 'What, is it a time to jest and dally now?' (Pt 1, V. iii. 55). Falstaff, an infantryman in an age of chivalry, enters the military world only on his own terms, and those terms do not always work. Nor are they always attractive. When Falstaff stabs the dead Hotspur, we see the logical consequence of his philosophy that 'to die is to be a counterfeit, for he is but the counterfeit of a man, who hath not the life of a man' (Pt 1, V. iv. 114–16). We may have applauded his assertion that life is the only reality, but if that is true it does not matter what you do to a corpse; and, when we see it done, we realize that it *does* matter. Our instinctive revulsion is triggered by one of the few jokes Falstaff makes unconsciously against himself: 'Nothing confutes me but eyes, and nobody sees me' (Pt 1, V. iv. 126–7). There is a flicker of shame here, an acknowledgement that this is a mean, furtive act; and we become aware that *we* are watching him, and judging him.[20] It is typical of Part 1 that the exposure of comedy's inhumanity comes in a single climactic moment. It is typical of Part 2 that the same point is made in a slower and more diffuse way. In Part 1 Falstaff could joke about his unfortunate recruits and we were not much disturbed, for we never saw them. In Part 2 we see them. Falstaff has fun with their names:

> *Fal.* Is thy name Mouldy?
> *Moul.* Yea, and't please you.
> *Fal.* 'Tis the more time thou wert used.
> *Shal.* Ha, ha, ha! most excellent, i'faith, things that are mouldy lack use: very singular good, in faith, well said, Sir John, very well said.
> *Fal.* Prick him. (Pt 2, III. ii. 104–10)

In the contrast between Shallow's rambling delight and Falstaff's curt order the joke suddenly goes cold. Despite their names, these figures are surprisingly resistant to caricature. Mouldy's complaint, 'My old dame will be undone now for one to do her husbandry and her drudgery' (III. ii. 112–13), sounds at first like a marriage joke, but we are made to listen to it again, and we glimpse an unfunny human reality: 'She has nobody to do anything about her when I am gone, and she is old and cannot help herself' (III. ii. 225–7). Feeble, the woman's tailor, cuts through the obvious jokes about his name and profession with his dignified acceptance of his fate. There is a nervous rattle in his voice, but he can say, as Falstaff cannot, 'we owe God a death' (III. ii. 229–30).

As Bergson warned us in his classic essay, laughter is like sea-foam, light and sparkling, 'But the philosopher who gathers a handful to taste may find that the substance is scanty, and the aftertaste bitter.'[21] It is the pause to analyse, to look closely at the cause of laughter, that makes the laughter die. Shakespeare does this with the gulling of Malvolio in *Twelfth Night*, and he does it increasingly throughout *Henry IV*. It is generally observed that in Part 2 Falstaff is losing his immunity to time, feeling age and disease creeping up on him. He is also becoming more analytical. One of his most effective ploys in Part 1 was the posture of innocence; in Part 2 he is more knowing and cynical. He comes to Gloucestershire as an urban con-man, sizing up Shallow and his servants: 'They, by observing of him, do bear themselves like foolish justices; he, by conversing with them, is turned into a justice-like servingman' (Pt 2, V. i. 63–5). Not only that, but he analyses his own comedy:

> I am not only witty in myself, but the cause that wit is in other men. I do here walk before thee like a sow that hath overwhelmed all her litter but one. If the Prince put thee into my service for any other reason than to set me off, why then I have no judgment.
>
> (Pt 2, I. ii. 8–13)

Falstaff is delivering a lecture on the subject of Falstaff. After answering the Lord Chief Justice at cross-purposes, he reveals his method like a magician showing how he does his tricks: 'it is the disease of not listening, the malady of not marking, that I am troubled withal' (Pt 2, I. ii. 120–1). He is also slower. His attack on the passengers at Gad's Hill included the splendid throwaway line, 'they hate us youth!' (Pt 1, II. ii. 81–2). Debating with the Lord Chief Justice, he moves at a much more deliberate pace: 'You that are old consider not the capacities of us that are young; you measure the heat of our livers with the bitterness of your galls; and we that are in the vaward of our youth, I must confess, are wags too' (Pt 2, I. ii. 172–6). Spun out and lacking surprise, the joke loses something the second time around. The lecture on sack seems designed as an encore to the lecture on honour, but, fine though it is, it is more relaxed, lacking the snap and tension of the original (Pt 2, IV. iii. 84–123). Falstaff, like Hal, has problems sustaining his role in a two-part play, and at one point he seems to grumble about being called back for a sequel: 'it was alway yet the trick of our English nation, if they have a good thing, to make it too common' (Pt 2, I. ii. 214–16).

As Falstaff reveals himself we see the consequences of his way of life more clearly, in the fuller view of his recruits, the more detailed treatment of his gulling of Quickly, and the sharper revelation of the mentality behind his trickery: 'Hook on, hook on!' (Pt 2, II. i. 160). The Eastcheap of Part 1 could be seen as an urbanized Robin Hood fantasy world; in Part 2, with its more detailed itemizing of material goods and the transactions they involve, it is more like the London of Middleton. Much of Falstaff's comic power depends on his sustaining a performance, and in Part 2 Hal, now overtly unsympathetic, looks forward to catching Falstaff offstage: 'How might we see Falstaff

bestow himself tonight in his true colours, and not ourselves be seen?'
(II. ii. 162–3). The result is II. iv, a deliberate reversal of II. iv in Part 1. In
place of the brilliant extempore play, we have the seedy theatrical rant
of Pistol; in place of a crowded stage, a small private encounter; and, in
place of the brazen and resilient Falstaff of Part 1, the maudlin appeals
for Doll's pity and the naked confession, 'I am old, I am old' (Pt 2, II. iv.
268). When Falstaff calls for sack and Hal and Poins burst from hiding
crying, 'Anon, anon, sir' (II. iv. 278–9), the old running gag temporarily
lifts the spirits of the scene; but it also reminds us that the best fun is in
the past and cannot be fully recovered. Time has had the last laugh
after all.


To our misgivings about Hal's artificially constructed role, then, we add
misgivings about Falstaff's artificially constructed world of comedy. In
both cases we see the machinery, and its neglect of human reality, a
little too clearly. But *Henry IV* has a third manner, close to comedy and
at times inseparable from it, yet embodying in the last analysis a
different kind of dramaturgy, one that was new to English drama in
Shakespeare's day and is still uncommon. There is a clue to it in the
different structures of the two parts: Part 1 is carefully shaped to the
climax of Shrewsbury (prominently advertised on the title page of the
Quarto); Part 2 is more loose and open.[22] There is another hint in the
language of Part 2. Here Shakespeare shows a new interest in the
rambling, illogical patterns of the human voice: 'Since when, I pray you,
sir? Gods light, with two points on your shoulder? Much!' (Pt 2, II. iv.
129–30). That is Doll attacking Pistol. Here is Bullcalf trying to buy out
his service:

> In very truth, sir, I had as lief be hanged, sir, as go. And yet for mine
> own part, sir, I do not care; but rather because I am unwilling, and, for
> mine own part, have a desire to stay with my friends; else, sir, I did not
> care, for mine own part, so much.                    (Pt 2, III. ii. 217–22)

The Nurse's first long speech in *Romeo and Juliet* anticipated this kind
of writing, but that was more a conscious *tour de force* ; here
Shakespeare seems to be simply standing back and letting his
characters talk. He has no particular designs on them; he does not try to
trigger laughs at particular moments; his own artistry disappears
(though its disappearance is, of course, part of its cunning). When he
comes to Shallow he lets him take all the time in the world, as though
there were no need to finish the play and get the audience home. If we
wanted to pin a label on this third manner we might call it realism, but

105

by its very nature it is better described than defined. It is the drama Chekhov called for: 'A play should be written in which people arrive, go away, have dinner, talk about the weather, and play cards. Life should be exactly as it is, and people as they are – not on stilts.'[23] By this standard, the scenes in Gloucestershire are the best Chekhov that Shakespeare ever wrote.

One function of this manner in *Henry IV* is to disturb any attempt, whether the characters' or ours, to reduce the action to simple paradigms. Whatever formula we or they come up with, there is always something outside it, something that doesn't fit. Given the great variety of *Henry IV* it is understandable that much critical ingenuity (including some of my own in this chapter) has gone into finding its internal connections, thereby reducing the play to a series of patterns. Here, for example, is one critic's reading of the Gad's Hill episode: 'The robbery is manifestly a comically scaled-down version of Bolingbroke's original crime, followed by a matching sequel in which a group of fellow-conspirators attempt to snatch the booty from their successful partners.'[24] Perhaps, but the word 'manifestly' troubles me. In reading or watching the play, do we really feel the pressure of one action on another so clearly as this suggests? There is common material, of course: the concern with honour in Part 1, the general sense of age and sickness in Part 2. But in the movement from one scene to another we are aware not so much of the unity of the play's components as of their independence. King Henry sums up his life with the decisive couplet, 'But bear me to that chamber; there I'll lie; / In that Jerusalem shall Harry die' (Pt 2, IV. v. 239–40), and Shallow immediately wanders on to the stage muttering, 'By cock and pie, sir, you shall not away tonight. What, Davy, I say!' (V. i. 1–2). 'Life goes on' is one way of putting it. (With Shallow, life goes on and on and on.) More important, however, is the sheer *other*ness of the King's subjects, their resistance to any kind of artistic packaging, their refusal to be enlisted in the service of a theme. This was hinted, as we saw, in *Henry VI*, but not much developed there; it is fully developed here. Our first clear example is the Carriers of Part 1, who are too busy complaining about the inn, the horses, the fleas, and the lack of chamber pots to contribute anything to the play's story or its themes. The King has his problems, they have theirs: 'Why, they will allow us ne'er a jordan, and then we leak in your chimney, and your chamber-lye breeds fleas like a loach' (II. i. 18–20). When in Part 2 Henry complains, 'How many thousand of my poorest subjects / Are at this hour asleep!' (III. i. 4–5), the Carriers are likely yawning, scratching, and preparing to set off for London in time 'to go to bed with a candle' (Pt 1, II. i. 42). But we do not have to think as far back as that. At the end of the previous scene we saw Falstaff send for Doll Tearsheet, and we know that two of the King's subjects are not asleep at all.

In Shallow's Gloucestershire the rhythms of life go on, far from the crises of history. Shallow does not attempt either to control time or to ignore it; he acknowledges it – admitting, for example, that Jane Nightwork 'cannot choose but be old' (Pt 2, III. ii. 202) – and lives within it. Old acquaintances are dying, young William is now at Oxford (to his father's cost) and the bucket needs mending. For all his foolishness, Shallow is the one character whose view of time is fully realistic. He touches briefly on one of the themes of Part 2, with its dying king, and then goes back to business: 'Death, as the Psalmist saith, is certain to all, all shall die. How a good yoke of bullocks at Stamford fair?' (III. ii. 36–8). In these scenes Shakespeare seems to be not so much writing a play as reading aloud from the diary of a countryman, an ancestor of Woodforde and Kilvert:

> *Davy.* . . . shall we sow the hade land with wheat?
> *Shal.* With red wheat, Davy. But for William cook – are there no young pigeons?
> *Davy.* Yes, sir. Here is now the smith's note for shoeing and plough-irons.
> *Shal.* Let it be cast and paid. Sir John, you shall not be excused.
> *Davy.* Now, sir, a new link to the bucket must needs be had; and sir, do you mean to stop any of William's wages, about the sack he lost the other day at Hinckley fair? (Pt 2, V. i. 12–23)

There is no judgement, no analysis, no pressure of events, just a savouring of the thing itself.

The contrast with what is happening in London is striking. It is a contrast not just in style or character but in dramaturgy. The new King is working up his most impressive and significant performance, the final triumphant shaping of his own image. He confronts the Lord Chief Justice (Falstaff's old sparring partner), who had committed the Prince for striking him and is understandably anxious about the new reign. Pretending to nurse his old grievance, the King challenges the Justice to defend himself, and the Justice does better than that: he defends the rule of law on which they both depend, the law Falstaff is so eager to set at naught. King Henry not only accepts the defence but submits to the Justice – 'You shall be as a father to my youth' (Pt 2, V. ii. 118) – in token of the King's dependence on the English law (something Richard II did not seem to grasp) and his rejection of his other substitute father, Falstaff. Their dialogue is firmly shaped to convey a message about Henry's view of his kingship, sharpening the message with a contrived but effective surprise; clearly, no one on stage expected the new King to behave like this. But we did, and we see in this moment the fulfilment of the strategy announced in Hal's soliloquy. The pattern is complete. The clarity of the scene tends towards allegory: 'You are right Justice and you weigh this well' (V. ii. 102).[25] The character, who has no proper name, becomes Justice itself; a far cry from Justice Shallow, who has a name of his own and a personality to match.

Justice is the second allegorical figure we meet in Part 2: the play opens with Rumour, who is a conscious throwback to the characterization of the morality plays. There was nothing as abstract as this in Part 1; but Part 2 separates more radically than its predecessor the realistic manner that simply reports on the play's characters and the artificial manner that shapes them into a conscious design. (The fusion of these two methods in Part 1 is best seen in the rebels' argument over the map: the division of the kingdom and the turning of Trent are clear images of the dangers of rebellion, but the style of the dialogue is unbrokenly fluid and realistic.) Rumour makes the audience self-aware:

> But what need I thus
> My well-known body to anatomize
> Among my household?
>
> (Pt 2, Induction, 20–2)

The Epilogue shares with us some now puzzling theatre gossip, including an announcement of Shakespeare's future intentions. In both cases we are made very conscious of being in the theatre – a consciousness that will be developed and extended in *Henry V*. And in V. ii we watch Henry and the Lord Chief Justice act out a brief morality play before our eyes. The scene is both decisive and artificial, and these qualities support each other.

The new King's manner is steady and confident. He is concerned to establish not just his responsibility as king but the continuity of the kingship itself, setting it against the vicissitudes of time, restoring what his father had violated:

> Brothers, you mix your sadness with some fear.
> This is the English, not the Turkish court;
> Not Amurath an Amurath succeeds
> But Harry Harry.                     (Pt 2, V. ii. 46–9)

This is the rhythm of the proclamation 'The King is dead, long live the King', and its air of reassurance is supported by the comforting

Englishness of the name 'Harry'. The new King also sees himself as part of the larger life of the nation:

> The tide of blood in me
> Hath proudly flow'd in vanity till now.
> Now doth it turn, and ebb back to the sea,
> Where it shall mingle with the state of floods,
> And flow henceforth in formal majesty.
>
> (V. ii. 129–33)

Yet here and there we detect a strain. Excusing his stealing of the crown, Hal declares, 'I put it on my head, / To try with it, as with an enemy' (IV. v. 165–6). There are many ways of dealing with an enemy, but making him sit on your head is not one of them. His command of language and imagery is no longer secure. And we see him censoring one of his own images when he tells his courtiers, 'My father is gone wild into his grave, / For in his tomb lie my affections' (V. ii. 123–4). The first line suggests, hauntingly, the old King's death as an unabsolved sinner. But that will not square with the picture of steady continuity Henry is trying to project, and so he gives it a forced interpretation that tidies it up. And his next confrontation will not be with the co-operative allegorical figure of the Lord Chief Justice but with Falstaff.

At this point History clashes with the opposing discipline of Comedy, and the relaxed, undisciplined world of Shallow's Gloucestershire is caught in the crossfire. Part 2, V. iii, opens as one of the pleasantest scenes in Shakespeare. Everyone is slightly muzzy with drink, Shallow is at his most amiable, and Silence blooms quietly and unexpectedly into song. Davy's line, 'I hope to see London once ere I die' (V. iii. 58), suggests the remoteness of the country from the political world. But as Shallow cries, 'Why, there spoke a king. Lack nothing! Be merry!' (V. iii. 67), there is a knock at the door. Pistol – urban, fantastic, spouting old play-tags – has come to announce the accession, and the word 'king' in Shallow's speech suddenly loses its pleasant looseness. Falstaff takes this as the fulfilment of his old dreams, but no messenger is better suited than Pistol to betray the emptiness of those dreams: 'A foutre for the world and worldlings base! / I speak of Africa and golden joys' (V. iii. 96–7). This scene is followed at once by the grimmest of the London scenes, as two beadles – one, evidently, the 'anatomy' of an actor who played the apothecary in *Romeo and Juliet* (V. iv. 29) – arrest Quickly and Tearsheet. After many failures the authorities have finally staged a successful raid on the Boar's Head Tavern. And the reason for the arrest, 'the man is dead that you and Pistol beat amongst you' (V. iv. 17–18), shows that the holiday world of Eastcheap, which is also the world of Shallow's Inns-of-Court memories, of all-night parties and 'bona robas', has shrunk to a grim and dangerous slum. The comic world, seen through the perspective of public, official morality, suddenly looks nasty. That view is dramatized on stage before us, while Falstaff's view of the public world remains a pathetic fantasy. Not only is the new King turning against him; so is the play.

I have said that Shakespeare emphasizes the separateness of the play's different worlds. Falstaff's mistake is to try to force them together, addressing the new King as 'King Hal' (V. v. 41), using a name that belongs only to Eastcheap and will never be heard again, and trying to turn his comic dream of a lawless England into reality: 'Let us take any man's horses – the laws of England are at my commandment. Blessed are they that have been my friends, and woe to my Lord Chief Justice!' (V. iii. 131–4). There is a flicker of resemblance between Jack Falstaff and Jack Cade. What Shakespeare emphasizes, however, is not the danger of Falstaff's ambition but its emptiness. Even as he approaches London, the beadles are at work, clearing the streets of garbage (Doll and Quickly) in preparation for the new King's progress. And Falstaff, waiting for the procession, is flustered and self-conscious as we have never seen him bere: 'O, if I had had time to have made new liveries, I would have bestowed the thousand pound I borrowed of you. But 'tis no matter, this poor show doth better, this doth infer the zeal I had to see him' (V. v. 10–14). He goes on in this vein for several lines, with Shallow reassuring him. When the politicians worry about how they look, they are trying to cope with a world in which such things really do matter. When Falstaff does it, we realize he has strayed into a world in which he is pathetically out of place.

The shameless pathos of 'My King! my Jove! I speak to thee, my heart!' (V. v. 46) releases King Henry's counter-attack:

> I know thee not, old man. Fall to thy prayers.
> How ill white hairs become a fool and jester!
> I have long dreamt of such a kind of man,
> So surfeit-swell'd, so old, and so profane;
> But being awak'd I do despise my dream.
> Make less thy body hence, and more thy grace;
> Leave gormandizing; know the grave doth gape
> For thee thrice wider than for other men.
> Reply not to me with a fool-born jest;
> Presume not that I am the thing I was.
>
> (V. v. 47–56)

Dangerously and unexpectedly, Henry's speech skirts the edge of the old Falstaff comedy. It is as though he is showing off his control by showing how close he can go. But the main effect is a terrible constriction of his own nature.[26] Other characters in Shakespeare have dreams; only Henry professes to despise his. There is also a grim attempt to control the nature of Falstaff, whose name, we notice, Henry never acknowledges; indeed, he reduces him, as he did in his first soliloquy, to a plural pronoun:

> For competence of life I will allow you,
> That lack of means enforce you not to evils;
> And as we hear you do reform yourselves,
> We will, according to your strengths and qualities,
> Give you advancement.                    (V. v. 66–9)

The promise of reform was one of Falstaff's recurring jokes. He was always *going* to reform, just as Henry IV was always going to liberate Jerusalem. But Falstaff truly penitent, secure and coming up in the world, would not be Falstaff at all. The imagination cannot cope with the idea, any more than it can really conceive of Mr Micawber doing well in Australia.[27] Each man tries to crush the other into a fantasy of his own making: King Hal on the one hand, a respectable Falstaff on the other. They have never really spoken each other's language, and now the break between them is complete. In the process the narrowness of each man's imagination, and of the view of life he represents, stands revealed.

'Master Shallow, I owe you a thousand pound' (V. v. 73). Falstaff's flat confession of his debt shows how much he has been drained by his ordeal. It also reminds us that the ruin of his dream includes damage to the peaceful, separate life of Gloucestershire. Standing helplessly on the sidelines in the rejection scene, Shallow looks lost and out of place. His attempts to bring Falstaff to his senses – 'A colour that I fear you will die in, Sir John' (V. v. 87) – and his pathetic appeals to have some of his money back, fall on deaf ears. Henry, of course, shows no awareness of him, and is quite unconscious that in rejecting Falstaff he is breaking Shallow's dream of a friend at court. Shallow has no place either in Falstaff's fantasy of eternal holiday (in his own world Shallow is a realist)[28] or in Henry's tightly controlled, theatrical vision of order. As History and Comedy clash in the persons of the King and Falstaff, Shallow's presence reminds us of a world elsewhere, narrow but palpable and comfortable – a world now painfully remote but clear enough in our memories to alert us to the fact that neither Falstaff nor Henry can stand for all of life, and neither has a full view even of England.

111

There remains one last puzzle, affecting our reading of Henry himself: the Lord Chief Justice's re-entry with the command, 'Go carry Sir John Falstaff to the Fleet; / Take all his company along with him' (V. v. 91–2). ('All', we note, includes Shallow.) Although in those days the Fleet was a comfortable and high-class place as prisons went, this last, unexpected kick delivered in private, after what looked like a decisive and sufficient public rebuke, leaves us wondering. Is Henry acting from a knowledge that Falstaff will not accept the rejection and needs to be held down longer? (Indeed, he seems to be trying to recover his fantasy just before the Lord Chief Justice enters.) Is he giving vent, as Bradley suggested, to an anger he did not show in public?[29] Is he reacting to an unresolved tension in himself? We do not know. Indeed, we cannot even be sure the order is Henry's own. The Bolingbroke paradox is with us again: Henry, in becoming a clear and decisive public figure, is simultaneously becoming more hidden than ever as a man. The two processes are one. It is worth nothing that, as his accession approaches, other characters speculate, as critics have been doing ever since, about what he is really up to in Eastcheap. Falstaff, recalling the gardening imagery of *Richard II*, subscribes to the theory that he is enriching his nature: 'for the cold blood he did naturally inherit of his father he hath like lean, sterile, and bare land manured, husbanded, and tilled, with excellent endeavour of drinking good and good store of fertile sherris' (IV. iii. 116–20). Warwick has a different theory of the self-education of the Prince: 'The Prince but studies his companions / Like a strange tongue' (IV. iv. 68–9); his father sees him as simply a man of mixed nature, potentially good but given to passion and needing careful handling (IV. iv. 20–41). As in the case of Hamlet, characters in the play, no less than readers and audiences, have their theories about the Prince.[30] But, as the explanations mount, the character disappears behind the public mask.

Falstaff and his company are carried to the Fleet. Doll and Quickly have already been cleared away. It is as though the whole vast, sprawling world of the *Henry IV* plays, so resistant to any kind of neat packaging, is being tidied up at last by force. Henry has called his dedication to the national life a return to 'the state of floods' (V. ii. 132); Pistol hears in the noise of the coronation the roaring of the sea (V. v. 40). But the impression of size and grandeur is offset by an impression of shrinkage. We are left with only two characters on stage, the Lord Chief Justice and John of Lancaster. The one, who has stood up to Falstaff with good temper and a wit of his own, is the attractive face of authority; the other, after Gaultree, is the unattractive one. Together they celebrate the new reign, but John's is the dominant voice. Even

Rumour, who opened Part 2 with a fine bit of chaos in the field of information, is brought under control when John says:

> I will lay odds that, ere this year expire,
> We bear our civil swords and native fire
> As far as France. I heard a bird so sing,
> Whose music, to my thinking, pleas'd the King.

(V. v. 105–8)

At the opening of Part 1 King Henry declared that the armies of England would 'March all one way' (I. i. 15), to Jerusalem. That was an impossible dream. But Henry V will revive that ideal in a more worldly and attainable form. He has just demonstrated his ability to shape his own career; he will now turn that ability to the shaping of a great national enterprise. But the cost to his own full humanity, and the full humanity of England, continues to disturb us. *Henry IV* shows the limits of any clear, shaping vision, whether that of History or Comedy, Hal's exercise in self-fashioning or Falstaff's eternal holiday. Even the two-part form is significant, for here (by contrast with the method of *Henry VI*) the first part seems complete in itself, and then the material spills over into a sequel longer and looser than the original. The problems of the dramatic form reflect the provisional nature of any achievement in a world where the final reality is time.

# 5

# *Henry V*

*Henry V* presents the anatomy of a war. We see the causes and the aftermath, the leaders and the common soldiers, the heroism that lives in legend and the grumbling, sickness, and petty crime that generally do not. Only strategy and tactics are underplayed. Shakespeare is more interested in the feelings and imaginations of his characters than in the way they move on a map – just as in *Richard II* he was more interested in the mentality that led the King to abuse his office than he was in the abuses themselves. The play's function as anatomy is connected with its episodic quality. We are not so much following an action as looking all round a subject, often in a discontinuous way. This includes not only characters and events but attitudes towards them, even ways of dramatizing them. *Henry V* provides evidence that can be used in a wide variety of readings, from romantic celebration to ironic satire. In that way it anatomizes not only its subject but the possible responses of its audience. In criticism and performance it becomes, perhaps more obviously than any other play of Shakespeare's, a way of revealing the biases of its interpreters.

As a patriotic pageant it gives a view of the past very different from the view in previous history plays. When York attacked Richard II for betraying the standards of his grandfather, Edward the Black Prince, the moment was typical in its contrast of a heroic past and a diminished present (*Richard II*, II. i. 171–85). Early in *Henry V*, on the other hand, Canterbury exhorts Henry:

> Look back into your mighty ancestors:
> Go, my dread lord, to your great-grandsire's tomb,
> From whom you claim; invoke his war-like spirit,
> And your great-uncle's, Edward the Black Prince.
>
> (I. ii. 102–5)

Edward can be revived; he is no longer a lost hero but an inspiration to

114

achievement in the present. In the process, the dynastic problem created by Bolingbroke's usurpation is forgotten. Ely, supporting Canterbury's exhortation, does not examine the lines of Henry's family tree in any detail. The blood is the same; that is enough:

> You are their heir, you sit upon their throne,
> The blood and courage that renowned them
> Runs in your veins.                    (I. ii. 117–19)

The continuity that matters lies in the office and the tradition of valour Henry has inherited. We are close to Henry VI's description of Richmond as framed by nature to be England's king.

Even the knockabout comedy of the scene where Fluellen forces Pistol to eat a leek ends with an assertion of the importance of the heroic past. Gower draws the moral as a lesson to Pistol to respect 'an ancient tradition, begun upon an honourable respect, and worn as a memorable trophy of predeceased valour' (V. i. 73–5). Henry represents that 'predeceased valour' come to life again. Recalling the terrible achievements of the Black Prince at Crécy, the French King warns his nobles, 'he is bred out of that bloody strain / That haunted us in our familiar paths' (II. iv. 51–2).[1] England itself becomes a magic kingdom. Scotland, Ireland, and Wales send representatives to support it;[2] even traitors profess delight at being caught (II. ii. 161–4). The divisions we have seen in previous plays are replaced, as at the end of *2 Henry IV*, by a common purpose: 'So may a thousand actions, once afoot, / End in one purpose' (I. ii. 211–12); 'Therefore let every man now task his thought, / That this fair action may on foot be brought' (I.ii.309–10). It is, we note, *action* that brings England together. England is unified not by what it is but by what it is doing: 'They sell the pasture now to buy the horse' (II. Chorus, 5). The land itself, a garden in *Richard II* and a suffering body in *2 Henry IV*, has become simply a resource to feed the action. The national imagination has been fired to the point of ecstasy: even before the war begins, the hearts of Henry's followers 'have left their bodies here in England / And lie pavilion'd in the fields of France (I. ii. 128–9). The French make their contribution to this patriotic fantasy. In *Henry VI* and *King John* the French, like all sensible people, speak English. In *Henry V*, especially when alarmed or excited, they break into French; and it seems to be Princess Katharine's native language. This sense of the Frenchness of the French has an initially comic effect, especially in Pistol's scene with Monsieur le Fer, but it also gives them a quality of otherness. Bickering and leaderless on the eve of Agincourt, they greet their first setback with 'The devil take order now!' (IV. v. 22), and the next we hear they have attacked the boys and the luggage. The contrast with the unity and control of the English under a strong leader is obvious. Against Henry's promise –

> he to-day that sheds his blood with me
> Shall be my brother; be he ne'er so vile
> This day shall gentle his condition.
>
> (IV. iii. 61–3)

– we set the concern of the French Herald Montjoy to separate the corpses into classes: 'For many of our princes – woe the while – / Lie drown'd and soak'd in mercenary blood' (IV. vii. 77–8). At certain points the French seem to be comic-book villains who make satisfyingly foreign noises when defeated. At others they display dignity and intelligence (this is true especially of the King and the Constable), but these qualities are clearest at moments when they show their respect for Henry and his followers.

Part of the excitement of Agincourt is the contrast between the small, tattered English army, 'warriors for the working-day' (IV. iii. 109), and the vastly greater numbers of the French, gorgeously overdressed and arrogant: 'let us but blow on them, / The vapour of our valour will o'erturn them' (IV. ii. 23–4). This is the eternal satisfaction of watching Jack kill the Giant. War is also the Great Game. Henry responds to the Dauphin's present of tennis-balls by challenging him to a set that 'Shall strike his father's crown into the hazard' (I. ii. 263), and tells his men at Harfleur, 'I see you stand like greyhounds in the slips, / Straining upon the start. The game's afoot' (III. i. 31–2). Excitement is not the only feeling to be played on. The deaths of York and Suffolk are frankly sentimental: 'The pretty and sweet manner of it forc'd / Those waters from me which I would have stopp'd' (IV. vi. 28–9). The French are allowed epic dignity when their King goes through a roll-call of the nobility, and the names themselves produce a sudden charge of excitement (III. v. 40–7).[3] The dignity turns sombre when Henry reads the names of the dead at Agincourt (IV. viii. 82–114). The disproportion in the casualties – 10,000 French to 29 English – produces a feeling of shock even in the victors. Henry's immediate reaction is to ascribe the victory to God, and there seems (on the evidence of the play) no other explanation. In *Richard II* God seemed deaf to all invocations, and York concluded bitterly, 'Comfort's in heaven, and we are on the earth' (II. ii. 78). Here, at a time of violent action, God seems to have drawn suddenly close to human affairs, and Henry, whose earlier invocations may have sounded perfunctory, is not just gratified but stunned:

116

> be it death proclaimed through our host
> To boast of this or take that praise from God
> Which is his only.                    (IV. viii. 116–18)

The campaign ends with a formal celebration of God's action: 'Do we all holy rites: / Let there be sung "Non nobis" and "Te Deum" ' (IV. viii. 124–5).

Fairy-tale excitement, epic dignity, religious awe: the play gives us all of these, drawn together in the myth of the hero-king. But we also see the grubby reality. The unglamorous side of the war is evoked in the stage direction '*Enter* KING HENRY ... *and his poor soldiers*' (III. vi. 89SD). Sickness spreads through the army (the historical Henry would die of camp fever), and Grandpré's gloating over the English includes a memorable description of their sick horses (IV. ii. 46–52). Faced with the prospect of carnage, Henry cleverly turns it into a threat that the smell of English corpses 'shall breed a plague in France' (IV. iii. 103), but in doing so he evokes a real horror, the stench of a battlefield when the game is over. France has its revenge in a small way when Doll dies 'i' the spital / Of malady of France' (V. i. 85–6); the nationality of the pox is an old joke, but in this case it connects the spread of disease with the war. Army surgeons do not just deal with wounds. The play also reminds us that between the crises of a war there are long, dreadful periods of waiting: the night before Agincourt seems to stretch for ever, and the French and English are equally on edge. The French while away the time with a convincing barrack-room conversation whose principal themes are sex and horses. The rhetoric of war in the largest sense includes not only patriotic speeches like Henry's great battle orations but a good deal of swearing and grumbling.[4] For every utterance on the level of 'Once more unto the breach' there must be thousands on the level of 'By Cheshu, I think a' will plow up all if there is not better directions' and 'By Chrish, la! tish ill done: the work ish give over' (III. ii. 67–8, 91–2). On this level of war, official history is generally silent; *Henry V* is not.

But at least Fluellen and Macmorris, authors of the complaints just quoted, are committed to the war. Pistol and his companions are in it for their own reasons, delicately suggested in Pistol's 'I shall sutler be / Unto the camp, and profits will accrue' (II. i. 111–12). But though Pistol exhorts his friends, 'Let us to France; like horse-leeches, my boys, / To suck, to suck, the very blood to suck' (II. iii. 56–7), they seldom rise above the level of stealing lute-cases and fire-shovels (III. ii. 44–9). The Boy has an even better idea: 'I would give all my fame for a pot of ale, and safety' (III. ii. 12–13). In *Henry IV* the low life of Eastcheap went its

117

own way till the final disaster. In *Henry V* the Eastcheap characters are more directly touched by history, enlisted in the great national enterprise. But they keep their own interests and voices. They die off one by one, as though history is determined this time to crush them slowly and thoroughly; but Pistol remains. Like Parolles in *All's Well That Ends Well* and Pompey in *Measure for Measure*, he is a survivor:

> Well, bawd I'll turn,
> And something lean to cut-purse of quick hand.
> To England will I steal, and there I'll steal:
> And patches will I get unto these cudgell'd scars,
> And swear I got them in the Gallia wars.
>
> (V. i. 89–93)

The grubby life of the underworld not only survives but retains its power to mock respectability. Pistol settles into a parody of the boasting old veteran of the St Crispin's Day speech.

As he did in *Richard II* and will do again in *Coriolanus*, Shakespeare gives us early in the play a set piece describing the ideal state. In each case the vision of perfection is at odds with the intractable human reality shown by the play as a whole. Appropriately for a play that presents an anatomy, the state is seen by Exeter as a body: 'While that the armed hand doth fight abroad / Th'advised head defends itself at home' (I. ii. 178–9). Exeter's concern with the state in action, each part in harmony with the others, leads into Canterbury's extended description of the bees' commonwealth:

> Therefore doth heaven divide
> The state of men in divers functions,
> Setting endeavour in continual motion;
> To which is fixed, as an aim or butt,
> Obedience: for so work the honey-bees,
> Creatures that by a rule in nature teach
> The act of order to a peopled kingdom.
> They have a king and officers of sorts;
> Where some, like magistrates, correct at home,
> Others, like merchants, venture trade abroad,
> Others, like soldiers, armed in their stings,
> Make boot upon the summer's velvet buds;
> Which pillage they with merry march bring home
> To the tent-royal of their emperor:
> Who, busied in his majesty, surveys
> The singing masons building roofs of gold,

> The civil citizens kneading up the honey,
> The poor mechanic porters crowding in
> Their heavy burdens at his narrow gate,
> The sad-ey'd justice, with his surly hum,
> Delivering o'er to executors pale
> The lazy yawning drone. (I. ii. 183–204)

The emphasis on action is characteristic of the play; everyone is *doing* something, and the penalty for doing nothing is death. The key word, isolated at the beginning of a line, is 'Obedience', for this is what such order depends on. The issue of obedience will return, however, in Henry's debate with his soldiers on the eve of Agincourt, and we shall see that it is not so simple a virtue for men as it seems to be for honey-bees. As the speech progresses, its tone becomes increasingly light and jocular, crossing the border from a serious political lesson to a comic fantasy like Mercutio's Queen Mab speech. The comedy does not, as in Menenius' fable of the belly, sharpen the lesson; it seems more a decoration, even a distraction. The fantasy is not the serious fantasy of Gaunt, taking us to a higher level of imagination. Like Drayton's *Nimphidia* it has about it a disconcerting touch of Walt Disney. In theory this speech presents a working model of the ordered, effectively functioning state that is the play's ideal for England; but when ranked with equivalent speeches in other plays – Gaunt's England, Cranmer's prophecy of Elizabeth – this is the hardest to take seriously.

Looking at the speech with twentieth-century eyes, we note that the bees are (as we would say) exploiting their environment. But pillaging the countryside is part of a system that includes creativity in town, 'The singing masons building roofs of gold'. There is no disturbance here. The play's second set piece about a kingdom, Burgundy's lament for France, gives us only ruin:

> Her vine, the merry cheerer of the heart,
> Unpruned dies; her hedges even-pleach'd,
> Like prisoners wildly overgrown with hair,
> Put forth disorder'd twigs; her fallow leas
> The darnel, hemlock and rank fumitory
> Doth root upon, while that the coulter rusts
> That should deracinate such savagery. (V. ii. 41–7)

The suggestion of human breakdown is developed in what follows:

> Even so our houses and ourselves and children
> Have lost, or do not learn for want of time,

119

The sciences that should become our country,
But grow like savages, as soldiers will
That nothing do but meditate on blood,
To swearing and stern looks, diffus'd attire,
And every thing that seems unnatural.

(V. ii. 56–62)

The picture of the disordered garden we saw in *Richard II* has become a larger picture of destruction embracing the land and the people. Henry has done what the Gardener wanted: he has ordered the garden of England – including, in the arrests at Southampton, some necessary pruning. But the result is that he has ruined the garden of France. In each case the effect of the set piece is not to summarize but to disturb, one by implication, the other directly. Canterbury's formula is too neat to account for our responses to the likes of Pistol and Bardolph, not to mention the late Sir John Falstaff, who would surely be executed as drones in this commonwealth – as some of them are in Henry's. Burgundy's speech disrupts our enjoyment of the English victory by reminding us that the French are people with a land and culture of their own, which the war has ruined.

The celebration of order is jocular and leaves us detached; the vision of ruin, taken by itself, is sombre and persuasive. Yet Burgundy has to compete with the charm and glamour of the victorious Henry. His speech, no less than Canterbury's, is challenged by its context. This throws the problem out to the audience: what is our final judgement of the war? Is Burgundy's speech a minority report, to be listened to respectfully and then shelved, or does it overturn the play's apparent satisfaction at Henry's achievement? The problem of interpreting the play, of judging between the heroic and the realistic visions, comes down to the question of how we put things together. It appears at the end – how do we relate Henry to Burgundy? – and it appears, most strikingly, at the very beginning, as we examine the cause of the war. After the stirring invocations of the Prologue, the play opens unexpectedly with a bit of backroom politicking by two very worldly sounding bishops. They are threatened with a bill that will strip the church of a large part of its possessions, applying the proceeds to such unchurchly ends as the King's honour and the relief of the poor, aged, and sick. They see their best hope in the favour of the King, who is not only 'a true lover of the holy Church' (I. i. 23) but has received an offer of massive clergy support for his war with France (I. i. 79–83). Through the bland ecclesiastical manner we glimpse the eternal cynicism of the backroom politician: they assume the King can be bought. Yet in the

120

following scene, when Canterbury expounds the Salic law to assure Henry he has a valid claim to France, there is no mention of the bill against the clergy. Holinshed makes the connection, telling us that in the excitement of war preparations the bill was set aside;[5] Shakespeare leaves the issue hanging. How, then, are we to judge Canterbury's encouragement of the King? Is it simply a piece of political jobbery? Or do we accept the legal argument as valid, dismissing his motives for putting it forward as secondary to the main question? This is bound up with the problem of the Salic law speech itself. It presents two perfectly clear arguments: that the Salic land is not France, and that French kings have in the past taken inheritance through the female line as valid. Put as baldly as this, the case is simple; but the speech is so overlaid with incidental detail that it *sounds* confusing, and the line 'So that, as clear as is the summer's sun' (I. ii. 86) seems to invite the laugh it usually gets. Which quality should be uppermost, clarity or muddle?[6] Finally, what do we make of the fact, never mentioned in the play, that if inheritance can pass through the female line then Henry has no right to the throne of England?

The play's episodic quality leaves us to make connections for ourselves, and leaves us wondering which connections to make. In theatrical tradition the Boy is killed onstage; but in the text he tells us at the end of IV.iv that he is going to guard the luggage, and Gower announces in IV. vii, ' 'Tis certain there's not a boy left alive' (IV. vii. 5). We have to make the connection ourselves. This case is relatively easy. But does Henry's order to kill the French prisoners mean that Pistol (who in the Quarto greets the order with a cry of 'Couple gorge!' but is not even on stage in the Folio) kills Monsieur le Fer? Assuming he does, Gary Taylor takes it as a surprising insight into his character, for in killing his prisoner Pistol is losing ransom money that would have set him up nicely; having exercised the play's key virtue of obedience, he returns to England destitute.[7] What do we make of the fact that Henry's attack on Scroop is framed by the two scenes of the death of Falstaff? What Robert Ornstein makes of it is that Quickly's affection for the man who mocked and cheated her shows up very well against Henry's unforgiving tirade.[8] Do we connect Henry's promise, in the St Crispin's Day speech, that the survivors will have something to boast of with his later order that boasting will be punishable by death (IV. viii. 116–18), and so accuse him of hypocrisy? Or do we conclude that Henry was not expecting a victory that was so obviously the hand of God, and that circumstances alter cases?

As the last two examples show, the more we put things together, the more critical and satiric the play becomes. The patriotic reading means

121

being swept along by the flow of the play, taking each moment as it comes; the critical reading means stopping and speculating, ferreting in the cracks between scenes, noting silences and omissions – like the conspicuous absence of the Dauphin in the last scene, when his inheritance is being given away. (Or is it conspicuous? Do we even think of him?) The whole play can be made decisively ironic by making a connection back to *2 Henry IV*, seeing Henry as taking his father's advice to busy giddy minds with foreign quarrels. On this reading, the fact that this motive is never mentioned only makes the cynicism deeper. There is also the question of how the comic characters function. There is a mischievous juxtaposition between the departure of Pistol and his comrades for the war and the opening of the next scene with the French King's announcement, 'Thus comes the English with full power upon us' (II. iv. 1). But if there is satire here it is not clear whether the English or the French are its targets. When Bardolph opens III.ii with 'On, on, on, on, on! to the breach, to the breach!' (1–2), we may take this as a parody of Henry's speech in the previous scene, or as a sign of that speech's power to inspire even the basest of Henry's troops. Other parallels between high and low life are equally uncertain in their effect. As Henry unifies England, Bardolph reconciles Pistol and Nym so that they can go to France as 'three sworn brothers' (II. i. 12). As at Harfleur, we wonder whether Henry's achievement is being parodied or confirmed by its low-life shadow. Fluellen admires Pistol's eloquence (III. vi. 64–5), as Canterbury and the audience admire the King's. But he is quickly disillusioned. Should we take this as simply a sign that Pistol's rhetoric and the King's are not to be compared, or should we take the parallel to its logical conclusion?

The play not only persists in raising such questions but at one point actually dramatizes the problem – possibly for our guidance. Fluellen's comparison of Henry with Alexander the Great may be a parody, as T. J. B. Spencer suggests, of the historical method of parallel lives Shakespeare found in Plutarch.[9] But it also plays on the whole critical activity of parallel-hunting, and the initial effect is ludicrous: 'There is a river in Macedon, and there is also moreover a river at Monmouth ... and there is salmons in both' (IV. vii. 27–32). Just as we are relaxing – and, if we have been doing this kind of thing throughout the play, starting to laugh at ourselves – Fluellen compares Alexander's killing of Cleitus with Henry's turning away of the old fat knight whose name Fluellen cannot remember. But we remember instantly. And, while our memories are working, Gower's apparently sensible objection, 'Our king ... never killed any of his friends' (IV. vii. 42–3), is answered by the voice of Mistress Quickly, earlier in the play: 'The king has killed his heart' (II. i. 88). Minutes before this, Henry has ordered the killing of the French prisoners, a desperate and controversial act that Shakespeare could easily have omitted if he had wanted our view of the King to be simple. The human cost of Agincourt is related to the human cost of the self-fashioning that has made Henry what he is. If this scene is a clue for the audience – and I think it is – what it tells us is that while the critical activity of making connections between unlike things may occasionally look silly it is always worth risking. We must discriminate, and be on the lookout for forced and arbitrary parallels; but our memories were given us for a purpose, and in watching this play we are meant to use them. Quite simply, the lapse in Fluellen's memory – 'I have forgot his name' (IV. vii. 52) – makes us aware of the functioning and the value of ours.

The Chorus also makes the audience self-aware, as we find ourselves comparing our readings with his. If we really are concerned with making connections, as I think we should be, we find him at times surprisingly unreliable. His claim that the French 'Shake in their fear, and with pale policy / Seek to divert the English purposes' (II. Chorus, 14–15) is too simple an account of the French response, which includes intelligent military preparation and over-confident boasting. The Chorus's announcements of what is coming are often baffled by events: he leaves us unprepared for the first bishops' scene, the first Eastcheap scene, and the leek-eating scene, all of which come immediately after he has told us (incorrectly) where the play is going next. The Chorus to Act II is particularly odd, with the announcement, 'the scene / Is now transported, gentles, to Southampton' (34–5), followed by clumsy second thoughts: 'But, till the king come forth, and not till then, / Unto Southampton do we shift our scene' (41–2). We find ourselves in Eastcheap. Granted that Shakespeare himself may have changed his mind in the course of writing, the effect of a crude patch-up could have been avoided so easily that we wonder if it is deliberate.

More overtly, the Chorus makes us compare what we are told to imagine with what we actually see, and thus alerts us to the inadequacies of the theatre:

> can this cockpit hold
> The vasty fields of France? or may we cram
> Within this wooden O the very casques
> That did affright the air at Agincourt?
>
> (Prologue, 11–14)

Agincourt itself, he complains, will be fought with 'four or five most vile and ragged foils' (IV. Chorus, 50). As in *Richard II*, theatre degrades. It also omits. The Chorus talks of things we cannot see – a fleet in the Channel, Henry's return to England, the opening of peace negotiations. Some of this we have no particular desire to see, and the Chorus to Act V especially makes us feel we are examining the chippings on the floor of a sculptor's studio. Some of it we see anyway, through the Chorus's words, and here his more positive function comes into play. The passages that work best – the descriptions of the fleet and of the two camps the night before Agincourt – do so because they fire our imaginations in response. The Chorus's function is not just to complain of the inadequacies of the theatre but to enlist us in the effort to overcome them: 'Piece out our imperfections with your thoughts . . . For 'tis your thoughts that now must deck our kings' (Prologue, 23, 28). He works on us as Henry works on his men.[10]

In the Chorus to Act III we are asked not only to imagine the English expedition but to join it:

> Follow, follow!
> Grapple your minds to sternage of this navy,
> And leave your England. (17–19)

The Chorus goes on to appeal like a recruiting sergeant to the audience's pride and manhood (20–4). Then, by a stage trick, the charm seems to work, and imagination begets reality:

> the nimble gunner
> With linstock now the devilish cannon touches,
>                   [*Alarum, and chambers go off.*
> And down goes all before them. Still be kind,
> And eke out our performance with your mind.
>                                          (32–5)

As Hippolyta puts it, it must be our imaginations and not theirs. But their stage effects, simple though they are, co-operate to make us believe that our imaginations are working, our minds and the performance are becoming one.

This is very different from the critical detachment, the standing back to put two and two together, that is, I have argued, an important part of our experience of the play. The Chorus's role as patriotic spokesman is connected with his technical function of sweeping us along, filling in the gaps between acts, precisely those gaps where our questions occur. A full reception of the play demands both engagement and questioning; and the common factor is that we are aware, as in *Richard III*, of our activity as audience. The play in a sense is about us – our judgements, our imaginations. The first tetralogy ended with the emergence of a great mythic figure. So does the second, but the differences are crucial, and they are not just the differences between villain and hero. Both are figures of considerable scale, and both are great manipulators. But while Richard III was stylized and simplified, and subject to a clear judgement from within the play, which included our own withdrawal from him, Henry is varied and elusive, and while the judgement of the play seems to go all one way – 'Praise and glory on his head!' (IV. Chorus, 31) – the judgement in the audience's mind is allowed to be more open and questioning. In *Henry IV* we found both Hal and his father hard to read, hard to judge. Here our difficulties are compounded, for the play is so thoroughly Henry's story that the problem of interpretation affects every area of it. To a degree unusual even for him, Shakespeare is setting the material before us, leaving its contradictions intact, and inviting us to make of it what we can. This effort must be centred on Henry himself.

The Chorus tells us that, if Shakespeare had a kingdom for a stage and princes to act,

> Then should the warlike Harry, like himself,
> Assume the port of Mars; and at his heels,
> Leash'd in like hounds, should famine, sword, and fire
> Crouch for employment.             (Prologue, 5–8)

This is the superhuman figure we hear of at the opening of *1 Henry VI*: 'His brandish'd sword did blind men with his beams: / His arms spread wider than a dragon's wings' (I. i. 10–11). But this is precisely the figure the stage cannot and will not show. On 'this unworthy scaffold' (Prologue, 10) there has to be an ordinary, life-sized actor. Shakespeare accepts – more gladly, I think, than the Chorus does – that to put Henry in the theatre is to make him human. The limits of time are also important. Henry commits himself to a single action, all or nothing:

> or there we'll sit,
> Ruling in large and ample empery
> O'er France and all her almost kingly dukedoms,
> Or lay these bones in an unworthy urn,
> Tombless, with no remembrance over them.
>             (I. ii. 225–9)

The myth Henry hopes to create concerns not his office but himself. Richard II was concerned with being a king; Henry is concerned with winning or losing a war. He will be, according to the outcome of his own efforts, a hero or a forgotten man.

Richard's range of performances was limited: the Lord's anointed and the suffering victim. He showed an actor's versatility only in his prison soliloquy, for him a nightmare of indecision. Henry is naturally, endlessly versatile. Canterbury describes him as a man for all occasions:

> Hear him but reason in divinity,
> And, all-admiring, with an inward wish
> You would desire the king were made a prelate:
> Hear him debate of commonwealth affairs,
> You would say it hath been all in all his study:
> List his discourse of war, and you shall hear
> A fearful battle render'd you in music:
> Turn him to any cause of policy,
> The Gordian knot of it he will unloose,
> Familiar as his garter; that, when he speaks,
> The air, a charter'd libertine, is still,
> And the mute wonder lurketh in men's ears,
> To steal his sweet and honey'd sentences.
>
> (I. i. 38–50)

What Canterbury emphasizes is the King's eloquence; he always has the right words. Like Tamburlaine, he conquers not just with his sword but with his language. But, while Tamburlaine was obsessed and single-minded, Henry is flexible. Tamburlaine swept across the map as an irresistible force; Henry works on different people in different ways. We have evidence of his ability to make just the right impression when Canterbury describes his reaction to the bill against the clergy:

> He seems indifferent,
> Or rather swaying more upon our part
> Than cherishing th'exhibiters against us.
>
> (I. i. 72–4)

The appearance of sympathy, but no real commitment – Henry is canny. And Fluellen might note that while Alexander cut the Gordian knot Henry unties it.

Arresting the conspirators at Southampton, he contrives a little morality play (recalling the scene with the Lord Chief Justice), which uses theatrical trickery and surprise to highlight his mercy and justice and their unworthiness. He insists there is nothing personal in it; he is doing what law and the kingdom's safety require (II. ii. 174–7). His most

126

bloodthirsty utterances are controlled by the demands of the occasion. His response to the Dauphin's insulting gift of tennis-balls may sound like a tantrum, but it is shaped by the wit of the tennis analogy and ends with an acknowledgement of the rights of ambassadors: 'So get you hence in peace' (I. ii. 294). His notorious threat to Harfleur, in which the fine fighting animals of 'Once more unto the breach' become murderous thugs who will run wild if the town does not surrender, is followed, once the surrender has been achieved, by Henry's command to Exeter, 'Use mercy to them all' (III. iii. 54), and his weary recognition of his real position: 'The winter coming on and sickness growing / Upon our soldiers, we will retire to Calais' (III. iii. 55–6). The terrible cruelty of the speech is introduced by Henry's statement of his role, 'as I am a soldier, / A name that in my thoughts becomes me best' (III. iii. 5–6), and switched off as soon as it has served its purpose. With Montjoy Henry plays, attractively, the gallant underdog, not glossing over his difficulties but putting the best face on them. His tribute to the herald, 'Thou dost thy office fairly' (III. vi. 145), is the greeting of one professional to another.[11]

Responsible statesman, bloody conqueror, good fellow – Henry plays them all. His most surprising and controversial performance is his last. Wooing Katharine, he presents himself, eloquently and at length, as a plain blunt man with no command of language. The last feat of eloquence, of course, is to make itself disappear. But this time we are more aware than usual of the pressure of a contrary reality behind the performance. With self-effacing charm Henry begs Katharine to accept him; but he has the whip-hand, and they both know it. The man who declared in the first act, 'France being ours, we'll bend it to our awe / Or break it all to pieces' (I. ii. 224–5), is now in a position to make that boast good. We see the true relations between Henry and the French when the French King, trying to preserve a shred of dignity, holds out on a small but significant piece of protocol, the addressing of letters. He will yield, he says, if Henry asks him to; the unspoken message is that it would be gracious of Henry not to ask. Henry's reply is soft but firm: 'I pray you then, in love and dear alliance, / Let that one article rank with the rest' (V. ii. 363–4). The disparity between the true relations of victor and vanquished and Henry's pose as wooer is made clear from the outset:

> *K. Hen.* Yet leave our cousin Katharine here with us:
>     She is our capital demand, compris'd
>     Within the fore-rank of our articles.
> *Q. Isa.* She hath good leave.

> [*Exeunt all but King Henry, Katharine, and Alice.*
>
> K. Hen.                                         Fair Katharine, and most fair,
>   Will you vouchsafe to teach a soldier terms
>   Such as will enter at a lady's ear
>   And plead his love-suit to her gentle heart?          (V. ii. 95–101)

This time we cannot miss the connection. The words 'capital demand' start an undercurrent that runs through the scene. In reply to Katharine's question, 'Is it possible dat I sould love de enemy of France?', Henry is cheerfully frank: 'in loving me, you should love the friend of France, for I love France so well that I will not part with a village of it; I will have it all mine' (V. ii. 174–80). Katharine's replies are for the most part guarded – 'I cannot tell wat is dat'; 'I cannot tell'; 'I do not know dat' (V. ii. 183, 203, 221) – and when she pays Henry a compliment it is somewhat backhanded: 'Your majesté 'ave fause French enough to deceive de most sage damoiselle dat is en France' (V. ii. 229–30). Actresses can play the Princess as charmed, attracted, even flirtatious; the words will allow that. But all the bare text conveys at her moment of surrender is a recognition of political reality combined with Canterbury's virtue of obedience:

> K. Hen. . . . wilt thou have me?
> Kath. Dat is as it shall please de roi mon père.
> K. Hen. Nay, it will please him well, Kate; it shall please him, Kate.
> Kath. Den it sall also content me.                    (V. ii. 260–4)

Her surrender is sealed with a significant gesture. Henry refuses to respect the French custom that unmarried ladies do not kiss; with the words 'therefore, patiently and yielding' (V. ii. 291) he kisses her on the mouth, and she is silent for the rest of the play.

Why did Shakespeare choose to end Henry's career in this way? The scene can look flat on the page, and critics frequently see it as a sad and puzzling let-down. But in the theatre, played by a witty and attractive actor, it is often the climax of the evening. It is not just the last in a string of Henry's performances; in a number of important respects it is special. Nowhere else in the play does the actor have so many chances to get laughs; this draws the audience to the character more directly than before, as we feel his control working on us.[12] At the same time we see more fully than ever that it *is* a performance: the disparities between role and reality are, I have suggested, unusually clear. On both counts it is an effective way of summing up the public Henry: a performance, but a powerful one. It is also an effective way of summing up the war with France. The Chorus has complained that the theatre cannot do battles properly; and in fact we never quite see Agincourt. At the centre of the great battle sequence in the Olivier film is a single combat between Henry and the Constable, in which Henry's victory stands for the English victory as a whole. Shakespeare could not give us anything like Olivier's cavalry charges and flights of arrows; but he could give us, as he did in *Richard III*, something like that scene. Instead, Henry sets out to battle, there are alarums and excursions, then Pistol captures Monsieur le Fer, then we see the French in panic and disarray – and we realize with a shock that Pistol and le Fer stand for the great English victory.[13] Our imaginations, we feel, may have to work overtime on this one. There are more alarums, and there is a certain amount of confusion. In one of the play's most realistic touches, Henry does not realize he has won until Montjoy tells him so (IV. vii. 85–8). He has barely started to savour his victory when he has to be polite to Fluellen, who is rattling on about the good service the Welsh did at Crécy (IV. vii. 94–119).[14] We see the tension before the battle, and the aftermath of victory; we never quite see the victory itself.

Where we see Henry win France is in V. ii, at the moment when he plants a kiss on the lips of the French Princess. The connection is suggested when Henry's victory at Harfleur is followed by a scene in which the Princess decides she had better learn English – 'il faut que j'apprenne à parler' (III. iv. 4–5)[15] – surveying the parts of the body and ending with bawdy puns on 'le foot et le count' (III. iv. 57). Henry has listed the rape of virgins among the atrocities he will unleash at Harfleur; after the town falls, the French complain that their women are threatening to 'give / Their bodies to the lust of English youth' (III. v. 29–30). Bourbon tries to rally his fellows after the first disaster at Agincourt:

> And he that will not follow Bourbon now,
> Let him go hence, and with his cap in hand,
> Like a base pandar, hold the chamber-door
> Whilst by a slave, no gentler than my dog,
> His fairest daughter is contaminated.
>
> (IV. v. 12–16)

Conquest and disgrace in battle have their sexual counterparts; and in V. ii. itself the word-play on 'maiden cities' that 'war hath never entered' (V. ii. 344, 340–1) encourages us to see the connection. Having conquered France, Henry conquers Katharine; the second event stands for the first, and is easier to show in the theatre. The peace is cemented by treaty, and Henry will marry Katharine, not rape her; yet we have seen an element of enforcement in both cases, and while there is much talk at the end of a marriage of kingdoms (V. ii. 366–86) the bride and groom, like Mortimer and his wife, do not speak the same language. The fact that the wooing is conducted mostly in English suggests the usual fate of a conquered people.

Henry impresses us, then, through a series of performances; and his climactic performance, like the opening performance of Richard of Gloucester, is a wooing scene, an act of persuasion. This also suggests something about the nature, and the means, of his victory. We hear little of the technicalities of war. Henry's principal strategy is summed up in the words 'All things are ready, if our minds be so' (IV. iii. 71). His petition to God is 'steel my soldiers' hearts' (IV. i. 295). His address to them at Harfleur reads like instructions to an actor, including a strong sense of decorum, of what is proper to the occasion:

> In peace there's nothing so becomes a man
> As modest stillness and humility:
> But when the blast of war blows in our ears,
> Then imitate the action of the tiger;
> Stiffen the sinews, conjure up the blood,
> Disguise fair nature with hard-favour'd rage.
>
> (III. i. 3–8)

The ferocity of the fighting man is a disguise, something laid on top of his ordinary nature. He expects of his men something of his own capacity to behave as the situation requires; and he knows that, if ferocity were to be man's normal state, life would sink to the level of horror described in Burgundy's speech. Agincourt presents a different problem, and requires Henry to inspire his men in a different way. Here the overwhelming odds and the fear of certain death pose a threat to morale. While Hotspur at Shrewsbury roused his fellows with the cheerful cry, 'Doomsday is near; die all, die merrily' (*1 Henry IV*, IV. i. 134), Henry asks his men to imagine themselves back in England, enjoying the 'pot of ale, and safety' the Boy longed for at Harfleur:

> He that shall see this day, and live old age,
> Will yearly on the vigil feast his neighbours,
> And say, 'Tomorrow is Saint Crispian':
> Then will he strip his sleeve and show his scars,
> And say, 'These wounds I had on Crispin's day'.
> Old men forget; yet all shall be forgot,
> But he'll remember with advantages
> What feats he did that day.                    (IV.iii.44–51)

Henry's phrasing implies a realistic admission that not everyone will survive; without that the speech would not be so persuasive. But its main effort is to make the idea of survival concrete. The scene is domestic and familiar, a far cry from the heroics of Harfleur, and the old veteran is made more convincing by Henry's joking suggestion that he will exaggerate a little. But like the scene at Harfleur it shows Henry's awareness that his principal task is not the arrangement of his soldiers on the field but the preparation of their minds.

Henry asks his men to imagine themselves as something different: tigers, greyhounds, old men. He asks of them, in other words, the versatility he shows himself. That versatility prompts the question: is there an essential Henry? Is there a man behind the public performances? One of his conversations with Fluellen raises the problem with special urgency:

> *Flu.* . . . the duke hath lost never a man but one that is like to be executed for robbing a church: one Bardolph, if your majesty know the man: his face is all bubukles, and whelks, and knobs, and flames o' fire; and his lips blows at his nose, and it is like a coal of fire, sometimes plue and sometimes red; but his nose is executed, and his fire's out.
>
> *K. Hen.* We would have all such offenders so cut off: and we give express charge that in our marches through the country there be nothing compelled from the villages, nothing taken but paid for, none of the French upbraided or abused in disdainful language; for when lenity and cruelty play for a kingdom, the gentler gamester is the soonest winner. (III. vi. 103–18)

As in his scene with the Lord Chief Justice, Henry stands for the principle of law, and he adds to it a principle of the conduct of war. But we feel like shouting at him, 'Dammit, it's *Bardolph*!' Of that fact, Henry shows not a flicker of recognition. Though Fluellen himself does not know it, his words 'if your majesty know the man' are a direct challenge. We know the importance of our memories; how good is Henry's? As Hal, he joined in the jokes about Bardolph's face that we are now hearing for the last time. Actors may fill in the moment with recognition of one kind or another;[16] what Shakespeare gives us is a deliberate silence, a refusal to acknowledge private life. Henry's own account of his self-control suggests it is enforced: 'our passion is as subject / As is our wretches fetter'd in our prisons' (I. ii. 242–3). But the control is so complete that no effort actually shows. There seems to be a formal surrender of private life in Henry's attack on Scroop. Scroop appeared to be the ideal friend – dutiful, grave, learned, noble, and, like

Horatio, no slave to passion (II. ii. 127–37). Scroop was also, Henry declares, a man who knew him intimately: 'Thou that didst bear the key of all my counsels, / That knew'st the very bottom of my soul' (II. ii. 96–7). The breaking of this ideal friendship is for Henry 'like / Another fall of man' (II. ii. 141–2). Throughout the play as a whole, Henry has no relationships; all his encounters with other characters are exemplary, designed to illustrate a point. Is Henry's relation with Scroop any different? The answer, I think, is no. Its sheer formality makes it hard to feel there was ever a real friendship to be betrayed; Scroop is not so much a man as an example. The scene is framed by the death of Falstaff, as though to remind us of a much fuller relationship, one whose course and end could not be seen so reductively.

We need to look for the private Henry, assuming there is one, on the eve of Agincourt. On the edge of action – 'Brother John Bates, is not that the morning which breaks yonder?' (IV. i. 85–6) – Henry tries to snatch a few minutes' solitude, and we realize that we have never seen him alone: 'I and my bosom must debate awhile, / And then I would no other company' (IV. i. 31–2). But solitude does not come easily; he keeps running into other people. Nor can he really shed his identity, despite his borrowed cloak. His encounter with Pistol may suggest a reversion to his Eastcheap past, but not if we remember that Hal and Pistol never met. When Henry introduces himself as 'Harry le Roy' we realize (assuming our French is better than Pistol's) that his present identity and public role are very much in place. Even his attempt to assert the King's common humanity is equivocal: 'I think the king is but a man, as I am: the violet smells to him as it doth to me; the element shows to him as it doth to me; all his senses have but human conditions: his ceremonies laid by, in his nakedness he appears but a man' (IV. i. 101–6). Only in that last touch, when he comes down to Lear's bare forked animal, does he see the King as simply 'a man'. But that is to go from one abstraction to another, from the role to the species. If somewhere in this process there is an individual, we have missed him. This apparently private scene only confirms that Henry is the King, and that his life consists in dealings with others. Those dealings involve a necessary distance, as we see when Williams speculates that the King will allow himself to be ransomed:

> *K. Hen.* If I live to see it, I will never trust his word after.
> *Will.* You pay him, then! That's a perilous shot out of an elder-gun, that a poor and a private displeasure can do against a monarch.
> (IV. i. 202–5)

Henry imagines that a common subject can pass judgement on a monarch, and the common subject finds the notion ridiculous.[17] The later development of the two men's relations confirms this distance: the glove trick is a practical joke conducted by remote control, and ends with Henry giving Williams a substantial tip.[18] The soldier's refusal of Fluellen's much smaller tip (IV. viii. 70) is in all likelihood the defiance he would like to utter to the King but knows he cannot.

The true relations of king and subject are authority and obedience. For Bates this is a comfort: 'If his cause be wrong, our obedience to the king wipes the crime of it out of us' (IV. i. 133–4). We see here that obedience is an equivocal virtue, freeing underlings from moral responsibility. Williams takes the argument a stage further, insisting that all responsibility for the carnage of war finally falls on the king: 'if the cause be not good, the king himself hath a heavy reckoning to make' (IV. i. 135–6). The subject may be free, but the king is trapped. At last Henry is touched on a nerve, and a number of other moments fall into place around this one. Throughout the play Henry is touchy on the question of responsibility, always trying to shift the burden – to Canterbury, for inciting him to war; to the Dauphin, for sending him the tennis-balls; to the French King, for resisting his claim; to the citizens of Harfleur, for presuming to defend their town (I. ii. 18–28; I. ii. 282–4; II. iv. 105–9; III. iii. 1–43).

His occasional deference to God (I.ii.289–90) may be another way of easing the burden. Henry has taken so much on himself that the thought of an authority above him may console him as it does Bates. Yet the burden of responsibility cannot finally be shifted; it can only be limited. Henry cannot, and does not, refute Williams's insistence that he is responsible for the war; he only jibs at the further implication that he is responsible for the souls of men who do not die in a state of grace: 'Every subject's duty is the king's; but every subject's soul is his own' (IV. i. 182–4). In the great doom picture that opens his speech, Williams imagines the soldiers as suffering victims with bereaved families, guilty only of the violence that war has made them commit (IV. i. 135–46). Henry imagines them, or some of them, as escaped criminals whom God will punish, using war as an opportunity to make good the lax judgements of men (IV. i. 163–74). Each man's view has its own narrowness; there is, as we see elsewhere, a distance between them. Williams's view is from the streets, Henry's from the bench. And their debate is conducted in general terms that make it seem, like Henry's other encounters, an illustration of a principle. But the fact that Williams has touched on something personal is hinted by the illustration Henry uses to begin his argument: 'So, if a son that is by his father sent about merchandise do sinfully miscarry upon the sea ...' (IV. i. 150–1).

The mercantile image is part of the Bolingbroke style we remember from *Henry IV*; but why son and father, not just master and servant? Is it because Henry himself has been sent on a dangerous errand by his father, who instructed him to busy giddy minds with foreign quarrels? Or is the mission his father gave him kingship itself? The recognition of Henry as not just king but son flickers only for a moment, and very lightly; it will return at the end of the scene.

Finally alone, Henry complains bitterly of Williams's attempt to put everything on him:

> Upon the king! let us our lives, our souls,
> Our debts, our careful wives,
> Our children, and our sins lay on the king!
> We must bear all. O hard condition!
> Twin-born with greatness, subject to the breath
> Of every fool, whose sense no more can feel
> But his own wringing.                    (IV. i. 236–42)

The echoes of Williams's speech (IV. i. 135–49) are direct, and his reference to Williams as a self-centred fool is bitter and unfair; Henry is giving way for once to an anger that makes him unreasonable. But he does not say this time that Williams is wrong. He goes on to complain that the only compensation for his burden is ceremony. Richard II saw the symbols of his office as essential signs of its divine sanction. Henry sees them as external trappings: 'The intertissued robe of gold and pearl, / The farced title running 'fore the king' (IV. i. 268–9).[19] He complains of ceremony, as Falstaff did of honour, that it hath no skill in surgery: 'Canst thou, when thou command'st the beggar's knee, / Command the health of it?' (IV. i. 262–3).[20] Like his father, he protests that the common people can sleep better than he does. All this is fairly generalized; but what follows is startlingly particular:

> Not to-day, O Lord!
> O not to-day, think not upon the fault
> My father made in compassing the crown!
> I Richard's body have interred new,
> And on it have bestow'd more contrite tears
> Than from it issued forced drops of blood.
> Five hundred poor I have in yearly pay,
> Who twice a day their wither'd hands hold up
> Toward heaven, to pardon blood; and I have built
> Two chantries, where the sad and solemn priests
> Still sing for Richard's soul. More will I do;

> Though all [that] I can do is nothing worth,
> Since that my penitence comes after all,
> Imploring pardon.                                    (IV. i. 298–311)

This man who keeps shifting responsibility to others is himself haunted by the guilt of a crime he did not commit. The lineal succession he boasted of at the end of *2 Henry IV* included more than the crown. On the eve of his great victory his mind goes back to the past, and he reveals that the problem created in *Richard II* has not been solved and may be insoluble. It seems to bother no one else in the play; but it bothers him. Why does Henry connect his inherited guilt and his war with France? He does not say explicitly, but we may make the connection ourselves. Kingship can never again be the sacred office it was for Richard; the best it can be is a vehicle for worldly achievement, and on those limited but real terms Henry is determined to restore it, to undo the damage his father did – if only the guilt incurred when the office was desanctified does not hold him back.

The look back to *Richard II* is the furthest reach of the play's historical vision. The furthest reach of its personal vision is the discovery of Henry's spiritual isolation. He is convinced that the ceremonies of prayer, like the ceremonies of kingship, are in his case worthless. To the official loneliness of a king is added the more terrible spiritual loneliness of a man convinced that his prayers are not being heard. Whatever he achieves in the world must be set against this. Surrounded by the praises of men, Henry is finally aware of the silence of God. Yet the routines of prayer go on, and Henry promises, 'More will I do'. At the end of the scene we have our final insight into him, when his brother Gloucester calls him: 'I know thy errand, I will go with thee: / The day, my friends, and all things stay for me' (IV. i. 313–14). He finally accepts, as calmly as his father accepted the role of scapegoat, that the whole burden of his kingship falls on him. There is none of the plaintiveness of Hamlet's 'The time is out of joint. O cursed spite, / That ever I was born to set it right' (I. v. 196–7). He has faced his pain, complained of it, found it incurable, and accepted it. This is what lies behind the panache and high spirits of his public performances: a man who has seen through his life to a point at which another man might despair, and is determined to carry on. He carries on alone; his own brother is merely a voice calling him to duty. Like Hotspur's last speech, his prayer ends with an incomplete line, but this time there is no one to finish it for him. The scene as a whole has insisted that Henry's kingship is inescapable; even the private man is defined by it. While Henry envies the life of the peasant, his own imagination – throwing up images like

135

'vacant mind' and 'distressful bread' (IV. i, 275–6) – tells him he could never live it. His father's references to 'smoky cribs' and 'loathsome beds' (*2 Henry IV*, III. i. 9, 16) show a similar realism; neither man sentimentalizes the life of the poor as Henry VI does. But of course the question goes deeper than class. Richard II's kingship was unremovable because of its sanctity; Henry's is unremovable because it is a lifelong duty. Like his subjects, he is a man under obedience.

As a hero who brings English history to a moment of triumph, he is like Richmond, but of course we never see into Richmond in this way. Nor does Richmond seem subject as Henry is to the workings of time. Shakespeare carries over from *Henry IV* the sense of time as ultimately ruinous, making any achievement provisional and temporary. Even at Agincourt the first flush of victory simply means new effort: 'Well have we done, thrice-valiant countrymen: / But all's not done; yet keep the French the field' (IV. vi. 1–2). We go to the deaths of York and Suffolk, the order to kill the prisoners, and the attack on the luggage. The follow-up to the first excited realization that the English are doing well is by turns painful, brutal, and squalid. When Henry himself jokingly claims a Falstaffian immunity to decay, the effect is to remind us of his mortality: 'But, in faith, Kate, the elder I wax the better I shall appear: my comfort is, that old age, that ill layer-up of beauty, can do no more spoil upon my face' (V. ii. 240–3). It didn't. Not long after his marriage to Katharine, he was dead. His achievements died with him. His astonishing victory at Agincourt may or may not be a sign that God has answered his prayer and released him from his father's guilt; it is one of those connections we are not sure whether to make. What is clear is that there was to be no release for England. Cambridge's hint of a deeper reason for his treachery than the gold of France (II. ii. 155–7) is a cryptic reference to the unsolved dynastic problem that will surface again in the Wars of the Roses. Later in the play, faint but deliberate memories of *Henry VI* are stirred. Henry's list of the heroes of Agincourt, 'Bedford and Exeter, / Warwick and Talbot, Salisbury and Gloucester' (IV. iii. 53–4), is also a list of names familiar from the earlier plays. Henry's dream of reviving the crusade, another inheritance from his father, produces the sharpest irony of all: 'Shall not thou and I, between Saint Denis and Saint George, compound a boy, half French, half English, that shall go to Constantinople and take the Turk by the beard?' (V. ii. 215–18). Henry, we notice, does not offer to go on a crusade himself; perhaps he senses that he has done all he can, and it is not for him to make John of Gaunt's dream a reality. But the boy they compounded was Henry VI. The marriage, technically a comic ending, produces a child who will preside over disaster.

136

One thing Henry envies in the peasant life is the simplicity of its relations to time:

> next day after dawn,
> Doth rise and help Hyperion to his horse,
> And follows so the ever-running year
> With profitable labour to his grave.

(IV. i. 280–3)

Like a Book of Hours, this sees country labour as a matter of regular cycles. For Henry time is more urgent. Exeter describes him as weighing it 'to the utmost grain' (II. iv. 138), as though he knows how little he has; the French King complains that he forces the pace (II. iv. 145–6). *Carpe diem* is one solution; another is to include posterity in the audience Henry is playing for: 'our history shall with full mouth / Speak freely of our acts' (I. ii. 230–1). He combines this with the idea of cyclical time in his prediction that

> Crispin Crispian shall ne'er go by,
> From this day to the ending of the world,
> But we in it shall be remembered.

(IV. iii. 57–9)

The secular achievement will go into the calendar as a saint's day, just as the day of the Queen's accession became an annual festival in Elizabethan England. In a way, Henry gets what he asks for. The play itself, less regular then a religious feast but still recurring, is a guarantee of his survival. That is why we are constantly aware, in *Henry V* as in none of the other histories, of the play as play. The Chorus began by complaining of the narrowness of the medium in which the great subject had to be confined. But when he declares, 'Small time, but in that small most greatly liv'd / This star of England' (Epilogue, 5–6), 'small time', in the movement of the speech, seems at first to refer to the brevity of the play rather than that of Henry's life. Finally, of course, it means both. The Chorus accepts that as a short life was enough for Henry, who weighed time to the utmost grain, two hours or so were enough for Shakespeare. As Henry has accepted his role, so the Chorus has finally accepted his medium, now that the play has demonstrated what it can do. The Epilogue is in the form of a sonnet, the form Shakespeare used elsewhere to insist on the permanent achievements of art.[21]

The Chorus also claims, as the Sonnets do, that only art survives:

Henry the Sixth, in infant bands crown'd King
  Of France and England, did this king succeed;
Whose state so many had the managing,
  That they lost France and made his England bleed:
Which oft our stage hath shown.          (Epilogue, 9–13)

If our memories stretch back – as they are now invited to – to the earlier plays, we may conclude that this is where we came in: a disunited group of nobles squabbling over the body of a hero who was 'too famous to live long' (*1 Henry VI*, I.i.6). History, which we normally think of as a straight line moving through time, turns back on itself and forms a circle, an image not of perfection but of futility. We keep coming back to the same point: loss and ruin. That is what Shakespeare's art shows us of our life in history. But the Chorus adds, 'and, for their sake, / In your fair minds let this acceptance take' (Epilogue, 13–14). Who are 'they'? The clearest reference seems to be to the cast of *Henry VI*; but perhaps they stand for all time's subjects as the history plays have shown them. And what is 'this' we are to accept? *Henry V*, and (I think) the whole historical vision that lies behind it. We are to accept the play, as Henry accepted his unrewarding role and the Chorus his imperfect medium. That is the last of our many responsibilities as audience. Our acceptance is our way of recognizing that the fusion of the hero with the art that creates him – however we may judge the imperfections of either – offers a chance to protect human achievement from the erosion of time. Taken together, Henry's prediction about Saint Crispin's Day and the Chorus's prediction about England's future imply that as history darkened again men would still remember this light from the past. As *Henry VI* shows, they did. The business of *Henry V* is to keep that memory alive through art, in a future even Shakespeare could not have imagined.

# 6

# *Julius Caesar*

*Henry V* is a play about a hero; so is *Julius Caesar*. But, while we see the climax of Henry's achievement in his conquest of France, Caesar's achievements are in the past. While Henry is tested and proven in action, Caesar has to emanate an aura of greatness without the deeds to match it. Henry is also the centre of a political structure his society takes for granted, one that gives him the key role: he is a king. Throughout the English history plays, whatever questions there may be about an individual's conduct in office, or his right to hold office, the office itself is always in place. In *Julius Caesar* we see Rome groping towards a new political structure in an effort to accommodate Caesar; the language of monarchy, dimly remembered from the past, is the only language they have for this new structure. But they use it uncertainly. Casca reports, 'I saw Mark Antony offer him a crown; yet 'twas not a crown neither, 'twas one of these coronets' (I. ii. 232–4). The phrasing of Brutus' 'My ancestors did from the streets of Rome / The Tarquin drive, when he was call'd a king' (II. i. 53–4) suggests that even then there was something unnatural about the term. Even the Senate, preparing to accept Caesar as king, leaves an important reservation: 'he shall wear his crown by sea and land, / In every place, save here in Italy' (I. iii. 87–8). In fact Rome would never be a monarchy in the English manner; the office of emperor as it later developed was quite different from that of king. (Something of this is suggested in the imperial election in *Titus Andronicus*, in which it is clear that Saturninus does not have an automatic title to the office just because he is the late emperor's eldest son, and Titus' selection of him is a serious mistake.) In the eyes of the English audience, Calphurnia's barrenness would be a bad omen for Caesar's kingship. Caesar's own worry about this problem shows in his attempt to use an old belief about Lupercal to put it right (I. ii. 6–9). He himself is the centre of a contrived ceremony using the crown, in effect an abortive coronation. Antony offers him a crown, he refuses it, and is obviously chagrined when the people cheer his refusal. Casca's sour irony makes him the perfect reporter: 'he put it by once; but for all that, to my thinking, he would fain have had it. Then he offered it to him again; then he put it by again; but to my thinking, he was very loath to lay his fingers off it' (I. ii. 235–8). This little piece of play-acting seems designed to do two things: to show Caesar's respect for the republic, and to goad the people into encouraging him to conquer his scruples and accept the crown. It fails on both counts; and Casca's report of Caesar's eagerness to touch the crown with his fingers recalls our uneasiness when Richard II, Bolingbroke, and Hal laid their hands on the crown. As in *Richard II* a public ceremony centred on kingship is degraded into play-acting: 'If the tag-rag people did not clap him and hiss him, according as he pleas'd and displeas'd them, as they use to do the players in the theatre, I am no true man' (I. ii. 255–8).

Casca's sense of himself as a 'true man' seems to oppose Roman integrity to the artifice of the new monarchical Rome that Caesar and his followers are trying to create. The play gives little sense of the republican constitution; Caesar seems to be not overturning an established order but moving into a political vacuum. Instead of a clear system we have an ideal of Romanness, something inherent in the blood, guaranteeing integrity of behaviour. Brutus tells his fellows:

> every drop of blood
> That every Roman bears, and nobly bears,
> Is guilty of a several bastardy,
> If he do break the smallest particle
> Of any promise that hath pass'd from him.     (II. i. 136–40)

It is an ideal not of how republicanism works, but why: the individual citizen can always be trusted. Shakespeare also suggests some of the social networks that sustain the republic. Family and ancestry matter. Cassius' clinching argument to Brutus is:

> O, you and I have heard our fathers say,
> There was a Brutus once that would have brook'd
> Th' eternal devil to keep his state in Rome
> As easily as a king.                          (I. ii. 156–9)

Portia sees her family as compensation for her sex: 'I grant I am a woman; but withal / A woman well reputed, Cato's daughter' (II. i. 294–5). This famous name is also invoked at Philippi by a young soldier who calls, 'I am the son of Marcus Cato, ho' (V. iv. 4), and is immediately struck down. The republic seems to die with him.

We also glimpse an old-school network: Brutus says of Casca, 'He was quick mettle when he went to school' (I. ii. 293), and, when he needs help in killing himself, appeals to Volumnius with the words, 'Thou know'st that we two went to school together' (V. v. 26).[1] School clings to them. When Caesar challenges Cassius to a swimming contest, it is a schoolboy's dare. The conspiracy itself is like a team or club, with its debates over who should be allowed to join. Portia is like a spirited girl who wants to prove she is as good as a boy. There are constant appeals to loyalty and affection, and there is a good deal of showing off. The latter point is particularly important. In the England of the Bolingbrokes, as we saw, appearances matter. So they do in Rome, but if anything more deeply. How the English politicians impress each other determines their place in an established structure; how the Roman politicians impress each other determines the structure itself,[2] since power here is a function of individuals, not offices. Casca has accused Caesar of play-acting; without seeming to notice the irony, Cassius points out that Casca's own bluntness is a calculated effect:

> This rudeness is a sauce to his good wit,
> Which gives men stomach to disgest his words
> With better appetite. (I. ii. 297–9)

The minor conspirators want Brutus and Cicero to join because they will make the conspiracy look better (I. iii. 157–60; II. i. 144–5). Antony complains that his reconciliation with the assassins must make him look either a coward or a flatterer (III. i. 191–3). Anxiety about one's appearance is a nerve that can always be touched. Cassius taunts Casca with his reaction to the storm: 'You are dull, Casca, and those sparks of life / That should be in a Roman you do want' (I. iii. 57–8). This is a preparation for the moment when, having revealed his true feelings about Caesar, Cassius draws back – 'I, perhaps, speak this / Before a willing bondman' (I. iii. 112–13) – and Casca refutes the charge and joins the conspiracy. Decius Brutus' manipulation of Caesar is based on the same principle: 'when I tell him he hates flatterers, / He says he does, being then most flattered' (II. i. 207–8). He gets Caesar to the senate house by pointing out that if he stays behind because of his wife's dreams he will be mocked for cowardice (II. ii. 96–101). One common factor in the contrasted orations of Brutus and Antony is that they both challenge the people to think well of themselves. Brutus appeals to their Roman integrity: 'Who is here so base, that would be a bondman? If any, speak; for him have I offended. Who is here so rude, that would not be a Roman? If any, speak; for him have I offended' (III. ii. 30–3). The people cry, 'None, Brutus, none' (III. ii. 36), savouring briefly the

141

sensation of themselves as freedom-loving Romans. Antony presents his appeal to their passions as an appeal to their humanity: 'You are not wood, you are not stones, but men' (III. ii. 144). Dimly remembering, perhaps, that the anti-Caesarian Marullus called them 'You blocks, you stones, you worse than senseless things' (I. i. 35), the mob goes with Antony.

When Cassius begins his seduction of Brutus he does so by stressing the importance of other men's view of him:

> Tell me, good Brutus, can you see your face?
> *Bru.* No, Cassius; for the eye sees not itself
> But by reflection, by some other things.

> *Cas.* . . . since you know you cannot see yourself
> So well as by reflection, I, your glass,
> Will modestly discover to yourself
> That of yourself which you yet know not of.  (I. ii. 50–2, 66–9)

This is a crucial moment. In the English histories all eyes were on Richard II, Henry IV, Hal, Henry V. There was a clear division of royal actor and common audience. In republican Rome, men on the same level eye each other. Everyone is actor, everyone is audience. Richard II studied his own face in a mirror; Brutus' mirror is the face of another man. We think of Donne's lovers, reflected in each other's eyes. More remarkable is Brutus' insistence that self-knowledge is impossible on any other terms. His sense of himself depends on what others think of him. Richard and the Bolingbrokes imitate the action of a king; Brutus feels called upon to imitate the Brutus other men expect.

This is not necessarily our view of what Brutus is capable of; the point is that it is Brutus' own. In fact his own will is always active in the process; he starts Cassius off by telling him how he likes to be seen, giving Cassius the image he wants him to reflect:[3]

> Set honour in one eye and death i' th' other,
> And I will look on both indifferently;
> For let the gods so speed me as I love
> The name of honour more than I fear death.
> *Cas.* I know that virtue to be in you, Brutus,
> As well as I do know your outward favour.
> Well, honour is the subject of my story.              (I. ii. 85–91)

Cassius pretends to oblige; but in fact honour is not the subject of his story at all. It is, if anything, envy. In the guise of appealing to Brutus' honour, he tries to get Brutus to feel his own resentment at the position

Caesar has attained. If the temptation works, as it seems to, Brutus thinks he is hearing one kind of appeal but the real work is being done by another. Cassius goes from pointing out his own common humanity with Caesar (indeed, his superior physical strength) to equating Caesar with Brutus in a way that appeals to Brutus' self-esteem, perhaps even his ambition: 'Brutus and Caesar: what should be in that "Caesar"? / Why should that name be sounded more than yours?' (I. ii. 140–1). He plans a further campaign:

> I will this night,
> In several hands, in at his windows throw,
> As if they came from several citizens,
> Writings, all tending to the great opinion
> That Rome holds of his name; wherein obscurely
> Caesar's ambition shall be glanced at.
>
> (I. ii. 312–17)

This time the appeal to Brutus' self-esteem is quite overt.

The letter-writing campaign is designed to give Brutus the impression that he is surrounded by the approval and expectations of his fellow Romans. As the eagerness of the other conspirators to have him join shows, this is not just an illusion. But his own sense of the importance of being Brutus, though it gets him into the conspiracy, produces trouble in the long run. His first reaction to Cassius' approach is guarded:

> Into what dangers would you lead me, Cassius,
> That you will have me seek into myself
> For that which is not in me? (I. ii. 62–4)

If this means that he has not entertained thoughts against Caesar, his reaction to the mob's offstage shout gives him the lie (I. ii. 78–81), and from that point he is more openly receptive to Cassius. But his initial guardedness is significant; it shows Brutus' constant insistence on doing things in his own time, in his own way. While Cassius sees him as the victim of seduction (I. ii. 305–9), Brutus insists that Cassius is only marshalling him in the direction in which he was going: 'What you would work me to, I have some aim' (I. ii. 161); and in fact this seems closer to the truth. Cassius has his own self-esteem, and gives himself more credit as a tempter than he may really deserve. From his idea that he sees himself only in the eyes of other men, Brutus goes to insisting that what he sees in those eyes must be approval and acquiescence. Shakespeare picks up from Plutarch's account a vein of stubbornness in Brutus: when he 'was moved to followe any matter, he used a kinde of forcible and vehement perswasion that calmed not, till he had obteyned his desire'.[4] Though Plutarch adds that what Brutus wanted was always good and honest, this suggests a hectoring quality that Shakespeare tones down. All the same, we cannot help noticing that as soon as he joins the conspiracy Brutus makes it his, overruling Cassius on every point – the oath, the enlisting of Cicero, the killing of Antony. His reason for rejecting Cicero is interesting: 'For he will never follow any thing / That other men begin' (II. i. 151–2). Brutus talks more often of principles, but here is a sharp insight into a personality, and it reveals in Brutus a desire to be surrounded only by good followers.

To see nothing but approval and obedience around you is to be cut off from reality. As Caesar is trying to construct an artificial kingship, Brutus (on republican principles) has constructed a more insidiously artificial world in which he is the custodian and exemplar of Roman values and the function of other men is to agree with him. It is not enough to be right; his rightness must be acknowledged and acted on. His detachment from reality is seen most strikingly in the soliloquy in which he argues himself into killing Caesar not because of what he is but because of what he might become if he were crowned: 'How that might change his nature, there's the question' (II. i. 13). What is remarkable is not so much the argument itself (that power corrupts, and therefore even a good man who is about to become powerful should be killed) as Brutus' insistence that there is nothing in Caesar's present behaviour to warrant killing him: 'I have not known when his affections sway'd / More than his reason' (II. i. 20–1). But we have already seen Caesar's arrogance and vanity, and the obsequiousness that surrounds him, in which even Casca joins; we have heard, and so has Brutus, that 'Marullus and Flavius, for pulling scarfs off Caesar's images, are put to silence' (I. ii. 282–3). The tyranny Brutus fears as a theoretical possibility in the future is a clear and present danger. Cassius has already insisted on it. Brutus is frequently chided by critics for killing a man for the sake of a theory; but Shakespeare is, I think, less concerned with the quality of Brutus' reasoning than with his inability to start with the evidence under his nose. He makes a similar mistake about Antony, though in this case only historical hindsight, not the evidence of the play itself, shows at the time that he is wrong. He has the theory that Antony 'is but a limb of Caesar', and it follows logically that 'he can do no more than Caesar's arm / When Caesar's head is off' (II. i. 165, 182–3). This in turn implies a theory of Caesarism – that, since everything depends on one man, when he goes his followers are powerless – that gives Antony no credit for will or initiative of his own. It is the projection into Caesar's camp of the structure Brutus has created in his own: one will, surrounded by obedience. Nor can he imagine what

144

Antony would do after Caesar's death; the word 'revenge' is not in Brutus' vocabulary of Roman values. As it turns out, to spare Antony is dangerous, and to let him speak to the people is fatal. In this case Brutus is blinded by self-esteem: 'I will myself into the pulpit first' (III. i. 236) seems to him sufficient guarantee that things will go well.

There is also something worked up and artificial in the way Brutus sees the assassination itself. In his rejection of the oath, he seems to be rejecting any kind of dressing up, insisting that the worth of the cause and the integrity of the men speak for themselves:

> What need we any spur but our own cause
> To prick us to redress? what other bond
> Than secret Romans, that have spoke the word,
> And will not palter?  (II. i. 123–6)

(Incidentally, if these really are secret Romans who will not palter, how do Artemidorus and Popilius Lena know so much?) But something tells Brutus that the act itself is not inherently pure; it needs to be performed in the right spirit, and correctly interpreted, if it is to look right: 'Let's be sacrificers, but not butchers, Caius' (II.i.166). Interpretation shades into deception:

> Let's kill him boldly, but not wrathfully;
> Let's carve him as a dish fit for the gods,
> Not hew him as a carcass fit for hounds.
> And let our hearts, as subtle masters do,
> Stir up their servants to an act of rage,
> And after seem to chide 'em.  (II. i. 172–7)

The split between the act itself and the way in which Brutus would like it to be seen leads him to admit a division between heart and hand, and to admit further an element of contrivance and deception in the heart's dealings with the hand. His final purpose is the usual one: get the appearance right:

> This shall make
> Our purpose necessary, and not envious;
> Which so appearing to the common eyes,
> We shall be call'd purgers, not murderers.
>
>  (II. i. 177–80)

As we shall see later, the act itself is anything but pure and is open to a wide variety of interpretations.

Brutus' insistence on controlling the way in which it is seen leads to precisely the sort of play-acting Casca has despised in Caesar. At the end of the scene, Cassius tells his friends to 'show yourselves true Romans' (II. i. 223), appealing to the sort of integrity Brutus appealed to in his rejection of an oath. But 'show' is a slippery word, and Brutus develops the suggestion of deception:

> Good gentlemen, look fresh and merrily.
> Let not our looks put on our purposes,
> But bear it as our Roman actors do,
> With untir'd spirits and formal constancy.

(II. i. 224–7)

Brutus and Cassius have virtually exchanged roles; the cynical manipulator now speaks for Roman integrity, and the man who began the scene remarking sourly on the concealment that conspiracy makes necessary (II. i. 77–85) now takes to that concealment with relish. Literally, all he is doing is offering good practical advice; but his concern to control appearances, even if it involves some wrenching of the truth, shows there is another and more dangerous sense in which Brutus has become a Roman actor.


Like Hal, Brutus attempts to control the way in which his nature and actions are seen by others. But he is much less conscious that this is what he is doing; he has no equivalent of Hal's first soliloquy. And while Hal has at least two roles, and they multiply when he becomes king, Brutus has only one: the noble Brutus. He cannot change. Caesar, we learn, has changed his mind about the importance of omens (II. i. 195–7). So does Cassius, and admits as much (V. i. 77–9). But when Brutus affirms his opposition to suicide, and in the next breath his determination not to be led in triumph through Rome (V. i. 98–113), he seems unaware of the deadlock.[5] The performance holds; the inconsistency it involves is not admitted. As in *Henry V*, the performer's insistence on keeping the mask on arouses our curiosity about what lies behind it, a curiosity that in this case extends beyond Brutus. We see these Romans posing for each other and for themselves, and we sense the effort it demands. Even Cassius' view of himself as a tempter involves a certain posturing. Is there anything but performance here? Do these people have private lives, private relationships, or are they on show all the time? We saw into Henry V only once, and we saw even then that the private man was preoccupied with the significance of his role. The treatment of private life in *Julius Caesar* is more pervasive, and explores over a wider range.

Our first impression may be that public concerns have seeped through all of life, and that there is no corner left for anything else. When Brutus describes his internal turmoil on the brink of decision, he uses political language:

> the state of man,
> Like to a little kingdom, suffers then
> The nature of an insurrection.
>
> (II. i. 67–9)

The image is commonplace, but in the context of the play it confirms an impression that everything is political. Cassius uses an appeal to Brutus' love as the hook to start a conversation about Caesar; Brutus says of his proposal to enlist Ligarius, 'He loves me well, and I have given him reasons' (II. i. 219). Love and argument are two counters in the transactions of politics. And love has a politics of its own, dependent, like the other politics, on show and observation. Cassius complains:

> Brutus, I do observe you now of late:
> I have not from your eyes that gentleness
> And show of love as I was wont to have.
>
> (I. ii. 31–3)

Brutus admits that he 'Forgets the shows of love to other men' (I. ii. 46), acknowledging the importance of show even if the love remains sincere. Love also has its ceremonies, and like other ceremonies they can become meaningless routines. Having publicly affirmed his trust in Cassius' friendship – 'He is not doubted' – Brutus speaks more confidentially to his messenger, and raises doubts:

> A word, Lucilius;
> How he receiv'd you, let me be resolv'd.
> *Lucil.* With courtesy and with respect enough,
> But not with such familiar instances,
> Nor with such free and friendly conference,
> As he hath us'd of old.
> *Bru.*                    Thou hast describ'd
> A hot friend cooling. Ever note, Lucilius,
> When love begins to sicken and decay
> It useth an enforced ceremony.          (IV. ii. 13–21)

In love as in politics, appearances count. And Brutus, in publicly affirming his trust in Cassius, then privately denying it, is guilty of just such an enforced ceremony as Cassius uses.

In this Roman world of ex-schoolboys the strongest emotional attachments are between men. In the case of Portia and Brutus we see,

147

played out in more severe language, what we have seen before in the case of Hotspur and Lady Percy: a marriage in which there is genuine love breaking under the strain of the man's involvement in public affairs. Portia complains of desertion, and Brutus at first puts her off with a lie she sees through easily: 'I am not well in health, and that is all' (II. i. 257). He promises to talk with her, and later it appears he has; but the theatrical emphasis is on the way he shelves her concern in order to deal with Ligarius. At the end of the scene the two men leave together. Portia's only contribution to the Ides of March is flustered and pathetic:

> Run, Lucius, and commend me to my lord;
> Say I am merry; come to me again,
> And bring me word what he doth say to thee.
>
> (II. iv. 44–6)

Knowing the importance of appearances, she proves her constancy by a significant gesture, giving herself 'a voluntary wound / Here, in the thigh' (II. i. 300–1), as though attacking her own sexuality. She goes from self-mutilation to suicide, swallowing fire. We think of the fires that sweep through Rome after Caesar's death. As Henry VI saw the red rose and the white branded on the faces of the victims of Towton, so Portia has made her body an image of the gutted city. Far from establishing a centre of private value, Portia symbolically involves herself with the public world, using two of its key images, sword and fire. The end is self-destruction.

Her death matters to Brutus as a way of displaying his Stoic integrity: 'No man bears sorrow better. Portia is dead' (IV. iii. 146). It is not that the sorrow is unreal; it is rather that Brutus feels it incumbent upon him to suppress it as part of his performance. The second account of Portia's death, and Brutus' public display of Stoic calm, may be a cancelled passage that appears by mistake in the text; if not – particularly in view of Brutus' pretence that he is hearing the news for the first time – it takes his display of self-command to the point of caricature.[7] Cassius' reaction, 'O insupportable and touching loss!' (IV. iii. 150), seems fuller and more human, as does his inability to put Portia out of his mind later in the scene when Brutus tries to get back to business (IV. iii. 165). We are the more struck by Cassius' natural emotion in that as a character he has had no previous relationship with Portia. But we have been prepared for it by an unexpected touch in the assassination scene, in which Cassius instructs an aged senator, 'leave us, Publius, lest that the people, / Rushing on us, should do your age some mischief' (III. i. 92–3). His ordinary humane concern, his ability to stand for a moment outside the great public event and tend to a small matter, is at this point something new for the play. In the last two acts Cassius comes to represent a spontaneous humanity that we can set against the self-dramatization of Brutus, and the sheer unexpectedness of this development is itself part of its effect.

In the early scenes the friendship of Brutus and Cassius cannot be distinguished from their political relations. They are looking together to a common goal. But, when their purpose fails, the division between them appears more sharply, and at the same time their emotional need for each other, and their ability to inflict real wounds because of it, stand revealed. Roman dignity breaks down as even Brutus resorts to crude insult: 'Away, slight man!' (IV. iii. 37). The careful rhetoric of argument and persuasion is replaced by:

> *Cas.*              I denied you not.
> *Bru.* You did.
> *Cas.*         I did not.                                      (IV. iii. 82–3)

This is the other side of schoolboy life. Cassius opens the quarrel in public with a frontal assault: 'Most noble brother, you have done me wrong' (IV. ii. 37). Brutus characteristically insists on keeping up appearances:

> Before the eyes of both our armies here,
> Which should perceive nothing but love from us,
> Let us not wrangle.                                      (IV. ii. 43–5)

Cassius accuses him, 'Brutus, this sober form of yours hides wrongs' (IV. ii. 40), but Brutus insists on maintaining the sober form, though it cracks and strains to the point of hypocrisy:

> I did sent to you
> For certain sums of gold, which you denied me;
> For I can raise no money by vile means.
>                                      (IV. iii. 69–71)

Cassius, it seems, must do the dirty work so that Brutus can afford to stay pure. In their reconciliation Cassius shows, as he has throughout, a remarkable emotional nakedness, while Brutus keeps his guard up, retreating behind dry wit:

> *Cas.* Have you not love enough to bear with me,
>       When that rash humour which my mother gave me
>       Makes me forgetful?
> *Bru.*                    Yes, Cassius; and from henceforth
>       When you are over-earnest with your Brutus,
>       He'll think your mother chides, and leave you so.
>                                      (IV. iii. 118–22)

149

When the poet invades their tent, Cassius, who has let his passions out, is amused and tolerant; Brutus is unexpectedly angry, betraying unresolved tension.[8]

There is never a final openness between them. They dispute the timing of the battle; Cassius, as usual, will be proved right by events, and Brutus, as usual, overrules him: 'Good reasons must of force give place to better' (IV. iii. 202). There is strained politeness in these words, and while Cassius accepts the decision he complains of it when Brutus is out of earshot (V. i. 74–6). Their last meeting is revealing. Brutus finds just the right words for parting – simple, eloquent, and nicely balanced. All Cassius can do is repeat them, unable to find words of his own (V. i. 117–22). The contrast is between a man who is moved beyond language and a man who is not. Brutus' reaction to Cassius' death, or rather his refusal to react, makes us wonder if he is retreating from feeling or covering up the lack of it:

> Friends, I owe moe tears
> To this dead man than you shall see me pay.
> I shall find time, Cassius, I shall find time.
> Come therefore, and to Thrasos send his body.
> His funerals shall not be in our camp,
> Lest it discomfort us. (V. iii. 101–6)

Cassius finally places his own relationship with Brutus, simply but revealingly, when he laments the fate of Titinius: 'O, coward that I am, to live so long, / To see my best friend ta'en before my face' (V. iii. 34–5). He and Titinius literally die for each other. We have seen Cassius pleading for Brutus' love and never quite getting it. All we see of his relationship with Titinius, earlier in V. iii, is two men simply working together, making no parade of their friendship. The revelation of the depth of that friendship is a flash of the unexpected, a touch of unprogrammed humanity in a world of controlled display.[9]

When we look for such a moment in Brutus, we find it not with Cassius or even Portia, but with the boy Lucius. Lucius' importance is signalled by the fact that he is the only minor character to cross the divide between the first three acts and the rest of the play. Henry V, we saw, could not relax with his inferiors; he was always the king. When Brutus is dealing with equals, he is controlled, on display, and somewhat overbearing. Alone with his servant, he becomes unexpectedly gentle. Two details matter: Brutus is in his gown,[10] and Lucius, unlike the servants of Caesar, has a name. For the first and only time in the play Brutus admits to having made a mistake:

150

> Look, Lucius, here's the book I sought for so;
>     I put it in the pocket of my gown.
> *Luc.* I was sure your lordship did not give it me.
> *Bru.* Bear with me, good boy, I am much forgetful.   (IV. iii. 251–4)

In its smaller way, 'I am much forgetful' is moving as Lear's 'I am old and foolish' is. Brutus, who has taken on the destiny of Rome with a masterful sense of purpose and supreme wrong-headedness, is now hesitant and apologetic with a servant. What from another man would be commands are shy requests:

>     Canst thou hold up thy heavy eyes awhile,
>     And touch thy instrument a strain or two?
> *Luc.* Ay, my lord, an't please you.
> *Bru*                                   It does, my boy.
>     I trouble thee too much, but thou art willing.
> *Luc.* It is my duty, sir.
> *Bru.* I should not urge thy duty past thy might;
>     I know young bloods look for a time of rest.
> *Luc.* I have slept, my lord, already.         (IV. iii. 255–62)

This time it is Lucius (who really is tired, for he falls asleep while playing) who has to be firm, and ensure that the master gets his music.

Brutus' last command is not so readily obeyed. He asks several friends to kill him, and they all refuse. Only Strato – who, like Lucius, has been asleep – agrees. We may contrast this with the behaviour of Pindarus, who readily obeys Cassius' order to kill him, saying nothing of his own regret until the job is done. There is something ambiguous in Brutus' insistence that he has had the perfect Roman friends: 'My heart doth joy that yet in all my life / I found no man but he was true to me' (V. v. 34–5). Does his friends' refusal of his last request confirm this, by showing their love, or work ironically against it? Lucilius has declared that suicide is the end expected of Brutus: 'no enemy / Shall ever take alive the noble Brutus' (V. iv. 21–2), and yet only a hitherto unknown minor character is willing to help him make this last gesture. Brutus dies as he has lived, consciously shaping his life to meet his own and others' expectations, showing no awareness of the intractable reality around him or the contradictions in his own statements.

But, if this were all that could be said, then Antony's tribute to the 'general honest thought / And common good to all' (V. v. 71–2) that led him to kill Caesar, and to the gentleness and fine balance of his life, would be merely ironic. We would be close to the sarcasm of Antony's earlier oration, in which the word 'honourable', the word by which

151

Brutus has defined himself, becomes increasingly poisonous. To find the ironic reading confirmed from that quarter should be enough to give us pause. It is true that Antony's final tribute is somewhat generalized; he does not mention Brutus by name.[11] It is also true that Shakespeare has shown in Brutus a pattern of failure so consistent that the characterization seems at times mechanical. But the fact that even after his last failure no one can bear to kill him points in another direction. In judging his motives, self-esteem and genuine dedication to Rome are hard to untangle; even so, in his posturing to himself and others there is a thin line between mere vanity and the need to shape and express a genuinely fine nature as an example to a crumbling world. That Brutus is at his very best when alone with a servant and not trying to impress anybody is an irony more subtle and compassionate than the hammering sarcasm of Antony's attack. Antony's last tribute, which he puts (we note) not into the mouth of Society or History but into the mouth of Nature, is simple and precise. Nature says not 'This was a hero' or 'This was a fool' but 'This was a man' (V. v. 75).

In the case of Caesar the relation of performance to reality looks more like simple irony. Shakespeare seems to have settled for a cruder solution than he found in *Henry V* to the problem of having a superhuman hero played by a life-sized actor. We see a frail and peevish man boasting of his courage and constancy:

> I rather tell thee what is to be fear'd
> Than what I fear; for always I am Caesar.
> Come on my right hand, for this ear is deaf,
> And tell me truly what thou think'st of him.
>
> (I. ii. 208–11)

At one point he projects himself into allegory:

> Danger knows full well
> That Caesar is more dangerous than he.
> We are two lions litter'd in one day,
> And I the elder and more terrible.
>
> (II. ii. 44–7)

He strikes poses like these even when alone with his wife.[12] His last boast, that he is 'constant as the northern star' (III. i. 60), is directly followed by his murder. His real achievements are not shown, and are talked of only in general terms. Marullus complains of the opening celebration, 'Wherefore rejoice? What conquest brings he home?'

(I. i. 32). The boasts look empty without the deeds to match them. In I. ii Cassius insists on Caesar's mortal frailty. He weakened when swimming and nearly drowned, he shook when he had a fever – this is the bare forked animal beneath the superman. And yet, like Antony's attack on Brutus in the funeral oration, Cassius' spiteful gloating should make us think twice about the easy ironic reading. Caesar's style is not all bombast. His insight into Cassius himself is remarkably shrewd: 'Such men as he be never at heart's ease / Whiles they behold a greater than themselves' (I. ii. 205–6). We catch a glimpse of the historical Caesar's generosity to old enemies in his gracious words to Ligarius (II. ii. 111–13), though admittedly the grace becomes strained a moment later when Brutus tells Caesar the time and he replies, 'I thank you for your pains and courtesy' (II. ii. 115).

Shakespeare does not depend solely on small touches of finer quality to gain respect for the character. Even the frailty need not be read as Cassius reads it. Shakespeare's Caesar is a convincing portrait of a great man seen in private. A little reading of history shows that men of genius who make this kind of impact are generally not modest, healthy, balanced, and reasonable people. They can be maddening, monstrous, and pathetic, as Caesar is. Their private lives and medical records do not bear examination. If Shakespeare goes daringly far in showing this aspect of Caesar the man, it may be because he wants to emphasize that his greatness consists not so much in what he says or does as in the mysterious impact he has on others. We see him, as Brutus sees himself, by reflection. For good or ill, he has a powerful effect on Rome. In the opening scene the people – to the annoyance of Flavius, who has a tidy mind and wants everyone labelled[13] – abandon the signs of their profession and make holiday for Caesar. It may be Lupercal for those who remember such things, but for them it is Caesar's day. The traditions of work and holiday alike make way for him. But while Henry V's greatness feeds others – 'A largess universal like the sun / His liberal eye doth give to every one' (*Henry V*, IV. Chorus, 43–4) – Caesar's greatness, according to Cassius, merely diminishes them:

> Why, man, he doth bestride the narrow world
> Like a Colossus, and we petty men
> Walk under his huge legs, and peep about
> To find ourselves dishonourable graves.

> (I. ii. 133–6)

This is the thinking of a republican; a royalist for whom Caesar was king would see his greatness very differently. In some respects the play confirms Cassius' thinking. It would strike a Renaissance audience with particular force that Cicero, for them one of the great figures of antiquity, is reduced to a minor character in Caesar's Rome.

While Caesar's greatness may be unhealthy for Rome, there is no doubt of his scale and importance. He is surrounded by supernatural portents. The storm that precedes his assassination is variously interpreted by Casca, Cicero, and Cassius, but Calphurnia gets it right: it both predicts Caesar's fall and confirms his scale: 'When beggars die, there are no comets seen; / The heavens themselves blaze forth the death of princes' (II. ii. 30–1). The portents, like those around Henry IV, all point to Caesar's death. Calphurnia's dream of the statue running blood is not, as Decius Brutus pretends, a sign that Caesar will give new life to Rome. Caesar's great action in the play – his only one – is to die. The assassination, like the Battle of Agincourt in *Henry V*, is consciously presented as a famous event, one that will live in history. The difference is that it is fully acted out onstage. Shakespeare uses shameless tricks to build the suspense: Portia's nervousness, the warnings of Artemidorus and the Soothsayer, the intervention of Popilius Lena. At the moment of his death Caesar speaks Latin, '*Et tu, Brute?* ', suddenly changing from a character in an English play to a figure from Roman history, fixed at a memorable moment. His next words, 'Then fall Caesar!' (III. i. 77), make the death his own willed act.[14] For the first time in the play Caesar *does* something. Normally passive, reacting to others, he makes of his death a dramatic action that will turn him into legend – and, as Cassius points out, into drama:

> How many ages hence
> Shall this our lofty scene be acted over,
> In states unborn, and accents yet unknown!
>
> (III. i. 111–13)

The play itself confirms this, just as *Henry V* confirms its hero's impact on posterity, simply by existing. Cassius' words, like Caesar's Latin, remind us that the story comes from another time and another culture; yet the illusion of drama keeps it alive. There is more to theatre than the vulgar play-acting Casca saw in Caesar.

But when Cassius continues –

> So oft as that shall be,
> So often shall the knot of us be call'd
> The men that gave their country liberty.
>
> (III. i. 116–18)

– the irony of history closes in. Like all great events, this one is open to intepretation, and Cassius' interpretation is proved wrong before the play is over. Nor has posterity always seen the conspirators even as noble failures; Sir Thomas Elyot, in *The Book Named the Governor*, paid tribute to the virtues of Brutus and Cassius but called their deaths 'A worthy and convenient vengeance for the murder of so noble and valiant a prince'.[15] Dante was even more severe, consigning the assassins to the very centre of Hell. Brutus' insistence that he and his followers smear their hands and weapons with Caesar's blood and present themselves to the people in that state, crying 'Peace, freedom, and liberty!' (III. i. 110), reflects his desire for a ritual sacrifice; but it also betrays the barbaric, violent, and irrational quality of the deed. Like Portia's swallowing fire, it has more than a touch of madness. Later in the play, as the event itself fades, we get new views of it. Brutus now claims Caesar was killed not for liberty but for justice, and because he supported robbers (IV. iii. 19–24). Arguing with Cassius, he is imposing (Bolingbroke-style) a new interpretation that suits his present purpose. Antony recalls the surface details of the killing accurately, but stresses the conspirators' cowardly fawning on Caesar (V. i. 41–4). He too emphasizes what he needs to emphasize. History is already being rewritten.

What is clear is that the assassination brings no new life to Rome. Memorable though it is, as an achievement it is even briefer than Agincourt. The omens that suggest otherwise prove false. Casca's 'Here, as I point my sword, the sun arises' (II. i. 106) implies new hope born of violence. This is countered when Octavius formally draws his sword to put an end to the conspirators (V. i. 50–1). Ligarius hails Brutus as a saviour who can heal the sick; the last order the mob gives itself is to burn Ligarius' house (III. iii. 37–8). In Ligarius' tribute, 'Thou, like an exorcist, hast conjur'd up / My mortified spirit' (II. i. 323–4), there is an ironic prediction of what will really happen. Brutus, who wishes he could kill the spirit of Caesar and spare the man (II. i. 167–70), kills the man and releases the spirit. Free of its mortal body, the spirit of Caesar dominates the second half of the play with new and frightening power. Like the dead Henry V, he can now be talked of as a superman, with nothing on stage to contradict this view, only the bloodstained body that (like Talbot's) makes the tribute poignant: 'Thou art the ruins of the noblest man / That ever lived in the tide of times' (III. i. 256–7).

The words are Antony's; and Antony becomes the custodian of Caesar's spirit. In one respect Caesar has not changed: the power of his spirit is not shown directly but reflected through other people. And reflection quickly becomes interpretation. When he shakes hands with the conspirators, Antony will get blood, Caesar's blood, on his own hands. The bloodstained assassins crying liberty are an incongruous sight. Antony's words go better with his appearance:

> Blood and destruction shall be so in use,
> And dreadful objects so familiar,
> That mothers shall but smile when they behold
> Their infants quartered with the hands of war,
> All pity chok'd with custom of fell deeds;
> And Caesar's spirit, ranging for revenge,
> With Ate by his side come hot from hell,
> Shall in these confines with a monarch's voice
> Cry havoc and let slip the dogs of war,
> That this foul deed shall smell above the earth
> With carrion men, groaning for burial.
>
> (III. i. 265–75)

Caesar has now the monarchy that eluded him in life; and Antony lifts him, as Caesar lifted himself, to the level of allegory. Yet what Antony predicts does not quite come to pass. Shakespeare's dramatization of the war shows none of the Guernica-like horror of this speech; we see only the armies, and we have no sense of a whole society suffering. And Antony's view of Caesar's spirit is very much his own. Its relation to Caesar the man is suggested when he reads the will and we learn that Caesar intended to bequeath to Rome not blood and destruction but

> all his walks,
> His private arbours, and new-planted orchards,
> On this side Tiber . . .
> > common pleasures,
> To walk abroad and recreate yourselves.
>
> (III. ii. 249–53)

This is Caesar at his most amiable; and we may wonder if this is one of the charges Antony means to cut out of the will (IV. i. 8–9).

The power of Antony's funeral oration stems not just from its tricky irony but from the way it overturns Brutus' appeal to abstraction and theory with an appeal to facts. This is what Caesar did, this is his torn mantle, this is his mangled body. For Brutus the incident is finished, and is already on the official record: 'The question of his death is enroll'd in the Capitol' (III. ii. 38–9). Antony breaks down this sense of distance and completion, and takes the action to its next stage. But, just as the conspirators have surprisingly little sense of what is to happen after they have killed Caesar, so Antony too does not seem clear about where he is going. Caesar, like Richard II, is unrevivable:

> Here was a Caesar! When comes such another?
> *1 Pleb.* Never, never! (III. ii. 254–5)

The mob seeks relief in violent but finally meaningless action, and Antony takes delight in watching them:

> *4 Pleb.* Pluck down forms, windows, any thing.
>
> [*Exeunt Plebeians . . .*
> *Ant.* Now let it work. Mischief, thou art afoot,
> Take thou what course thou wilt! (III. ii. 261–3)

There is a certain desperation in the citizen's 'any thing', and it is matched by Antony's surprising lack of direction. Even the clear purpose of vengeance no longer seems to be in his mind. His sense of triumph is made ironic when he echoes the Fourth Plebeian: 'Fortune is merry, / And in this mood will give us any thing' (III. ii. 268–9). He began by seeing himself releasing the spirit of Caesar to take vengeance on his enemies. He now delivers himself to the whims of Fortune. We know what Fortune does to great men, what that 'any thing' can include.

Shakespeare's Roman commoners, unlike his English ones, have no names, only numbers. Even in moments of relaxation they are halfway to becoming that single organism, the mob. In the aftermath of Brutus' oration, they can be discriminating:

> *2 Pleb.* Give him a statue with his ancestors.
> *3 Pleb.* Let him be Caesar.
> *4 Pleb.*                    Caesar's better parts
> Shall be crown'd in Brutus. (III. ii. 51–3)

We should not let the obvious irony of Number 3's cry blind us to the more intelligent proposal of Number 4 or Number 2's recognition of the sort of honour that really would please Brutus. But under the spell of Antony the citizens are reduced to monosyllables: 'Seek! – Burn! – Fire! – Kill! – / Slay!' (III. ii. 206–7). The cobbler's puns on mending and fixing (I. i. 10–26) become the more sinister word-play that leads Cinna the Poet to his death. For a mob to tear a poet to pieces, recalling the fate of Orpheus, may look like a final and decisive image of the breakdown of civilization. To modern directors this seems a good place for an interval. But Shakespeare goes on, and to break the play at this point is to lose one of his most telling juxtapositions. From watching the mob kill in hot blood, we go to watching the second triumvirate – Antony, Octavius, and Lepidus – kill in cold blood, by remote control and with clinical detachment. The mob has a reason, if a crazy one, for killing Cinna. The triumvirs, as far as we can tell, simply kill. And we hear later that, while the mob has killed a now-forgotten poet, the triumvirs kill Cicero (IV. iii. 176–9). The violence of the mob has not burned itself out but is channelled in a new and more dreadful way through Caesar's successors.

Brutus wanted a tight, clear, finished action. Antony has broken the play open and set history going in new, unpredictable directions. This accounts for some odd features in the play's structure: the early placing of its climactic event, the discontinuity that sees all the conspirators but Brutus and Cassius disappear halfway through to be replaced by a new supporting cast. Even in the final scene new names keep cropping up. The most telling of these effects involves Octavius, who is not even referred to until after Caesar's death. The timing of his first appearance suggests a way of reviving Caesar that is quite different from Antony's mighty spirit of vengeance. This new Caesar is colder, lower, but deadly effective. We do not need to know later Roman history to sense that in giving him his opportunity Antony has sealed his own doom. The cracks in the alliance show early, as Octavius develops Brutus' habit of overruling his senior partner. Antony's energy, which flared suddenly and brilliantly in the third act, starts to die. In the play's final irony, the Caesarians compete for the privilege of honouring Brutus, with Antony giving the oration and Caesar claiming the body. The echo of Caesar's funeral orations, in which Brutus had fine and dignified words but Antony had the body, bodes ill for Antony now. And it is Caesar, not Antony, who takes the practical step of enlisting Brutus' friends in his own service. The future belongs to a character we had not even heard of till the play was half over.

The closely defined Rome of the early scenes – the streets and houses, the Capitol, the Forum, the statues – is replaced by an open, featureless countryside, a neutral setting for camps and battles. The reasoned action of the conspiracy is replaced by something like the nightmare of *Henry VI*: competition and conflict for their own sakes, with no end in sight.[16] The long anticlimax is a dangerous but legitimate device on Shakespeare's part, to remind us, as he did after the Battle of Shrewsbury, that nothing in history is ever quite finished. Set against this are the characters' own attempts to see shape in their lives. These too have their equivalent in the shaping of the play itself, which can suggest an open future but must find a way for its own action to end. The last scenes are full of references to closing up a circle. But the effect is not, as at the end of *Henry V*, ultimate futility; it seems rather an attempt to see order, if only an aesthetic order, in one's existence. Cassius sees it in the fact that he is dying on his birthday:

> This day I breathed first. Time is come round,
> And where I did begin, there shall I end.
> My life is run his compass.                    (V. iii. 23–5)

The repetition in the speech itself suggests the character trying to fix the idea in his mind. In the same spirit, Brutus sees the larger action completing itself: 'this same day / Must end that work the ides of March begun' (V. i. 113–14). In his last scene he tries to see himself as fulfilling an inherent destiny: 'my bones would rest, / That have but labour'd to attain this hour' (V. v. 41–2). The conspirators' most powerful ally at this point is Caesar himself. As Antony edits Caesar's will, so he and Octavius begin to leave even the spirit of Caesar behind, and the real issue becomes the power struggle between them. It is Brutus and Cassius who need Caesar now, and who call on him most often. Cassius' death closes a circle in more ways than one: 'Caesar, thou art reveng'd, / Even with the sword that kill'd thee' (V. iii. 45–6). Brutus picks up the idea:

> O Julius Caesar, thou art mighty yet!
> Thy spirit walks abroad, and turns our swords
> Into our own proper entrails.               (V. iii. 94–6)

He marks his own death with the same invocation: 'Caesar, now be still; / I kill'd not thee with half so good a will' (V. v. 50–1). The ironic upshot of the assassination is that Brutus and Cassius both require Caesar to give a final sense of form to their lives.[17]

Brutus also sees himself as doing Caesar a final service, letting his spirit rest. The relation between Caesar and the other characters continues to be reciprocal: Caesar's spirit lives through others' invocations of it, changing shape to meet their different needs. When it appears as an independent entity, Brutus' first impression is of something formless:

> Art thou any thing?
> Art thou some god, some angel, or some devil,
> That mak'st my blood cold, and my hair to stare?
> Speak to me what thou art.
> *Ghost.* Thy evil spirit, Brutus.              (IV. iii. 277–81)

The spirit names itself in relation to the person it appears to; it does not call itself Caesar. Though it has an objective reality for the audience, there is a stronger suggestion than is usual in Elizabethan ghost scenes that it is a function of Brutus' mind.[18] Brutus himself says as much: 'I think it is the weakness of mine eyes / That shapes this monstrous apparition' (IV. iii. 275–6). Antony told the mob, 'Brutus, as you know, was Caesar's angel' (III. ii. 183). Now the relationship works in reverse, as Caesar becomes Brutus' evil spirit. His promise to appear again is not kept to the audience, only to Brutus; it is as though Brutus and Caesar have an intense, private relationship from which we are excluded. Caesar in life had constantly insisted on his own name: 'For always I am Caesar' (I. ii. 209). In death he surrenders his name and borrows one from Brutus. It is the play's sharpest image of the interdependence of its characters, who find not just the meaning of their actions, but their very identities, in the eyes of others. Rome could not find a political structure for Caesar; kingship was a dead institution. Instead Caesar finds himself, as Brutus does, in other people.

# 7

# *Antony and Cleopatra*

IN *Julius Caesar* the title character casts a giant shadow. There is the Caesar the actor is given to play, and there is the Caesar other characters talk about; the play is in the end more concerned with the latter. Shakespeare's interest in this doubleness of character, shadow and substance, can be traced back to Talbot's encounter with the Countess of Auvergne; it finds its most elaborate development in *Antony and Cleopatra*. The Soothsayer who warns Antony that in any contest with Octavius Caesar he is bound to lose puts it in this way:

> Thy demon, that thy spirit which keeps thee, is
> Noble, courageous, high, unmatchable,
> Where Caesar's is not. But near him, thy angel
> Becomes afeard; as being o'erpower'd.　　(II. iii. 18–21)

The attendant spirits are in fact projections of the men themselves; behind the political drama, with its closely observed personalities, is a shadow-play of demigods. At that level, as the Soothsayer insists and Antony confirms, Caesar wins because he is lucky:

> 　　　　The very dice obey him,
> And in our sports my better cunning faints
> Under his chance: if we draw lots, he speeds.
> 　　　　　　　　　　　　(II. iii. 32–4)

In her death scene Cleopatra mocks 'The luck of Caesar' (V. ii. 285). But in the historical action the play shows luck has nothing to do with it. Caesar is crafty and skilful; Antony is inept. At the start of the war, Antony's astonishment at the speed with which Caesar has captured Toryne shows he is simply outgeneralled (III. vii. 20–57). As a negotiator Antony is equally out of his depth. Through his ambassador he 'Requires to live in Egypt, which not granted, / He lessens his requests'

161

(III. xii. 12–13). This is not the way to open a bargaining session with a tough opponent. The play's action offers what looks like a full explanation of the course of the war in the relative skill of the antagonists. The Soothsayer's insistence that Caesar is simply lucky seems to refer to another action on another plane of reality, one in which men's fates are made not by themselves but by Fortune. In that respect it is like the apocalyptic speeches of Margaret in *Richard III*, which give the political action a dimension of myth it could not attain on its own.

Characters are likewise idealized in defiance of what the play actually shows. Cleopatra's dream of the Emperor Antony, 'His legs bestrid the ocean, his rear'd arm / Crested the world' (V. ii. 82–3), is not the Antony we have seen, any more than the giant Henry V we hear of in the opening of *1 Henry VI*, whose 'arms spread wider than a dragon's wings (I. i. 11), is the skilled role-player and leader of men Shakespeare will later put on the stage. Cleopatra knows this as well as we do. Her dream is presented in a defiant, even quarrelsome spirit, introduced by one of those passages of sharp comic observation so characteristic of this play. Dolabella tries to impress her:

> *Dol.* Most noble empress, you have heard of me?
> *Cleo* I cannot tell.
> *Dol.*                     Assuredly you know me.
> *Cleo* No matter, sir, what I have heard or known:
>      You laugh when boys or women tell their dreams,
>      Is't not your trick?
> *Dol.*                     I understand not, madam.
> *Cleo.* I dreamt there was an Emperor Antony.
>      O such another sleep, that I might see
>      But such another man!
> *Dol.*                          If it might please ye, –
> *Cleo.* His face was as the heavens, and therein stuck
>      A sun and moon, which kept their course, and lighted
>      This little O, the earth.                (V. ii. 71–81)

Cleopatra's first reaction to this self-important fool is icy; then she decides that he will do to stand for the prosaic, diminished world against which she sets her dream. She casts him in the role of sceptic, overrides his interruptions, and then, when she has quite finished, dares him to contradict her:

> *Cleo.* Think you there was, or might be such a man
>      As this I dreamt of?
> *Dol.*               Gentle madam, no.

*Cleo.* You lie up to the hearing of the gods.
But if there be, or ever were one such,
It's past the size of dreaming: nature wants stuff
To vie strange forms with fancy, yet to imagine
An Antony were nature's piece, 'gainst fancy,
Condemning shadows quite.                    (V. ii. 93–100)

At the most literal level, the play supports Dolabella's 'Gentle madam,
no.' His reply is given extra force by its attractive balance of courtesy
and firmness, so unlike the silliness of his first address to Cleopatra;
unexpectedly, she is bringing out the best in him. At first she simply
gives him the lie; then her language suddenly becomes difficult as she
admits he could be right ('if' and 'were' make the dream conditional, not
absolute) and goes on to argue her case by changing the meanings of
words. Shadow and substance, as normally conceived, are reversed:
the imagined Antony is the work of nature; it is prosaic reality that is a
fantasy-world of shadows.

Cleopatra's dream is not an isolated aria but arises from a dramatic
situation, and is one side of a real debate. Dolabella's 'no' is a simple way
of stating the case for prose, for history, for fact. Caesar makes the
same point – again, with unexpected courtesy – when he hears of
Antony's death:

> The breaking of so great a thing should make
> A greater crack. The round world
> Should have shook lions into civil streets,
> And citizens to their dens.                    (V. i. 14–17)

He misses the portents that really did surround the death of Julius
Caesar;[1] there is a distinct note of regret as he registers the fact that the
world he now lives in does not recognize the greatness of men in this
way. There are no miracles; man is on his own. The play's one
supernatural moment is offstage music signalling the departure of a
god. If there is to be a supernatural dimension in life, men and women
are responsible for creating it themselves, in their own minds and
imaginations. And they must do it not by imagining gods but by seeing
what is godlike in each other. Caesar and Dolabella cannot or will not
make the effort; Cleopatra can, and does.

She presents her Antony as a dream; that is one way of challenging
the facts of nature. Another is through the creations of art. Earlier in
the play Cleopatra has been exalted as she exalts Antony here: this is
done not by Antony but by Enobarbus, in a speech that, having nothing
literally supernatural about it, none the less challenges reality in its own
way:

163

The barge she sat in, like a burnish'd throne
Burn'd on the water: the poop was beaten gold;
Purple the sails, and so perfumed that
The winds were love-sick with them; the oars were silver,
Which to the tune of flutes kept stroke, and made
The water which they beat to follow faster,
As amorous of their strokes . . .
                    At the helm
A seeming mermaid steers: the silken tackle
Swell with the touches of those flower-soft hands,
That yarely frame the office. From the barge
A strange invisible perfume hits the sense
Of the adjacent wharfs.                    (II. ii. 191–7, 208–13)

A barge is a throne, fire burns on water, perfume hits with the impact of something *felt*. Where a sensible shipbuilder would use wood and rope we have silver and silk. Instead of real sailors there are women with 'flower-soft hands', and they in turn impersonate sea-nymphs and mermaids. The impersonation extends to 'pretty dimpled boys, like smiling Cupids' (202) and Cleopatra herself, 'O'er-picturing that Venus where we see / The fancy outwork nature' (200–1). The speech is not overtly about Cleopatra, yet in a deeper sense she is its centre and subject. Though she is hidden beyond description, glimpsed only in the role of Venus, the sensual artifice of the whole scene radiates outward from her, expressing her power to delight and fascinate through deception. And Enorbarbus, the realist, is clear that all this *is* a deception. From the opening line he deals in similes, not metaphors. He himself is impressed and delighted but never fooled; he knows the barge is steered by a 'seeming' mermaid. He admits that fancy can outwork nature, but they do not change places for him as they do for Cleopatra. As we listen to the speech, the categories of reality seem to dissolve and the senses melt into each other; but Enobarbus' phrasing makes it clear that all this is the product of human art. It is also, like Cleopatra's debate with Dolabella, offered as a challenge and defiance to his listeners. Maecenas has taken a vulgar tourist's view of Egypt: 'Eight wild-boars roasted whole at a breakfast, and but twelve persons there, is this true?' (II. ii. 179–80). He is fascinated by quantity; he imagines the delights not of the epicure but of the glutton. The words that begin Enobarbus' speech, 'I will tell you' (II. ii. 190), give it the quality of a set piece designed to impress. He is out to dazzle his listeners, and in the process to expose the feebleness of their own attempts to imagine Egypt.

The speech also has the effect of bringing Cleopatra and Egypt to the mind's eye during a long Roman sequence. For all the vast distances its action covers, this is a play in which one land impinges on another quickly and easily. Geographically much smaller, the England of *Henry IV* was a fragmented place where the flow of information was blocked and twisted by rumour. *Antony and Cleopatra* is full of messengers, who always tell the truth. The flow of information is clear and constant, and annihilates distance. But the crucial factor is the mind itself, which can call up instantly an absent character or an absent world. Cleopatra complains of Antony, 'He was dispos'd to mirth; but on the sudden / A Roman thought hath struck him' (I. ii. 79–80). As in *Julius Caesar* characters found their identities in the eyes of others, so in *Antony and Cleopatra* characters seem most vivid and powerful when they are absent, living in the imaginations of those who remember them. We see the greatness of Antony through Cleopatra, the glamour of Cleopatra through Enobarbus. In the first three scenes, when Antony and Cleopatra are together onstage, she plays manipulative games in which he can do nothing right; once he is safely in Rome, he can do nothing wrong:

> *Cleo.*                   What, was he sad, or merry?
> *Alex.* Like to the time o' the year between the extremes
>       Of hot and cold, he was nor sad nor merry.
> *Cleo.* O well-divided disposition!                   (I. v. 50–3)

Even their sexual relationship thrives on absence; Cleopatra's strongest erotic feelings for Antony come when all she can do is daydream.[2] At this level even the eunuch Mardian can have a rich sex life: 'Yet have I fierce affections, and think / What Venus did with Mars' (I. v. 17–18).

Idealizing others, the characters reveal their own natures. Everything we hear about Antony's wife Fulvia indicates that the world is a simpler and pleasanter place without her. But as soon as she is dead Antony takes a generous view – 'There's a great spirit gone!' – and adds, revealingly, 'she's good, being gone' (I. ii. 119, 123). Enobarbus may be right when he insists, 'the tears live in an onion, that should water this sorrow' (I. ii. 167–8), but Antony's reaction, whatever it tells us about Fulvia, is a clear sign of his own chivalry and courtesy. When Caesar idealizes Antony for his heroic endurance, he inadvertently tells us something about himself:

> When thou once
> Wast beaten from Modena, where thou slew'st
> Hirtius and Pansa, consuls, at thy heel

> Did famine follow, which thou fought'st against,
> Though daintily brought up, with patience more
> Than savages could suffer. Thou didst drink
> The stale of horses, and the gilded puddle
> Which beasts would cough at. (I. iv. 56–63)

His admiration of Antony is genuine; but, where Cleopatra's dream-Antony overflows with power and generosity, Caesar's is grotesquely degraded. He pictures Antony in defeat, and his own imagination lingers over foul images, taking the speech in a direction very different from his overt intention. If we are inclined to think of Caesar as simply cool and rational, we have to think again.

The recurring device of celebrating an absent character in a set speech takes an ugly turn here; and it is subject to direct parody when Cleopatra and the messenger between them reconstruct the absent Octavia:

> *Cleo.* Is she as tall as me?
> *Mess.*                    She is not, madam.
> *Cleo.* Didst hear her speak? is she shrill-tongu'd or low?
> *Mess.* Madam, I heard her speak; she is low-voic'd.
> *Cleo.* That's not so good: he cannot like her long.
> *Char.* Like her? O Isis! 'tis impossible.
> *Cleo.* I think so, Charmian: dull of tongue, and dwarfish!
>      What majesty is in her gait? Remember,
>      If e'er thou look'st on majesty.
> *Mess.*                    She creeps:
>      Her motion and her station are as one:
>      She shows a body, rather than a life,
>      A statue, than a breather. (III. iii. 11–21)

Lear's reference to Cordelia's low voice as 'an excellent thing in woman' shows what the conventional attitude was. But Cleopatra takes Octavia's virtues as well as her neutral qualities, and turns them to malicious caricature. The messenger quickly sees the game she is playing and joins in. This is Cleopatra at her most petty and vindictive; and yet the sheer brazenness of it is irresistible. The very next scene shows us the 'real' Octavia, a woman of feeling with a deep sense of responsibility, concerned as no one else in the play is for the suffering the war will cause, and offering to act as peacemaker. In *Henry IV* the full reality of the characters overshadowed the caricatures they made of each other; but that is not what happens here. Such is the unfairness of Shakespeare's art at this point that we find it hard to concentrate on

Octavia's virtues. A nice girl, of course, but terribly dull; our minds, like Antony's, turn back to Cleopatra, and the caricatured Octavia overrides the 'real' one.

Elsewhere in Shakespeare, the idealizing set pieces are about the state: Gaunt's England, Canterbury's commonwealth of bees, Menenius' body politic, Cranmer's vision of Elizabeth. Here they are about people. Apart from Cleopatra's parody of Octavia, they celebrate the greatness of the great. The common people, who make vivid contributions of their own elsewhere, have all but vanished. (There is, as we shall see, one important exception.) Octavia's concern for the casualties of war, 'As if the world should cleave, and that slain men / Should solder up the rift' (III. iv. 31–2), finds no echo. While Enobarbus shows a similar awareness of the scale of the conflict, he views it with equanimity:

> Then, world, thou hast a pair of chaps, no more,
> And throw between them all the food thou hast,
> They'll grind the one the other.          (III. v. 13–15)

There is no hint there of the pain and outrage of the Towton allegory. When the great make war, they consume their subjects; the process is as natural as eating. It is the same when they make love: Cleopatra talks of consuming her whole nation to create a messenger service: 'He shall have every day a several greeting, / Or I'll unpeople Egypt' (I. v. 77–8). The focus on the great individual rather than the general community has another effect. Speeches like Gaunt's and Canterbury's arise from particular dramatic situations, and support particular interests; but as they express an ideal of the state they have, or claim, qualities of timelessness and impersonality we do not find in the idealizing speeches of *Antony and Cleopatra*. Here the needs of the characters and the demands of the moment are more in the foreground, and the speeches have an impulsive, improvised quality. There is no sense of permanent reality, larger than any of the characters, to which a final appeal can be made. The characters' own tendency to live intensely for the moment – 'There's not a minute of our lives should stretch / Without some pleasure now' (I. i. 46–7) – is reflected in the dramaturgy of the play, as several critics have pointed out. For Julian Markels each action of Antony's 'seems uncaused, self-generated, a new creation whose spontaneity disarms our challenge'.[3] For Maynard Mack, this leads to difficulties of interpretation, since we are unsure 'how to reconcile one action with the next'.[4] As in *Henry V*, the problem of knowing how to make connections is compounded by the lack of knowledge of the characters' inner states of mind.[5] What is Cleopatra really up to with Thidias, with Seleucus, even with Antony? Does

Antony seriously want to make his marriage with Octavia work? Does Caesar really hope that it will? Do the characters themselves know what they want? As knowledge of them eludes us, so self-knowledge seems to elude them. They respond to the needs and desires of the moment, not to some consistent inner reality.

There is no sense of a fixed political state; no sense, either, of a fixed private self. Nor is there a fixed perspective from which to judge the action. As Margery M. Morgan has argued, Cleopatra's line about Antony, 'Though he be painted one way like a Gorgon, / The other way's a Mars' (II. v. 117–18), suggests a perspective-trick painting, 'contrary distortions imposed one upon another'.[6] We recall the perspective tricks of *Richard II*. Which is the real Antony, Cleopatra's or Dolabella's? Which is the real Caesar, the skilled general and politician or the minion of Fortune? And how do we grasp the quicksilver that is Cleopatra? The play's first two words suggest an ongoing debate: 'Nay, but' (I. i. 1). Philo and Demetrius are arguing about Antony even as they come onstage. The first words belong to Philo, who tells us to use our eyes:

> Look, where they come:
> Take but good note, and you shall see in him
> The triple pillar of the world transform'd
> Into a strumpet's fool: behold and see.

(I. i. 10–13)

His perspective is firm, and he appeals to the stage picture we see before us. He sees what Bernard Shaw was to see: 'a faithful picture of the soldier broken down by debauchery, and the typical wanton in whose arms such men perish'.[7] But later, if we take Lear's advice and look with our ears, we see Cleopatra's barge burning on the water and Antony bestriding the ocean. Nor is this a simple conflict between picture and word. Within the dialogue itself the debate goes on. We hear it in the first words of the lovers. Having been told to look, we listen:

*Cleo.* If it be love indeed, tell me how much.
*Ant.* There's beggary in the love that can be reckon'd.
*Cleo.* I'll set a bourn how far to be belov'd.
*Ant.* Then must thou needs find out new heaven, new earth.

(I. i. 14–17)

Playing the realist, Cleopatra challenges Antony to express his love within the limits of language. He declares language inadequate to express that love and the present world too small to contain it; but of course he uses words to say this. The characters' imaginations are constantly trying to create new heaven, new earth, in which Caesar and Antony are at war in the realm of the spirit and Antony and Cleopatra are avatars of Mars and Venus. But the dream of 'What Venus did with Mars' is also the prurient fantasy of a eunuch, and the characters have to live, act – and dream – in a world of hard reality in which the voices of Philo and Dolabella can be argued against, but not silenced. This does not mean, however, that Philo has the last word; he only has the first. And Shakespeare is no more content here than he was in *Richard II* to play perspective games and leave it at that. Having looked at the play's idealizing visions, we should now consider more closely the 'reality' out of which they arise.

The play's political scenes have a remarkable quality of sharp, close observation. We see not demigods but men between five and six feet tall (closer to five, as a rule) with recognizable faces. The relations of Caesar and Lepidus are caught in a matter of seconds:

> *Lep.* Farewell, my lord; what you shall know meantime
> Of stirs abroad, I shall beseech you, sir,
> To let me be partaker.
> *Caes.*                              Doubt not, sir,
> I know it for my bond.                                                  (I. iv. 81–4)

Legally they are equal partners in the triumvirate; but their relative strength and authority as men have created a very different relationship. Against Caesar's curt acknowledgement of legal obligation we can set the kindness of Antony:

> *Ant.*                              Let us, Lepidus,
> Not lack your company.
> *Lep.*                              Noble Antony,
> Not sickness should detain me.                                    (II. ii. 168–70)

A small matter, perhaps, but, as Granville-Barker observes, 'The little man is grateful.'[8] If Lepidus is a nonentity, Pompey seems at first a man seduced by his own rhetoric. He begins his first scene full of self-confidence, celebrating his own achievements and pouring scorn on his opponents. His reaction to bad news is 'Where have you this? 'tis false' (II. i. 18). But he betrays his real view of his own enterprise when he learns of Antony's return to Rome:

> I did not think
> This amorous surfeiter would have donn'd his helm
> For such a petty war.                              (II. i.  32–4)

There is nothing petty about taking on the rulers of the known world. Pompey shows here the small-scale thinking that leads him to make peace on very modest terms and to refuse Menas' offer to make him lord of all the world.

The real contest is between Caesar and Antony; the smaller figures are there to help establish the scale. For these natural enemies, nothing is too small to cause a power struggle:

> *Caes.* Welcome to Rome.
> *Ant.*                              Thank you.
> *Caes.*                              Sit.
> *Ant.*                                        Sit, sir.
> *Caes.*                                        Nay, then.      (II. ii. 28)

Caesar lets Antony win this round; and in the ensuing confrontation he seems at first on the defensive, offering complaints Antony can easily deny. But he soon has Antony driven into a corner, admitting he has 'Neglected' (89) the commitments that go with his oath. When the marriage with Octavia is proposed, he forces Antony's hand, refusing to speak 'till he hears how Antony is touch'd' (II. ii. 140). Caesar is guarded and calculating. When he feasts his army, it is only after checking the budget: 'we have store to do't, / And they have earn'd the waste' (IV. i. 15–16). Antony's style in such matters is rather different. We have seen their differing treatments of Lepidus; and Antony will defy Pompey only after thanking him for past courtesies (II. ii. 154–8). His attention to such niceties is of a piece with the old-fashioned chivalry that looks so pathetic in the war sequence, as he challenges Caesar to single combat and his followers shake their heads in disbelief. Hal, though a pragmatist, was prepared to meet Hotspur on his own terms, hero against hero, letting the whole enterprise depend on him. Caesar does not work in that way. In a small touch – 'I do not know, / Maecenas; ask Agrippa' (II. ii. 16–17) – we hear the voice of an administrator who is quite comfortable about delegating responsibility. There is no discernible affection between him and his associates, but they work together easily. Antony does inspire affection, and it causes practical problems: the messenger who brings him bad news at the start of the play can hardly bear to speak, and Antony has not only to wring the message from him but to complete it himself (I. ii. 91–102). It is easier doing business with Caesar; his messengers report bad news briskly

170

and frankly, and he accepts it in the same spirit (I. iv. 34–40). Working for the most part in small details, Shakespeare builds a decisive picture of the two men, pointing to Caesar's ultimate victory.

As in *Julius Caesar*, and in the England of the Bolingbrokes, appearance and reputation count. The final breaking of the triumvirate is preceded by a propaganda war in which accusations are hurled back and forth (III. vi) and Caesar, in order to make Antony look bad, pretends that Octavia has 'come / A market-maid to Rome' (III. vi. 50–1), though she has entered '*with her Train*' (38SD) and 'To come thus was I not constrain'd, but did it / On my free will' (56–7). Octavius, I think, genuinely loves his sister. But the needs of propaganda come first. Finally, Caesar consolidates his victory by offering evidence of

> How hardly I was drawn into this war,
> How calm and gentle I proceeded still
> In all my writings. (V. i. 74–6)

In fact the great men spend a remarkable amount of their time and effort on propaganda, while much of the real work is done by underlings. Ventidius, having just won a victory on Antony's behalf, declares, 'Caesar and Antony have ever won / More in their officer than person' (III. i. 16–17). He goes on to point out that if the underlings do too much their superiors become jealous and turn on them; hence his own refusal to exploit his present victory. This not only exposes the inner workings of war but casts an ironic light on the great men themselves. Subordinates like Ventidius have to make a conscious effort not to outdo them.

What begins as realistic observation of the political world becomes increasingly critical and deflating. The famous names of Pompey and Caesar establish the current crop of politicians as second-generation and second-rate. Menas' complaint, 'Thy father, Pompey, would ne'er have made this treaty' (II. vi. 82–3), identifies this character as Pompey the Less. Julius Caesar was known for his generosity to old enemies, and we saw a touch of this in the earlier play in his gracious words to Ligarius (II. ii. 111–13). The new Caesar is different:

> Plant those that have revolted in the vant,
> That Antony may seem to spend his fury
> Upon himself. (IV. vi. 9–11)

Antony himself is a link with a more glorious past,[9] but this only sharpens the contrast between his former achievement and his present failure. He accuses Caesar of 'harping on what I am / Not what he knew I was' (III. xiii. 142–3) and thus admits his own decline. As in the second

171

tetralogy, we are acutely aware of the ruinous effects of time, against which no achievement can stand. With his usual frankness Caesar tells Pompey, 'Since I saw you last, / There is a change upon you' (II. vi. 52–3). Even this younger Pompey is starting to look old. Caesar's own victory was one of the great achievements of history; but Maecenas says, of his reaction to Antony's death, 'When such a spacious mirror's set before him, / He needs must see himself' (V. i. 34–5). As in *Julius Caesar*, men see themselves through each other; Caesar, Maecenas speculates, sees in Antony his own mortality.

Reputation, on which so much depends in politics, is constantly related to the uncertain favour of

> Our slippery people,
> Whose love is never link'd to the deserver
> Till his deserts are past.               (I. ii. 183–5)

Even success has a way of turning sour. Enobarbus, a realistic observer of love and politics alike, makes a pragmatic decision to follow Caesar, and finds, when he sees how Caesar treats turncoats, that he is worse off than before. He dies of a broken heart, but what could have been a sentimental effect has a sardonic edge: Enobarbus has betrayed his better self *and* made a practical blunder. The shadowy, unreal nature of worldly achievement is most fully dramatized for us in the party on Pompey's galley. In the phrasing of Menas' offer to Pompey, what could have been momentous becomes farcical:

*Men.* Wilt thou be lord of all the world?
*Pomp.*                                              What say'st thou?
*Men.* Wilt thou be lord of the whole world? That's twice.

                                                      (II. vii. 60–1)

Pompey's refusal, 'In me 'tis villainy, / In thee 't had been good service' (II. vii. 73–4), not only reveals scrambled values but confirms the effect created by Menas' comic exasperation. A world that can be tossed so easily from hand to hand cannot be taken seriously. The servant who carries off the drunken Lepidus is called a strong fellow because "A bears the third part of the world' (II. vii. 89), and later in the scene we see the whole world drunk as the great men dance hand in hand, presumably in a circle, singing 'Cup us till the world go round' (II. vii. 116).[10] Later, when we are told that Antony used to have 'superfluous kings for messengers' (III. xii. 5) and that 'realms and islands were / As plates dropp'd from his pocket' (V. ii. 91–2), the power of the world is made to look trivial. Antony, on the point of losing that world, orders:

> Fall not a tear, I say, one of them rates
> All that is won and lost: give me a kiss,
> Even this repays me. (III. xi. 69–71)

We might see this as lover's hyperbole; but the play has already shown dramatically how trivial the world is. The economy of the theatre, which brings great men on to the stage as life-sized figures exposed in ordinary daylight, has let us see them 'as it were, down the wrong end of the telescope'.[11] The closer we look at them, the smaller they become.

The lovers too are closely and realistically observed. As in *Julius Caesar*, love has its own politics, in which appearances count. When Cleopatra accuses Antony of betraying her, she claims she can see it in his face: 'Thou blushest, Antony, and that blood of thine / Is Caesar's homager' (I. i. 30–1). Her manipulation of him is based on countering his appearance with hers:

> If you find him sad,
> Say I am dancing; if in mirth, report
> That I am sudden sick. (I. iii. 3–5)

That is an obvious trick, to be played when she is working through underlings. Moments later he enters, evidently Roman and serious, and she makes a snap decision: 'I am sick, and sullen' (I. iii. 13). It is hard to cope with a player who keeps changing the rules like this. And it is hard for Antony, that most artless of men, to deal with a great actress who keeps insisting that *he* is giving a performance:

> Good now, play one scene
> Of excellent dissembling, and let it look
> Like perfect honour.
> *Ant.* You'll heat my blood: no more.
> *Cleo.* You can do better yet; but this is meetly. (I. iii. 78–81)

There is, however, a crucial difference between the politics of love and the politics of the world. The Romans are constantly explaining, defending, and excusing themselves. The conference on Antony's return to Rome, and the mutual accusations that precede the outbreak of war, are prolonged exercises in self-justification on both sides. Antony and Cleopatra, on the other hand, do not deal in explanations or excuses, however much they wrong each other. Cleopatra does not demand, nor does Antony offer, the reasons for his marriage to Octavia. He simply returns to her, and she simply takes him back. (There is a gap in the action here, but we are not encouraged to fill it in;

for the purposes of the play, anything we do not see or hear about does not happen.) Through the war sequence Antony has every reason to accuse Cleopatra of betraying and destroying him; but, when the accusations come, Cleopatra does not counter them with arguments but simply waits till Antony's passion blows over, as she knows it will: 'I must stay his time' (III. xiii. 155). When she goes on to protest her loyalty, it is because she senses that Antony will now be receptive. Antony accuses her of betraying him in the last battle, and will not hear her speak; but when told she is dead he declares, 'I will o'ertake thee, Cleopatra, and / Weep for my pardon' (IV. xiv. 44–5). He says nothing of pardoning her. When, having wounded himself fatally, he learns that she is alive after all – learns, in fact, that her last trick has caused his death – there is no resentment or recrimination, merely a businesslike order: 'call my guard, I prithee . . . . Bear me, good friends, where Cleopatra bides' (IV. xiv. 128, 131). Behind the repeated accusations, even the real betrayals, the fundamental principle of their love is an unconditional acceptance of each other. To this they always return in the end, quickly and simply, with no need for the lengthy negotiations that precede reconciliation in the political world. By contrast, the politicians are bound together only by temporary expediency, however they may protest (and even want to believe) otherwise. If the final principle of love is unconditional acceptance of the other person, the final principle of politics, as this play shows it, is kill or be killed. The game is over when only Caesar is left standing.

Unconditional acceptance is not a practical or sensible attitude. It avoids analysis, judgement, and justification. But it is the attitude of a poet, and we have encountered it before in Shakespeare: 'Man is but an ass, if he go about to expound this dream.' It is a pervasive attitude in Egypt, and Antony and Cleopatra apply it to more than each other. When Caesar speaks of the people it is to analyse and judge their fickleness (I. iv. 41–7). Antony and Cleopatra just watch them: 'To-night we'll wander through the streets, and note / The qualities of people' (I. i. 53–4). At Pompey's party there is a particularly revealing discussion of things Egyptian. Antony enters, evidently in conversation with Caesar, who has apparently been asking practical questions about the economic significance of the Nile:

> Thus do they, sir: they take the flow o' the Nile
> By certain scales i' the pyramid; they know,
> By the height, the lowness, or the mean, if dearth
> Or foison follow. (II. vii. 17–20)

The great, mysterious river is here analysed for its usefulness. If Caesar has indeed started this conversation, he is getting information helpful to someone who will one day administer Egypt. The practical attitude is linked with the desire for control. But this sensible conversation is interrupted by Lepidus, drunk and as belligerent as he is capable of being, insisting that 'the Ptolemies' pyramises are very goodly things' (II. vii. 33–4) – not useful or significant, just goodly. He is silenced by Antony's description of the crocodile: 'It is shap'd, sir, like itself, and it is as broad as it hath breadth: it is just so high as it is, and moves with its own organs. It lives by that which nourisheth it, and the elements once out of it, it transmigrates' (II. vii. 41–4). A crocodile is a crocodile is a crocodile. It was so commonly an emblem of deceit that the audience must have noticed a deliberate suppression when Antony says not 'the tears of it are treacherous' but simply 'the tears of it are wet' (II. vii. 48). Divided as he is, Antony can have a practical Roman conversation with Caesar, analysing the significance of the river; and an Egyptian conversation with Lepidus, simply accepting the crocodile for what it is. This is also a key to the differing views of sex in Rome and Egypt. Agrippa's reference to Julius Caesar's affair with Cleopatra, 'He plough'd her, and she cropp'd' (II. ii. 228), describes the movement of the sexual act as seen by an observer, and judges its significance by results. Cleopatra's line, 'O, my oblivion is a very Antony, / And I am all forgotten' (I. iii. 90–1), is not overtly sexual at all; but in its sudden surrender to annihilation it evokes and savours the feeling of an orgasm.

This enjoyment of the thing itself is the key to the way in which Shakespeare dramatizes Egypt. The local colour his audience would have expected is all there: the wealth and feasting, for which Egypt was famous; the pyramids, the serpents, the insects; and above all the mysterious, fertile river, breeding monsters generated by the sun.[12] Iras' palm presages chastity 'as the o'erflowing Nilus presageth famine' (I. ii. 47). Antony swears 'By the fire / That quickens Nilus' slime' (I. iii. 68–9). His return to Cleopatra is predicted in Enobarbus' 'he will to his Egyptian dish again' (II. vi. 123), and his sharpest attack on her is 'I found you as a morsel, cold upon / Dead Caesar's trencher' (III. xiii. 116–17). In Egypt, as in Shallow's Gloucestershire, the routines of life go on: music, billiards, drinking, fishing, and making love. The Roman scenes are full of information and business, but in Egypt there is a more palpable texture, a stronger sense of felt life. The politicians talk of ruling the world, but a few place-names and a couple of disparaging references to the fickle people do not add up to a world that one can see, much less a world that sounds worth ruling. Rome itself, a palpable city in *Julius Caesar* and *Coriolanus*, complete with streets, shops, public places, houses, famous hills, and a great river, is here as neutral and unatmospheric as a committee room. Its entire political structure seems to consist of Caesar and his entourage. If we recall the formula *Senatus Populusque Romanus*, we notice that the people are a distant rumour and the Senate has vanished completely.[13] There are three images in the play of a land sinking into a river, and they are worth comparing. In Antony's 'Let Rome in Tiber melt, and the wide arch / Of the rang'd empire fall!' (I. i.33-4) Rome simply disappears, and the Tiber, characterless in itself, is merely the thing into which it vanishes. In Cleopatra's 'Melt Egypt into Nile! and kindly creatures / Turn all to serpents!' (II. v. 78-9) the life of Egypt does not disappear but returns transformed from the river, low and ugly but still alive. And there *is* life in Egypt; Rome is just empty scenery, if that. Later in the same scene Cleopatra wishes the messenger were lying about Antony's marriage 'So half my Egypt were submerg'd and made / A cistern for scal'd snakes!' (II. v. 94-5). Here the kingdom sinks only halfway, and the serpents, whose hissing can be heard in the sound of the line, are more alive than ever. In history, Rome absorbed the kingdom of the Ptolemies and the empire Caesar built lasted for centuries. In the play, the empire is spun into the drunken round dance on Pompey's galley, and for theatrical purposes disappears, while Egypt is alive and vivid to the end. Antony's crocodile, we remember, does not die; it 'transmigrates'. The economy of the theatre has made its own judgement: compressed and foreshortened, the business of history begins to look trivial, while the frivolities of Egypt, dramatized in a relaxed and detailed way, look solid and real. And it seems to be Egypt, not Rome, that has found a way to resist the ruin of time.

The play, having brought us to this point, is only half over. Shakespeare still has to relate his contrasted visions of Rome and Egypt to the contrast between the heroic and realistic visions we noted earlier. The relation is not a simple one, and demands a look at the mixture of triumph and defeat in the fates of the two lovers. Antony, a practical failure for most of the play, wins the second battle; for once his greatness can be celebrated as something seen and proven, not just talked about. His victory is preceded by the desertion of Hercules; this warns us that his success will be temporary,[14] but also establishes that, if he is a failure, he is a failure on a very high level; a man favoured by a god, and deserted by a god. The scene also lifts the action as a whole to a mysterious, supernatural plane: how, for example, does the soldier *know* that the music is Hercules (IV. iii. 15-16)? This prepares us for the arming of Antony. In *Henry IV*, Part 2, comedy, realism, and allegory were deliberately kept apart: there was a sharp difference between Henry's exemplary encounter with the Lord Chief Justice and the aimless ramblings of Justice Shallow; and there could be no final meeting between Eastcheap and Westminster. In the arming of Antony comedy, realism, and allegory are fused in a seamless whole:[15]

> *Cleo.*                     Nay, I'll help too.
>     What's this for?
> *Ant.*                     Ah, let be, let be! thou art
>     The armourer of my heart: false, false; this, this.
> *Cleo.* Sooth, la, I'll help: thus it must be.
> *Ant.*                                         Well, well,
>     We shall thrive now. Seest thou, my good fellow?
>     Go, put on thy defences.
> *Eros.*                     Briefly, sir.
> *Cleo.* Is not this buckled well?
> *Ant.*                     Rarely, rarely:
>     He that unbuckles this, till we do please
>     To daff't for our repose, shall hear a storm.
>     Thou fumblest, Eros, and my queen's a squire
>     More tight at this than thou: despatch. O love,
>     That thou couldst see my wars to-day, and knew'st
>     The royal occupation, thou shouldst see
>     A workman in't.                          (IV. iv. 5–18)

With obvious allegory, Antony is armed as the warrior of love, flanked by Cleopatra and Eros. But the scene is ballasted by realism and comedy: in Cleopatra's fumbling, her childish pride, Antony's amused, affectionate condescension, and Eros' (we may imagine) discreet silence. The scene is not just airy and fantastic; practical business is going on all through it, and Cleopatra's hands are on Antony's body. Antony is not just a hero but a 'workman', 'master of his craft'.[16] Even the fact that he has an attendant called Eros is not a detail Shakespeare made up but one he found in Plutarch.

We need this practical ballast, for the scene in other respects moves out of history. Before this battle Antony speaks not of fighting Caesar but of fighting death and fortune (III. xiii. 192–4, IV.iv.4–5). By association with the spirit of the morning, Antony seems younger: 'This morning, like the spirit of a youth / That means to be of note, begins betimes' (IV. iv. 26–7). Time seems not just halted but reversed. Wounds do not hurt: Scarus notes with interest, 'I had a wound here that was like a T, / But now 'tis made an H', and adds, 'I have yet / Room

177

for six scotches more' (IV. vii. 7–8, 9–10). But the real magic is in Antony himself. For most of the play he has followed initiatives taken by Caesar or Cleopatra. In the war, his followers complain, 'our leader's led, / And we are women's men' (III. vii. 69–70). He loses the first day's battle by following her retreat. Now at last he leads: 'You that will fight, / Follow me close, I'll bring you to't' (IV. iv. 33–4). In the process, as realism and allegory are fused, so Antony's different roles are fused. From Philo's opening speech onwards, we are told that Antony's love has destroyed his generalship. Now the warrior and the lover are one, and he celebrates his victory in powerfully erotic language:

> O thou day o' the world,
> Chain mine arm'd neck, leap thou, attire and all,
> Through proof of harness to my heart, and there
> Ride on the pants triumphing!            (IV. viii. 13–16)

In Cleopatra's 'O happy horse to bear the weight of Antony!' (I. v. 21) Antony as horseman, traditionally an image of military victory and the control of the lower passions, is transformed into Antony as lover. It is a quick summary of how Cleopatra has changed him. Now he imagines her riding him; in a further act of poetic fusion, triumph and submission become one.

Caesar too is lifted to a new level, but only briefly. He begins the battle by announcing,

> The time of universal peace is near:
> Prove this a prosperous day, the three-nook'd world
> Shall bear the olive freely.            (IV. vi. 5–7)

For a moment the future opens out, and we see the real scale of his achievement. But at once we descend to examine the means he uses, in his ugly trick of putting Antony's ex-followers in the forefront of the battle (IV. vi. 8–11). The bringer of universal peace looks small and shabby. More remarkably, he has no reaction to his day's defeat. We may take this on a realistic level and say that Caesar is the sort of politician who never acknowledges failure; or we may conclude that Antony's battle, and his victory, do not take place in the world of history Caesar inhabits. Antony's enemies are time, death, and fortune. We do not see Caesar's defeat because at his plane of reality it never happens. That is a harder reading; but it fits with the most disturbing fact about the victory, the absence of Enobarbus. The sequence is framed by his desertion and death, so that we cannot help noting that the familiar figure is missing from Antony's side. This means that, for all its air of realism, Antony's victory cannot carry full conviction, for it has not been tested against the commentary of Enobarbus, who may not stand for the whole truth but whose viewpoint, with its nice balance of sympathy, irony, and pragmatism, is an indispensable part of the truth. His absence alerts us to something shadowy in Antony's achievement: it is too close to being a matter of talk alone, and it is not quite of this world. As Antony opens the third day's battle, we know instantly that the trick cannot be played twice:

> I would they'ld fight i' the fire, or i' the air,
> We'ld fight there too. But this it is; our own foot
> Upon the hills adjoining to the city
> Shall stay with us (order for sea is given . . .).
>
> (IV. x. 3–6)

The cosmic poetry is suddenly empty; we are back in history. The heroic and practical visions had seemed for a while to come together; now they fall apart.

Antony loses, as we have always known he would. What he fears through the play is not just the loss of kingdoms but the loss of self: 'These strong Egyptian fetters I must break, / Or lose myself in dotage' (I. ii. 113–14). At the realistic level this means a loss of his Roman identity, even his sexual identity. Octavius declares he

> is not more manlike
> Than Cleopatra; nor the queen of Ptolemy
> More womanly than he. (I. iv. 5–7)

Cleopatra reports that they have played transvestite games (II. v. 22–3), and, when Antony celebrates his victory by imagining himself as the passive sexual partner, the misgivings of conventional Romans would be confirmed. His ultimate fear, however, is not the loss of an old or conventional identity, but the loss of any identity: 'Haply you shall not see me more, or if, / A mangled shadow' (IV. ii. 26–7). This is the fear that comes to a head in the aftermath of the final battle, when Antony imagines himself dissolving like the clouds of sunset:

> *Ant.* That which is now a horse, even with a thought
>   The rack dislimns, and makes it indistinct
>   As water is in water.
> *Eros.*                 It does, my lord.
> *Ant.* My good knave Eros, now thy captain is
>   Even such a body: here I am Antony,
>   Yet cannot hold this visible shape, my knave. (IV.xiv.9–14)

The eerie calm of the whole passage suggests that Antony has reached 'the very heart of loss' (IV. xii. 29), where there is nothing left but the final peace of annihilation. But the scene begins with Antony's question, 'Eros, thou yet behold'st me?' (IV. xiv. 1), and even after announcing his dissolution he can still say, 'here I am Antony'. Antony's dissolving into nothing is something that can be talked of, but not seen; at the simplest level, the actor's body gives his words the lie. His loss of self, like his victory the previous day, is not quite real; Antony is still before us, as real as he ever was.

It is worth noting that if he has been submissive in Egypt –

> I go from hence
> Thy soldier, servant, making peace or war,
> As thou affects. (I. iii. 69–71)

– he has been equally submissive in Rome, making under pressure a marriage that puts him in a false position in which he behaves with less than his usual chivalry. Cleopatra taunts him with being at Caesar's beck and call –

> 'Do this, or this;
> Take in this kingdom, and enfranchise that;
> Perform't, or else we damn thee.'
> (I. i. 22–4)

– and, more humiliating, at Fulvia's (I. iii. 20–1). This is a caricature, but based on truth: in the political scenes Antony is generally passive, following initiatives taken by others. Caesar insists that a showdown between them was inevitable – 'we could not stall together, / In the whole world' (V. i. 39–40) – and the Soothsayer predicts that Antony is bound to lose. He has, in other words, the choice of being destroyed in Egypt or destroyed in Rome. It may be worth pausing at this point over the fate of Alexas. Charmian utters a comic curse on him, praying he will be cuckolded fiftyfold by a succession of bad wives; what actually happens is that he betrays Antony for the sake of Caesar, and Caesar hangs him (IV. vi. 11–16). The political humiliation is worse than the sexual one.

Nor is Antony's choice simply two methods of destruction. It is in Rome that things disappear, including Rome itself; in Egypt they are transformed. This is what happens to Antony. After one of the most lyrical death scenes in English drama – 'Unarm, Eros, the long day's task is done, / And we must sleep' (IV. xiv. 35–6) – he fails to kill himself. The workman has bungled: 'I have done my work ill, friends' (IV. xiv. 105). And we know even as we watch his attempted suicide that he is acting on a false report of Cleopatra's death. He has to die not as a Stoic

Roman in the manner of Brutus and Cassius, but as Cleopatra's lover, held for the last time in her arms. And there has to be more than lyricism in his last moments, or they will not be a full summary of him. The aftermath of his bungled stroke is cruel and embarrassing: he writhes on the stage, no one will finish him off, and Decretas steals his sword to give it to Caesar. The business of raising him to the monument exalts him, together with Cleopatra, above the ordinary Romans on the main stage; but it is also physically difficult, even grotesque and ludicrous. In the revised version of Samuel Daniel's *Cleopatra*, there is a detail that, according to Margaret Lamb, may reflect business in the King's Men's production: Antony gets stuck halfway up and dangles in mid-air, dripping blood on the spectators below.[17] Even without this detail, there is in the stage picture a recollection of Cleopatra's earlier joke about herself as a fisher of men: 'I'll think them every one an Antony, / And say "Ah, ha! y'are caught"' (II. v. 14–15). Anyone who has seen a Crucifixion play knows that the sheer physical difficulty of getting Christ raised on the cross has powerful dramatic impact. Shakespeare aims for a similar impact here, as Antony is drawn up to the monument, but he leavens it with comedy, some of which is sexual: 'Here's sport indeed! How heavy weighs my lord!' (IV. xv. 32). Antony, now physically passive as never before, is restored in the language to his dominant role as lover. In the sequence as a whole he is at once exalted and humiliated, and the tone of the scene veers between the grand –

> O sun,
> Burn the great sphere thou mov'st in, darkling stand
> The varying shore o' the world.          (IV. xv. 9–11)

– and the pragmatic: 'None about Caesar trust but Proculeius' (IV. xv. 48). The scene summarizes the full range of Antony, in a way in which the second day's victory and the dissolving clouds did not. But the remarkable thing is that we never see him die. Editors usually place a stage direction for his death around Cleopatra's 'O, see, my women: / The crown o' the earth doth melt' (IV. xv. 62–3), but there is no stage direction in the Folio. The effect Shakespeare wants, I think, is that at some point, as Cleopatra talks, he fades out, so quietly that we do not see it happen. To steal another actor's death scene is, we might say, a feat that only Cleopatra could manage. But she does it for a reason. As the physical Antony fades, he is replaced by the heroic Antony for whom Cleopatra is the spokesman, the Antony we hear of in her speech to Dolabella. For Antony, loss is a final step to transformation.

The realistic and heroic Antony are finally separate: one is seen, the other talked of. The heroic Antony, like the heroic Julius Caesar in the earlier play, is securely in place only after the other Antony is dead. Cleopatra goes one stage further. She has defined the heroic Antony for us; she must create for her own death a convincing heroic image of herself, something not just talked of but shown. She does this not by selection, as Hal defines his kingship by cutting out his former life, but by a fusion of everything she has been, high and low, grand and comic. She centres it on a political point: it matters now, as never before, that she is Queen of Egypt. Earlier, whatever political significance her affair with Antony may have had was blurred by a concentration on the affair itself. When she and Antony adopted royal images, we saw this only through Caesar's unsympathetic eyes, as a vulgar display in the market-place (III. vi. 2–12). They were surrounded by 'all the unlawful issue that their lust / Since then hath made between them' (III. vi. 7–8), suggesting not the fertility of a true royal line but the casual, prolific breeding of animals. In later negotiations with Caesar, when Cleopatra requests 'The circle of the Ptolemies for her heirs' (III. xii. 18), the idea of preserving a royal line becomes more serious. After Antony's death she demands 'conquer'd Egypt for my son' (V. ii. 19). In the end, however, Cleopatra's royalty matters more as a means of self-assertion, institutionalizing her grandeur and surrounding it with imagery that is not a matter of words alone. When she orders, 'Show me, my women, like a queen' (V. ii. 226), she emphasizes the importance of the stage picture. Characteristically, Caesar appreciates not the symbolism but the triumph of the will, saying that Cleopatra 'being royal / Took her own way' (V. ii. 334–5). But at least he recognizes that Cleopatra's nature in this respect is a function of her office. Charmian makes another political point: 'It is well done, and fitting for a princess / Descended of so many royal kings' (V. ii. 325–6). Against this regal past, Caesar is a mere republican upstart, as diminished as Napoleon among the pyramids. However we judge his victory, we know that like the Bolingbrokes he had to work for it; Cleopatra simply *is* a queen, as a crocodile simply *is* a crocodile. Thidias calls Caesar 'The universal landlord' (III. xiii. 72), and we may recall John of Gaunt's rebuke to his nephew: 'Landlord of England art thou now, not king' (*Richard II*, II. i. 113). We have seen in *Julius Caesar* how uneasily regal imagery sits in Rome, and this Caesar never attempts to use it.

If that were all that could be said, we would conclude that Cleopatra and Caesar have won separate victories on different terms. But Cleopatra has also beaten Caesar on his own terms, something Antony never managed to do. When Antony advises her, 'None about Caesar trust but Proculeius', she replies, 'My resolution, and my hands, I'll trust, / None about Caesar' (IV. xv. 48–50). Events prove her right and Antony wrong. Proculeius betrays her; Cleopatra does better on her own – enlisting, of all people, Dolabella. Given that politics deals in appearances, Caesar wants to bolster his appearance by adding Cleopatra to his train of captives: 'her life in Rome / Would be eternal in our triumph' (V. i. 65–6). This is not, as we shall see, the sort of eternity Cleopatra wants. Proculeius asks her to co-operate:

> let the world see
> His nobleness well acted, which your death
> Will never let come forth. (V. ii. 44–6)

At the same time Caesar tries to cut down her appearance of grandeur; he insults her, as the Countess's messenger insulted Talbot, by claiming not to recognize her: 'Which is the Queen of Egypt?' (V. ii. 112). But he has met his match. Grovelling before him, she puts him off his guard, and buys the time she needs to cheat him of his triumph. She imagines the asp calling 'great Caesar ass, / Unpolicied!' (V. ii. 306–7), and once again we hear the hissing of the snakes of Egypt, those symbols of indestructible life. One of the guards sums up the last phase of the political action in two words: 'Caesar's beguil'd' (V. ii. 322).

Nor is Cleopatra content with a royal Egyptian triumph over republican Rome. She takes over Rome itself, as she has taken over Antony, using her gift for transformation to embody in herself what was best in the Rome of legend: 'Let's do it after the high Roman fashion' (IV. xv. 87). The low Roman fashion of the present is indicated when Caesar talks blandly of corrupting a Vestal Virgin for money (III. xii. 29–31). Cleopatra, I think, savours the irony of being in the end the noblest Roman of them all. In the process she dismisses finally the conventional Roman view of herself and Antony, Philo's view. If she is taken to Rome in triumph, then

> saucy lictors
> Will catch at us like strumpets, and scald rhymers
> Ballad us out o' tune. The quick comedians
> Extemporally will stage us, and present
> Our Alexandrian revels: Antony
> Shall be brought drunken forth, and I shall see
> Some squeaking Cleopatra boy my greatness
> I' the posture of a whore. (V. ii. 213–20)

The Romans become dirty old men, their view of Antony and Cleopatra

183

a vulgar play of a drunk and a whore. Shakespeare, through Cleopatra, invites us to compare that play with his, and its third-rate boy actor with the brilliant lad he trusted with this part (and with this line). The theatre that degrades, this time at least, is not Shakespeare's theatre, which has presented Cleopatra, as it presented Henry V and Julius Caesar, in a form that, though not uncritical, is full and rich and refuses the easy route of caricature.

As true theatre defies time – 'we'll strive to please you every day' – so does kingship. Cleopatra's order, 'Give me my robe, put on my crown, I have / Immortal longings in me' (V. ii. 279–80), implicitly connects kingship with immortality (and with theatre, for she is dressing the part, though in her case this is no impersonation). The Queen is dead, long live the Queen. However, she does not aim at the immortality that is mere survival through time. Henry V, not anticipating some recent developments in Shakespeare criticism, could be confident about how England would remember St Crispin's Day. But, as history is written by the victors, Antony and Cleopatra will survive through history as part of Caesar's story. Caesar himself says as much in the speech that ends the play:

> No grave upon the earth shall clip in it
> A pair so famous: high events as these
> Strike those that make them: and their story is
> No less in pity than his glory which
> Brought them to be lamented. Our army shall
> In solemn show attend this funeral,
> And then to Rome.                                    (V. ii. 357–63)

Having paid his tribute, he pulls the focus to himself, and, leaving the lovers in their graves, turns to the next stage in the story of Rome. This would not do for Cleopatra. Enobarbus' way of surviving is even worse. Having promised himself 'a place i' the story' (III. xiii. 46) for his loyalty to Antony, he predicts a future of infamy for his betrayal: 'let the world rank me in register / A master-leaver, and a fugitive' (IV. ix. 21–2). After death, survival in this world is a chancy business, dependent on the interpretation of posterity. Antony thinks of going to another world:

> Where souls do couch on flowers, we'll hand in hand,
> And with our sprightly port make the ghosts gaze:
> Dido, and her Aeneas, shall want troops,
> And all the haunt be ours.                          (IV. xiv. 51–4)

In some ways this is a legitimate reflection of their life together, especially the idea of playing out their love in public, before an audience.[18] Antony and Cleopatra, in striking contrast to Romeo and Juliet, are never alone. But couching on flowers does not seem quite the style of the love we have seen, nor does strolling hand in hand sound as though it will satisfy the Cleopatra who cried, 'O happy horse to bear the weight of Antony!' This is to say nothing of Antony's sentimental view of Dido and Aeneas, and his revision of their last painful encounter in the underworld, a story Shakespeare's audience would have known from Virgil.

We have, then, no satisfying image of a life beyond death, in this world or the next. Cleopatra's solution is simple, or at least simply phrased: 'I am again for Cydnus, / To meet Mark Antony' (V. ii. 227–8). She imagines herself not beginning a new life but starting the old one again; she takes time and twists it in a circle, like an asp coiled in a basket.[19] It is repetition like that of the theatre, where the players time and again can go back to the same starting point. If Antony's dream of immortality is a wistful fantasy, Cleopatra's, being rooted in the repeatability of the theatrical occasion itself, has greater substance. This is in line with the conscious dressing-up and role-playing of her last moments, and her scorn for the Roman theatre's shabby imitation of her. As her first appearance to Antony in the pageant of the barge was the product of art, so her last appearance in the play is consciously artistic, consciously theatrical. In her words, 'I am again for Cydnus', the one occasion circles back into the other, and we see before us the splendour we only heard of. Shadow and substance are joined. Cleopatra's immortality is not a dream of the future but something acted out before us, concretely, now; and something that can be acted over and over whenever the play is presented. At the end of *Henry V* the circling of time suggested the futility of history; in *Julius Caesar*, the characters' attempts to find significant form in their lives. For Cleopatra, the circle means a chance to have the same life over again, cheating time not by getting out of it but by going through it, finding transcendence as she always has, in the here and now, not shaped or analysed but felt intensely: 'Eternity was in our lips, and eyes' (I. iii. 35). We have been fairly prepared for this. Egypt has already disrupted our normal sense of time: in the long sequence from II. v to III. iii it seems that weeks pass in Rome while minutes pass in Egypt.[20] We have seen Antony briefly restored to youth on the morning of his one victory; and the Antony Cleopatra imagines in defiance of Dolabella expresses the fertility of nature in a way that ordinary time would make impossible:

> For his bounty,
> There was no winter in 't; an autumn[21] 'twas
> That grew the more by reaping.
>
> (V. ii. 86–8)

Antony has imagined banks of unchanging flowers; Cleopatra imagines a harvest that happens over and over.

At the start of her last scene, Cleopatra seems to be trying to stop the world of time, change, and fortune, the world of Caesar:

> it is great
> To do that thing that ends all other deeds,
> Which shackles accidents, and bolts up change;
> Which sleeps, and never palates more the dung,
> The beggar's nurse, and Caesar's.             (V. ii. 4–8)

She sees her own nature as transformed: 'now from head to foot / I am marble-constant' (V. ii. 238–9). But marble is not her true medium: she has always appealed by change, variety, and action, not by any fixed achievement. As Susan Snyder puts it, to hop forty paces through the public street (II. ii. 229) 'is surely no way to *arrive* anywhere'.[22] Enobarbus, early in the play, gives us a clue as to how her death scene will really work: 'Cleopatra catching but the least noise of this, dies instantly. I have seen her die twenty times upon far poorer moment: I do think there is mettle in death, which commits some loving act upon her, she hath such a celerity in dying' (I. ii. 137–42). Enobarbus' jokes connect her play-acting with her capacity for multiple orgasms; the cumulative effect is to make death, like sex, a game that can be played over and over, taking away its sting by taking away its finality. By the end of the play Enobarbus is gone. But if we take his view of Cleopatra into the final scene we will find it does not destroy that scene but helps us see it more clearly. The Clown who brings the asp gives us a comic view of death. His warning, 'there is no goodness in the worm' (V. ii. 265–6), is offset by his jokes: 'his biting is immortal: those that do die of it, do seldom or never recover' (V. ii. 245–7). A recent victim 'makes a very good report o' the worm' (V. ii. 254), though the Clown suspects that her report of her death may be a little exaggerated. Death as described here hardly sounds final, and immortality is a matter of easy chat among neighbours. The Clown is the play's only commoner; his effect is not just to take the sting out of death[23] but to bring immortality down to earth.

He also combines two of Egypt's principal activities, sex and feasting, when he says, 'I know, that a woman is a dish for the gods, if the devil dress her not' (V. ii. 272–4). The asp and the figs are sexual symbols. Antony has already declared,

> I will be
> A bridegroom in my death, and run into't
> As to a lover's bed.                    (IV. xiv. 99–101)

Cleopatra makes the same connection, but in a more intimate and physical way: 'The stroke of death is as a lover's pinch, / Which hurts, and is desir'd' (V. ii. 294–5). She encourages the asp as she might a clumsy lover: 'poor venomous fool, / Be angry, and despatch' (V. ii. 304–5). Though she is robed and crowned, she dies not on a throne but on a bed (V. ii. 354); her last moments are full of touching, kissing, and handling. Her action in applying the asp to her breast makes us conscious of her body as an ordinary stabbing or poisoning would not. That body is anything but marble: 'Dost thou not see my baby at my breast, / That sucks the nurse asleep?' (V. ii. 308–9). Nor is her nature really altered. She is, as before, putting on a performance for Antony as audience: 'I see him rouse himself / To praise my noble act' (V. ii. 283–4). And she is already getting ready for the next quarrel, saying of Iras, who is dead before her,

> If she first meet the curled Antony,
> He'll make demand of her, and spend that kiss
> Which is my heaven to have.                    (V. ii. 300–2)[24]

As she talks through Antony's death she talks through her own: 'O Antony! Nay, I will take thee too. / What should I stay –' (V. ii. 311–12). Death interrupts her, but we may imagine she goes on talking on the other side. Nor is there a stillness on stage when she dies: Charmian's 'your crown's awry, / I'll mend it, and then play' (V. ii. 317–18) suggests that Shakespeare wants the small fussy movements, the touching and handling, to continue.

This is an intensely physical scene, alive with the full language of the theatre. It uses royal symbols as 'visual verification of the claims of the poetry',[25] allowing us to see what Enobarbus in his description of the barge only talked about. The royal Cleopatra, the crafty politician who outwits Caesar, and the sensual woman come together. As its suggestions of marriage and fertility link it with the traditional ending of comedy,[26] so the style moves easily between grandeur and laughter. The tone of the scene is caught in Cleopatra's words to Charmian, 'when thou has done this chare, I'll give thee leave / To play till doomsday' (V. ii. 230–1). *Antony and Cleopatra* is like *Richard III* in giving a mythical dimension to the world of history. The difference is that while in *Richard III* myth took over history, fixing it in simple shapes that no historian would see as true, *Antony and Cleopatra* allows us glimpses of human grandeur working through the vicissitudes of time and through closely observed reality. Its method is not selection but fusion. *Henry IV* ended with a great king publicly dismissing a representative of the sensual life, history overriding comedy. *Antony and Cleopatra* ends with a great queen, robed, crowned, and triumphant, joking with her attendants and handling her own body as she waits in bed for her lover.

# 8

# *Coriolanus*

In Cleopatra's dream of the emperor Antony there was a recognizable connection between the demigod whose bounty was a harvest that 'grew the more by reaping' and the naturally generous man we saw before us. But the difference in scale was more striking, and our main impression was of the distance between Cleopatra's idealized Antony and the flawed character the actor was given to play. In *Coriolanus*, when Cominius celebrates the deeds of the hero, the connection between ideal and reality is much tighter:

> He stopp'd the fliers,
> And by his rare example made the coward
> Turn terror into sport; as weeds before
> A vessel under sail, so men obey'd
> And fell below his stem: his sword, death's stamp,
> Where it did mark, it took; from face to foot
> He was a thing of blood, whose every motion
> Was tim'd with dying cries: alone he enter'd
> The mortal gate of th'city, which he painted
> With shunless destiny, aidless came off,
> And with a sudden reinforcement struck
> Corioles like a planet. (II. ii. 103–14)

It is almost supernatural, almost inhuman. But we can say of it, as we cannot say of Cleopatra's vision, that we have seen it with our own eyes.[1] Point by point, Cominius recounts what has already been acted out on the stage. He exaggerates only to simplify, to bring out the essence of the scene. Gloucester, mourning Henry V, created a similar picture of that hero, whose 'brandish'd sword did blind men with his beams' (*1 Henry VI*, I. i. 10), concluding, 'His deeds exceed all speech' (15). Cominius' first words are 'I shall lack voice' (II. ii. 82). What was conventional hyperbole about a character we never saw is now a

189

genuine question about whether language can match what we have just been shown.

The split this time is not between imagination and reality, but between two areas of reality, war and civil life. We see not so much a man who is, and is not, heroic, as a man whose heroism affects us differently in different contexts. As Antony is at home in the realm of the imagination and at a loss in the business of the world, so Martius is at home on the battlefield – when war breaks out he is frankly delighted (I. i. 224) – and out of place in the political arena. That at least is our first impression. There is a fine simplicity about war as Martius experiences it: the enemy is the enemy, and the task at hand is to beat him.[2] Lesser spirits like Cominius can take a balanced view of a retreat, congratulating the army on being 'neither foolish in our stands / Nor cowardly in retire' (I. vi. 2–3). Martius is absolute: 'Are you lords o'th' field? / If not, why cease you till you are so?' (I. vi. 47–8). It is this extra edge of the unreasonable that drives him to achievement against impossible odds. Though Cominius is in command, Martius pulls the focus to himself by his greater achievements, and this produces not a flicker of resentment from his colleagues. Henry V's achievements, theatrically speaking, were those of language: we never saw him strike a blow. Hal showed his heroism before our eyes when he killed Hotspur. Martius in this respect is more like Hal; but the focus is not so much on what he does as on what he is. He is a striking figure. When he was younger, his mother tells us, 'youth with comeliness plucked all gaze his way' (I. iii. 7–8), and what we see in battle is an extension of that. After his single-handed attack on Corioles he becomes, as Cominius later calls him, a thing of blood. Cominius asks, 'Who's yonder, / That does appear as he were flay'd?' (I. vi. 21–2), and recognizes him only by the voice (25–7). Martius himself declares, 'To Aufidius thus / I will appear and fight' (I. v. 19–20). He seems quite conscious of the power of his appearance; he will not just fight his adversary but display himself to him. In this state he can also excite his own soldiers: when he calls for volunteers *They all shout and wave their swords* (I. vi. 75SD).

That moment of excitement is shown, acted out. The excitement of the crowd on his return to Rome, like the greatness of Antony, is only described, and seems a little less real. There may even be unconscious irony in the messenger's report, 'I have seen the dumb men throng to see him, and / The blind to hear him speak' (II. i. 260–1). We are reminded of another saviour around whom the crowds gathered; but in the presence of Coriolanus the dumb remain dumb and the blind remain blind. He does not reach out and touch the people. It is emphasized, over and over, that his achievement at Corioles is a solitary one: 'he is himself alone, / To answer all the city' (I. iv. 51–2). That line reverberates through the play, as we see him alone against Rome, against Antium, and then against Rome again. '*They all bustle about Coriolanus*' (III. i. 183) is a stage direction from a political scene that would fit equally well in the war sequence. When his soldiers lift him in their arms he cries, 'O me alone! Make you a sword of me!' (I. vi. 76).[3] This is exact: he is not the sword-arm of Rome but the sword, not a part of the body politic but an instrument the body politic uses – and later throws away, only to find it in other hands. As long as he can fight he is comfortable; but in human relations of other kinds he is prickly. In striking contrast to Henry V, he rallies his troops by insult and abuse. When he leads it is by a temporarily inspiring example rather than by any natural rapport with his followers. Cominius insists that his deeds must be recognized: 'Rome must know / The value of her own' (I. ix. 20–1); but even this form of contact offends him, and his rejection of praise passes quickly from irritation to absurd anger as he accuses his friends of flattery (I. ix. 42–3). Yet the new name, Coriolanus, seems to please him, since his acceptance of it is (for him) gracious and good-humoured:

> I will go wash;
> And when my face is fair, you shall perceive
> Whether I blush or no: howbeit, I thank you.
>
> (I. ix. 66–8)

Why does the name please him? Perhaps because he can see it as *his*, something he can possess, while the voices of other men belong finally to themselves. The name recognizes not his family or tribe but his achievement; it is therefore his in a special sense. Yet it is bestowed by Cominius. As the gift of another man, it is a constant reminder of his dependence on other people for his identity;[4] this is a theme we have seen before in the Roman plays. In a complementary moment a few lines later Coriolanus, having got a new name for himself, forgets the name of the poor man who sheltered him in Corioles and whose kindness he would now like to return (I. ix. 80–9). The impulse of generosity is surely genuine; but it is blocked by something funda-mental in his nature, the fact that 'Other people are not quite real to him.'[5] In battle Martius can be a thing of blood, a sword; but in the focus on names towards the end of the war sequence we feel the relationships of civil life returning (Martius evidently visited his poor host at a time of peace), and we see that for him these relationships are difficult.

Aufidius' servants will later describe peace as an unhealthy state (IV. v. 225–38). For the tribunes it is comforting to see 'Our tradesmen singing in their shops and going / About their functions friendly' (IV. vi. 8–9), but this attractive picture is shadowed by the servants' claim, heard moments earlier, that peace 'makes men hate one another . . . because they then less need one another' (IV. v. 236–8). Peace, in this play, is not an unmixed blessing. Its return after the first campaign is signalled by a new diffuseness in the theatrical idiom: a cooling of the play's temperature, a slowing of its pace, and a general sense of anticlimax. The town we have just seen Coriolanus win in such exciting fashion will be 'deliver'd back on good condition' (I. x. 2). The striking battle poetry of Cominius' tribute to Coriolanus is preceded by a cool prose scene in which two officers construct a balanced picture of the hero's relations with the people – realistic, analytical, and rather deflating (II. ii. 5–35). They are presumably civil, not army, officers, for as they speak they are laying cushions: a simple theatrical sign of a return to civil life. Volumnia, 'as if plotting a heroic biography',[6] takes it for granted that there will be a role for her son in this life: 'there will be large cicatrices to show the people when he shall stand for his place' (II. i. 146–8) ('when', we notice, not 'if'). The wounds that made him a thing of blood have now hardened into scars, and even these are no longer badges of heroism but counters to use in the political market-place.[7]

Coriolanus has the wisdom to see what is wrong with his mother's plan: 'I had rather be their servant in my way / Than sway with them in theirs' (II. i. 201–2). This shows remarkable shrewdness and self-knowledge. For him, military service is freedom, and political power would be servitude. His failure to act on this insight is arguably his worst blunder. His misgivings are amply justified by his own behaviour. When praised on the field of battle, he protests but stands his ground; when merely threatened with praise in the Capitol (by the same man, Cominius), he walks out, remarking, 'When blows have made me stay, I fled from words' (II. ii. 72). He seems eager to show his bleeding body to Aufidius, but to show his scars to the people is another matter. Set upon by Volscian soldiers, he is in his element; set upon by peaceful Romans who just want him to be polite and ask for their voices, he very nearly retreats before the encounter is over:[8]

> Rather than fool it so,
> Let the high office and the honour go
> To one that would do thus. I am half through,
> The one part suffer'd, the other will I do.
>
> (II. iii. 120–3)

We never see him vacillate like this in battle. Translated from war to politics, he loses in translation.

192

After the victory at Corioles, Cominius offers him tribute 'In sign of what you are, not to reward / What you have done' (I. ix. 26–7), and it is on precisely this point – his identity, what he *is* – that he feels most threatened in politics. Friends and enemies alike insist that he wear the gown of humility and beg the voices of the people because it is a custom. Sicinius declares the people will not 'bate / One jot of ceremony', and Menenius tells him, 'Take to you, as your predecessors have, / Your honour with your form' (II. ii. 140–1, 143–4). As a soldier, Coriolanus is used to doing what has to be done, rather than what is traditionally done, and he objects to the blind following of custom for its own sake (II. iii. 116–20); later, Sicinius (ironically, for his own office is a recent creation) will denounce him as 'a traitorous innovator' (III. i. 173). But his real objection is to the compromising of his own identity. To do what his predecessors have done, because they have done it, is to surrender the individual to the office, the man to the role. Henry V can do this gladly, letting the stream of his own life 'mingle with the state of floods, / And flow henceforth in formal majesty' (*2 Henry IV*, V. ii. 132–3). But the temporary and elected office of consul has none of the mystique of kingship; republics do not work in that way. Coriolanus, as he himself sees it, would not be entering a larger life but simply losing his own. The need for approval, recognized by Hal as one of the conditions of kingship after the deposition of Richard II, is built into the Roman political system as an absolute necessity, without which the office cannot be held at all. As a result Coriolanus is forced to 'crave the hire which first we do deserve' (II. iii. 113), as though his desert is not his own but bestowed by the people.

There was an element of performance and display in the military scenes: the mere appearance of the hero was enough to generate excitement, and he seemed quite conscious of this. But that performance reflected his authentic self. The performances of civil life are different. The ceremony of begging the people's votes demands that Coriolanus play-act, pretend a humility he does not feel, wear a standard-issue costume instead of being clothed, as at Corioles, in his own blood. He calls this 'a part / That I shall blush in acting' (II. ii. 144–5), and when told that he has passed the test asks immediately, 'May I change these garments?' (II. iii. 145). It is play-acting that is uppermost in his second attempt to win the people. His mother coaches him:

> Go to them, with this bonnet in thy hand,
> And thus far having stretch'd it – here be with them –
> Thy knee bussing the stones – for in such business
> Action is eloquence, and the eyes of th'ignorant
> More learned than the ears. (III. ii. 73–7)

As the scene proceeds, the theatrical language becomes overt to the point of self-mockery, as though Coriolanus and his friends are trying to deal with something intolerable by making a joke of it:

> *Cor.*                                       ... To th' market-place!
>     You have put me now to such a part which never
>     I shall discharge to th'life.
> *Com.*                              Come, come, we'll prompt you.
>
> (III. ii. 104–6)

The fact that the performance has to be given in the market-place equates acting with commercial bargaining.[9] Coriolanus is not even a gentleman amateur but a tradesman (like Richard Burbage) doing it for pay. It is a small step from that to prostitution: 'Away my disposition, and possess me / Some harlot's spirit!' (III. ii. 111–12). He goes on to imagine himself impersonating a enunch, a virgin, a schoolboy, and a beggar (112–20). The actor's versatility, a nightmare for Richard II and an opportunity for Hal, is several different kinds of degradation for Coriolanus. He imagines himself losing his social position, his physical strength, and his sexual identity, in a loss of self more specific and detailed than anything Antony feared. Small wonder that when he gets to the market-place his pretence of humility cracks almost at once, to his own palpable relief.

In war, then, Coriolanus is a myth come to life, acting out before us heroism of a sort that in *Julius Caesar* and *Antony and Cleopatra* was only talked about. When he comes back to Rome we see, in the words of Eugene M. Waith, 'the impossibility in this world, as in the world of Bussy d'Ambois, of reliving a myth'.[10] Chapman's hero operates in a corrupt and trivial court, Shakespeare's in a city that works by rules of compromise and pretence to which he cannot and will not adjust. But there is more to the problem than a conflict between a straightforward hero and a devious, sophisticated political world. We need to look more closely at that world, and at Coriolanus' place in it. For he does have a place there, no less than in the Roman army. When he first confronts the citizens whose voices he needs, the encounter goes surprisingly well:

> *Cor.* ... You know the cause, sir, of my standing here?
> *Third Cit.* We do, sir; tell us what hath brought you to't.
> *Cor.* Mine own desert.
> *Second Cit.* Your own desert?

*Cor.* Ay, but not mine own desire.

*Third Cit.* How, not your own desire?

*Cor.* No, sir, 'twas never my desire yet to trouble the poor with begging.

*Third Cit.* You must think, if we give you anything, we hope to gain by you.

*Cor.* Well then, I pray, your price o' th'consulship?

*First Cit.* The price is, to ask it kindly.

*Cor.* Kindly, sir, I pray, let me ha't.                    (II. iii. 64–76)

There is wit and frankness on both sides here, and through the banter there is a meeting of minds. Neither party can pretend to like the other, but a rough working arrangement seems possible. 'Kindly' in Coriolanus' last line seems to refer both to his kindness in asking and their kindness in granting, and the word itself embodies a pun that catches the quality of the scene. Coriolanus and the citizens are being themselves, true to their kind; but they are also being as gracious as it is in their nature to be. Above all, they are being honest with each other. Rough and prickly though it is, the dialogue shows a limited but genuine rapport. Later Coriolanus warms to his task and puts on a smooth, ironic, self-mocking performance in which he pretends to be accepting the requirements of the ceremony: 'For your voices I have fought, / Watch'd for your voices' (II. iii. 125–6). This time there is no dialogue; he does not let the citizens get a word in edgeways. And this time he is lying. The Third Citizen, who has earlier said that the people are obliged to give Coriolanus their voices if he asks for them (II. iii. 5–9), consolidates his own misgivings and those of his fellows by asking, 'Was not this mockery?' (II. iii. 171). Indeed it was; and there was mockery even in that first encounter. But that also showed that Coriolanus and the citizens could make contact with each other by stepping outside the strict requirements of the occasion. It is when he plays by the rules that Coriolanus descends to play-acting and sarcasm, and the citizens are nonplussed, confused, and finally indignant. If Coriolanus could speak to the people as himself, without pretending humility, without pretending that he fought simply for their voices, but admitting that on this occasion he needs them, he might get somewhere. He might even find himself listening to and appreciating the citizens when their frankness matches his own; indeed, we almost see this happen. But politics, no less than war, has its own simplicities. Like a play within the play, the vote-begging routine casts Coriolanus and the people in set roles that freeze their relationship and block any possibility of real contact.

195

The people when left to themselves are capable of an open view of their awkward hero. In the very first scene they debate his faults and achievements, and speculate about the motives that drive him, in a way that shows real understanding of the issues and the difficulties (I. i. 29–45). They speak neither in monosyllables nor in Mummerset but in the thoughtful, sophisticated, sometimes difficult prose of Shakespeare's late period: 'though soft-conscienced men can be content to say it was for his country, he did it to please his mother, and to be partly proud, which he is, even to the altitude of his virtue' (I. i. 36–9). It is Menenius who in the fable of the belly reduces the body politic to a simple system for the distribution of benefits, in which the belly only gives and the other parts only receive. Gaunt's England and Canterbury's commonwealth of bees stressed the variety of national achievement, and Canterbury especially insisted on the 'divers functions' (*Henry V*, I. ii. 184) of the beehive. For Menenius only one organ matters, and it does only one thing. Of all Shakespeare's set speeches describing an ideal state, this is the most brutally reductive. It is one of the citizens who sees every part as having a function:

> The kingly crown'd head, the vigilant eye,
> The counsellor heart, the arm our soldier,
> Our steed the leg, the tongue our trumpeter.
>
> (I. i. 114–16)

Recognizing a dangerous adversary here, Menenius tries to dispose of him with mockery, calling him 'the great toe of this assembly' (I. i. 154) and, with more insidious irony, declaring, ''Fore me, this fellow speaks!' (I. i. 119), as though an articulate citizen were an astonishing prodigy. But the citizen in a few lines has done more with the idea of the body politic than Menenius in his long oration.

In a way the plebeians complement Coriolanus: as he shows up badly in peace, they show up badly in war, sneaking away in comic cowardice when Martius ironically offers to recruit them (I. i. 247–50) and putting much of their energy into looting. Though the common soldiers take part in the final attack on Corioles, the general effect of the war sequence is that Coriolanus, unlike Talbot, wins his own battles with little help from 'that article'. But, just as his single-mindedness makes him unfit for politics, so the sheer variety of their opinions, their ability to hold real debates among themselves, could be a strength to a free republic. Though their own attitude to this variety is ruefully self-mocking (II. iii. 15–36), their arguments among themselves offer some of the play's shrewdest and most interesting commentary. In the first scene they arrest their own rebellion in mid-flight 'because it is

196

important to them to inquire exactly what they are doing, and why'.[11]
But they are betrayed, no less than Coriolanus is, by the political forms
Rome makes available to them. In the first scene they have a problem –
starvation – and at least one of them has a solution: 'What authority
surfeits on would relieve us' (I. i. 15). The First Citizen accuses the
patricians not just of permitting the dearth but of benefiting from it:
'our sufferance is a gain to them' (I. i. 21). But as the scene progresses
the question of whether or not the patricians have corn they could
distribute is lost sight of. Menenius blames the dearth on the gods and
assures the people, 'The helms o'th'state … care for you like fathers' (I. i.
71–6). The issue becomes not distribution but information. The belly
tells the members:

> Though all at once cannot
> See what I do deliver out to each,
> Yet can I make my audit up, that all
> From me do back receive the flour of all,
> And leave me but the bran.               (I. i. 141–5)

To the citizens' claim that they are starving, Menenius replies in effect
that they aren't really; they just don't realize they're being fed. Martius'
contribution is to pour scorn on the people's claim that they know there
is corn to spare, ranking it with their general penchant for foolish
political gossip (I. i. 189–99). He does not deign to say whether they are
right or wrong. As Menenius denies their capacity for knowledge,
Martius denies their right to it. What began as a practical question of
survival becomes a political question about the flow of information in
the state. This is reflected in the upshot of the rebellion: the people ask
for bread and are given tribunes.

It is not a particularly good bargain. Though we learn later that corn
has been distributed, we never learn whose idea it was (III. i. 112–3).
What Shakespeare emphasizes about the tribunes is not their service to
the people but their concern for their own office. This makes them
jealous of the people's adulation of Coriolanus (II. i. 203–11) and gives
them a reason for opposing his consulship: 'Then our office may, /
During his power, go sleep' (II. i. 220–1). In place of the citizens' full and
balanced view of the hero, the tribunes think in partisan and competitive
terms, in which Coriolanus is simply the enemy. Their function is not to
express the people's wills but to ensure that the people express theirs.[12]
When the people elect Coriolanus, Brutus rebukes them for not
following orders: 'Could you not have told him / As you were lesson'd'
(II. iii. 174–5). Their mistake of leaving the people to themselves is not
repeated; in the crisis after the revoked election, the people are herded

here and there by the Aediles, and Sicinius reduces their voices to monosyllabic echoes of his own: 'let them, / If I say fine, cry "Fine", if death, cry "Death" ' (III. iii. 15–16). In the end, sheer noise becomes a political instrument, used by the tribunes to 'Enforce the present execution / Of what we chance to sentence' (III. iii. 21–2). ('Chance' is interesting; it is the will that matters, not the reason.) We have heard the citizens' voices debating state affairs in a shrewd, thoughtful, and open way; those voices are now reduced to a group chant of 'It shall be so, it shall be so!' (III. iii. 119). They get what they want, of course, or rather what the tribunes want. Whether it is to their advantage is another question, and it could be said that they have expelled their enemy at some cost to their political freedom. As the consequences of the banishment become clear in Coriolanus' threat to Rome, the Third Citizen declares, 'though we willingly consented to his banishment, yet it was against our will' (IV. vi. 145–6). In his flustered and pathetic way he is making a real point: the wills of the people have been confused and lost in the will of the tribunes.

Menenius claims that as magistrates the tribunes are incompetent and serve the people badly (II. i. 67–79). Perhaps we should take his gibes with a grain of salt; but we see them as out of their depth in war as Coriolanus is in peace. Brutus reacts to the news of the latest Volscian threat by refusing to face reality: 'Go see this rumourer whipp'd. It cannot be / The Volsces dare break with us' (IV. vi. 48–9). What they are good at is partisan conflict, and they bend everything to that purpose:

> *Bru.*           You speak o'th'people
>      As if you were a god to punish, not
>      A man of their infirmity.
> *Sic.*                               'Twere well
>      We let the people know't.                    (III. i. 79–82)

Brutus utters one of the most telling criticisms levelled at the hero through the entire play, and Sicinius, with no sense of incongruity, turns it into a meanly childish threat for political ends. Sicinius has an exchange with Menenius that reveals how his own instincts operate:

> *Sic.* Nature teaches beasts to know their friends.
> *Men.* Pray you, who does the wolf love?
> *Sic.* The lamb.                              (II. i. 5–7)

His reply is automatic and unthinking, ignoring the logic of his first statement and revealing that for him this is a world of predators.

Roman politics is not a search for the best solutions but a competitive game. The tribunes play it in that spirit, and they are not alone. Each side identifies the state with itself. Menenius advises the people not to oppose 'the Roman state' (I. i. 68). The implication is that they are not part of it, a point he makes crystal clear later in the scene: 'Rome and her rats are at the point of battle' (I. i. 161). Rome is his own class, and that alone. When the mob cries, 'The people are the city' (III. i. 198), they are echoing Sicinius; but they are also echoing Menenius. Party thinking leads the patricians to take undisguised satisfaction at the impending destruction of Rome because they can blame it on the plebeians. Cominius' taunt, 'He'll shake your Rome about your ears' (IV. vi. 100), plays neatly on the plebeians' identification of the city with themselves, but forgets that it is his city too. Though Menenius acts occasionally as a conciliator, his essential partisanship is undisguised. His reputation as 'one that hath always loved the people' (I. i. 50–1) is sustainable, it would seem, only because his jocular manner means they do not take his insults seriously. Falstaff made the same mistake with Hal. The phrasing of his comic self-description is interesting: 'I am known to be a humorous patrician, and one that loves a cup of hot wine, with not a drop of allaying Tiber in't; said to be something imperfect in favouring the first complaint' (II. i. 46–9). He is describing not his nature but his reputation, which includes a reason for laughing off his insults: 'What I think, I utter, and spend my malice in my breath' (52–3). But when Brutus replies that they do indeed know him Menenius retorts, 'You know neither me, yourselves, nor any thing' (II. i. 67). As Coriolanus scorned the people's claim to know about the corn supply, Menenius scorns the tribunes' claim to know his true nature. The pose of public buffoon is just that: a pose. It seems to deny him a serious role in the state; Brutus tells him, 'Come, come, you are well understood to be a perfecter giber for the table than a necessary bencher in the Capitol' (II. i. 80–2). But it also means that when the patricians need a conciliator they can always use him. In the competitive game that is Roman politics Menenius has a clear, set role.

As in *Henry IV*, the partisans caricature each other and so fail to take each other seriously. The people are not just the rats Menenius calls them; nor is Menenius quite the harmless old buffoon the tribunes think him. But this time the jocularity also suggests the possibility of a final tolerance, as it does not quite do in *Henry IV*. For people who despise each other, Menenius and the tribunes spend a lot of time meeting socially. Partisan conflict is always pushing Rome to the brink of self-destruction, but there is a collective instinct in place – if only just – that prevents a final breakdown.[13] 'That is the way to lay the city flat' (III. i. 202) is the ultimate threat and the ultimate fear. Menenius speaks for the pragmatic streak in the patricians when he declares, 'this must be patch'd / With cloth of any colour' (III. i. 250–1). The citizens and the tribunes are less articulate on this point, perhaps because in the central confrontation they are flushed with the excitement of victory. But though Sicinius at first insists on Coriolanus' death because 'To eject him hence / Were but our danger' (III. i. 284–5), and events prove him right, something in the tribunes makes them settle for exile instead. There is a clue when Brutus, preparing to meet the banished hero's family, tells his colleague,

> Now we have shown our power,
> Let us seem humbler after it is done
> Than when it was a-doing. (IV. ii. 3–5)

His humility, like that of Coriolanus earlier, will only be an appearance; but his reluctance to crow over his victory suggests an awareness that after all he and Volumnia have to live in the same city.

That final instinct for conciliation, however, appears only in moments of extremity. The normal state of Roman politics is war. There is more than one reason for Coriolanus to be uncomfortable with the charade of begging the people's voices. It is a lie about himself; it is also a lie about the state. It presupposes a co-operative society in which the classes understand each other, recognize each other's interests, and are prepared to bargain. At the same time, by codifying the bargaining process in such a theatrical way, it implicitly admits that the process is not natural. What is natural is class war. This means that the view of Coriolanus as a man who can function in war but not in politics is only half true. In so far as politics is war, he has a recognized place in it. The play's very first reference to him is 'First, you know Caius Martius is chief enemy to the people' (I. i. 6–7). The phrasing suggests an office. In that office he can be the focus for their hate, the representative of everything that has gone wrong. 'Let us kill him, and we'll have corn at our own price' (I. i. 9–10) may not sound like a sophisticated economic policy, but it shows the sort of thinking that goes with the politics of confrontation. Here, as in battle, Coriolanus is the cynosure of all eyes: in the first scene the people spend as much time talking about him as about the famine. He brings to politics the mentality of the battlefield. The only occasion on which he seems quite happy in the political action is when, after a long passage in which the others shout at each other and he remains silent, he suddenly draws his sword: 'I'll die here. / There's some among you have beheld me fighting' (III. i. 221–2). We have beheld him too, and we realize that he is prepared to repeat his feats at Corioles. The kind of voting he understands is captured in the line 'Stand fast. / We have as many friends as enemies', at which even

Menenius is shocked: 'Shall it be put to that?' (III. i. 229–31). If politics is war, there is logic and a certain grim honesty in his willingness to make a real fight of it. But he does not fight on that level alone. In the war of words he is remarkably shrewd, articulate, and quick-thinking. It is true that his political discourse can be on the level of 'Hence, old goat!' and 'What should the people do with these bald tribunes?' (III. i. 175, 163). These are battlefield taunts. But he is also alert to the exact significance of words. When Sicinius dares to say 'shall', he rages for several lines, hammering away at the offending word (III. i. 85–106). This may look like touchiness over trifles; but it shows that Coriolanus has a soldier's eye for the significance of even a small movement in the enemy's ranks.

Nor does he fight just for the sake of fighting. For him this is not a game in which the conflict is arbitrary and finally limited. He sees himself opposing brute reaction with thought – 'I'll give my reasons / More worthier than their voices' (III. i. 118–19) – and he does indeed think. As soon as he appears in the first scene, the range of political issues expands beyond the immediate cause of the riot, as he gives a full account of his reasons for hating the people: their cowardice in war, their fickleness, their tendency to favour the undeserving, and their need to be kept in awe lest they prey on one another (I. i. 167–87). He has reasons, too, for refusing to distribute corn: the people do not deserve it, and to give in to the pressure of mere numbers will debase political life (III. i. 119–38). He thinks pragmatically, as a soldier should, seeing the practical disadvantage of a mixed state:

> my soul aches
> To know, when two authorities are up,
> Neither supreme, how soon confusion
> May enter 'twixt the gap of both, and take
> The one by th'other.                    (III. i. 107–11)

He adds, 'Purpose so barr'd, it follows / Nothing is done to purpose' (III. i. 147–8). The upshot is that the state will be stymied, 'Not having the power to do the good it would / For th'ill which doth control't' (III. i. 159–60). No one else on the patrician side is so articulate about the reasons why the class war is worth fighting; in this respect Coriolanus is matched only by a few of the more articulate citizens – such as the one who, when Menenius asks, 'Will you undo yourselves?', replies, 'We cannot, sir, we are undone already' (I. i. 62–3). And no one on either side is so committed to the conflict. He lacks that final tolerance, that willingness to declare the game over, that we see in the other Romans. The conflict is not finally as serious for them as it is for him. While

201

Menenius and the other patricians, we feel, are committed to their side because it is their side, Coriolanus is committed to an idea of how the state should be run, and promotes the interest of his class because it serves that idea. Party loyalty as such does not matter to him. This may account for a recurring trick in his language. Characters throughout this play indulge in hyperbole; it is as natural as breathing. The special form it takes with Coriolanus is a tendency to imagine allegiances loosened and rearranged. He says of Aufidius:

> Were half to half the world by th'ears, and he
> Upon my party, I'd revolt to make
> Only wars with him.                                   (I. i. 232–4)

He will not accept his soldiers as Romans unless they behave as Romans should: 'He that retires, I'll take him for a Volsce, / And he shall feel mine edge' (I. iv. 28–9). He makes a similar point about the mob:

> I would they were barbarians – as they are,
> Though in Rome litter'd; not Romans – as they are not,
> Though calv'd i'th'porch o'th'Capitol.         (III. i. 236–8)

In that speech we can actually hear him changing the meanings of words, so that the terms 'barbarian' and 'Roman' become functions of behaviour, not birth. This ability to loosen traditional identities leads to his climactic defiance of the people: 'I banish you!' (III. iii. 123). Seemingly absurd, this takes to its logical conclusion the habit each Roman party has of identifying the state with itself: the people are the city, the patricians are the city. Coriolanus says, in effect, '*I* am the city.' It is also the logical outcome of his gift for solitary achievement. Most important, it shows his insistence on living by his own standards, to which all other allegiances are secondary.[14] If the rest of Rome betrays those standards, then he is all of Rome that matters.


Dr Johnson's complaint that 'There is, perhaps, too much bustle in the first act, and too little in the last'[15] embodies an astute observation about the way in which the play moves from an external to an internal drama, from the body politic that is Rome to the body politic that is Coriolanus. Its examination of Rome shows that the forms and habits of Roman politics are reductive: instead of a free, intelligent political life we see a competitive game in which everyone belongs to one team or another, and goes with the team. The effect is like the civil war sequence of *Henry VI* or the political scenes of *Antony and Cleopatra*; but while in *Henry VI* particularly the dramatic idiom was also reductive and simplified, creating an ironic distance from the political figures, in *Coriolanus* it remains, as in *Henry IV*, open, sophisticated, and realistic. In certain speeches of Coriolanus and the plebeians, we glimpse what a more open political life, concerned with issues rather than loyalties, would look like. Irreconcilably at odds, each party none the less claims some of our respect. In the internal drama of Coriolanus himself that ends the play, we see an equivalent problem. Coriolanus' nature becomes limited and simplified, while we remain aware of its larger possibilities. The hero's radical isolation of himself is compelling and logical; it recalls Richard of Gloucester, and it may also be linked to Cleopatra's insistence that reality is what she makes it.[16] But we are also aware that Coriolanus, like Hal, is creating an oversimplified image of himself, one that is not fully in tune with reality.

Here as in *Richard III* the final issue goes deeper than politics narrowly conceived, but Shakespeare does not resort to the myth-making stylization of that play: he examines the nature and consequences of the bond of common humanity in a more searching, realistic, and ironic way. Coriolanus cuts off his ties from the city, quickly and simply. As he goes into exile he still seems concerned for his family and friends, and promises to write to them (IV. i. 51–3). But he breaks that promise (IV. vi. 18–19), and comes to rank the nobles among his enemies (IV. v. 76–7). The scene in which he goes into exile shows an identity in flux:

> though I go alone,
> Like to a lonely dragon that his fen
> Makes fear'd and talk'd of more than seen, your son
> Will or exceed the common, or be caught
> With cautelous baits and practice.          (IV. i. 29–33)

The smooth flow of the speech does not conceal its confusion. It merely makes us wonder if Coriolanus realizes how confused he is. The son, the dragon, the hero, the dupe; invisible and the centre of attention; lonely and still having to do with men. Already we see that in being cut off from Rome he is losing certainty about himself, far more than he seems to realize. He is a more social creature than he thought, and his attempts to create a new, asocial identity for himself are fumbling.

He also loses the intense commitment that made him distinctive in both war and peace. With no apparent discomfort, he disguises himself *'in mean apparel'* (IV. iv. SD) of the sort that galled him when he had to wear the cloak of humility in Rome. When he offers allegiance to Aufidius, his statement of purpose is childishly flat and simple:

in mere spite
To be full quit of those my banishers,
Stand I before thee.                                            (IV. v. 83–5)

This reflects his own cool, ironic appraisal of his change of allegiance as simply the way of the world:

so fellest foes,
Whose passions and whose plots have broke their sleep
To take the one the other, by some chance,
Some trick not worth an egg, shall grow dear friends
And interjoin their issues. So with me.            (IV. iv. 18–22)

Later he will hear the laughter of the gods; here he regards himself with calm detachment, seeing his treachery as absurd, but not, apparently, bothered by the absurdity. In the previous scene the spy Nicanor has been cool and matter-of-fact about his betrayal of Rome; Coriolanus seems to be following his example. The man who argued passionately that there was only one right course of action now offers Aufidius a choice – accept him or kill him – and seems indifferent about the outcome:

But if so be
Thou dar'st not this, and that to prove more fortunes
Th'art tir'd, then, in a word, I also am
Longer to live most weary, and present
My throat to thee and to thy ancient malice;
Which not to cut would show thee but a fool.
                                                            (IV. v. 93–8)

Again there is a final indifference, a sense of absurdity. The decision of life or death belongs to Aufidius, and Coriolanus offers it to him with an ironic shrug.

His claim to be tired of life seems more than just rhetoric: his sense of identity, his commitment to the meaning of his actions, even his confidence that life itself has a meaning, seem all to have broken down. He is a *tabula rasa* on which a new identity may be drawn. In effect, he asks Aufidius to define his life for him: either finish him off or set him moving again. Aufidius does the latter, and starts to re-forge on his own terms the human bonds Coriolanus has severed. But the way in which he does this contains an element of parody that makes us uneasy. In the fight for Corioles, Martius had greeted Cominius with the physical eagerness of a bridegroom on his wedding night:

> Oh! let me clip ye
> In arms as sound as when I woo'd; in heart
> As merry as when our nuptial day was done,
> And tapers burn'd to bedward. (I. vi. 29–32)

This conveyed the erotic excitement of battle and the loyalties it creates. Aufidius picks up the idea, and develops it into an extended fantasy in which he accepts Coriolanus not just as a friend or ally but as a bride (IV. v. 114–19), not just in the excitement of the moment but as the fulfilment of the erotic dreams that have haunted him since their last meeting:

> I have nightly since
> Dreamt of encounters 'twixt thyself and me –
> We have been down together in my sleep.
>
> (IV. v. 123–5)

Elsewhere in Shakespeare – at the end of *Richard III*, for example – marriage has its traditional function as a basic symbol of the human bond. Coriolanus will later be reminded that he has a wife in Rome. What Aufidius offers is not an alternative to that bond but a parody of it. And the intense excitement of this moment does not last; it is doubtful if Coriolanus himself even feels it. Aufidius has said, from early in the play, that he will strike at his enemy by craft if he has to (I. x. 15–16), and that determination is soon reawakened. Even before Coriolanus surrenders to his mother, Aufidius is gathering evidence to use against him (IV. vii. 17–26). They do not even have the intense bond of true enemies: our expectation of a single combat between Hal and Hotspur is satisfyingly fulfilled, but Aufidius, who has raged at the 'condemned seconds' (I. viii. 15) who rescue him at Corioles, finally sets on his enemy with a gang. And Coriolanus, whose first greeting to Aufidius is 'I do hate thee / Worse than a promise-breaker' (I. viii. 1–2), breaks promise with him. The notion that Coriolanus can find a new identity and new integrity with Aufidius, either as friend or as enemy, leads nowhere.

When he returns to destroy Rome, he seems to have made a new identity on his own, an inhuman one; but in fact his identity is still unresolved:

> He is their god. He leads them like a thing
> Made by some other deity than nature,
> That shapes men better. (IV. vi. 91–3)

Again there is confusion in the language: a god, or something made by a

god? something other than man, or a better form of man? He is
between one name and another:

> 'Coriolanus'
> He would not answer to; forbad all names:
> He was a kind of nothing, titleless,
> Till he had forg'd himself a name o'th'fire
> Of burning Rome.                                    (V. i. 11–15)

The speaker in both cases is Cominius, and this is no accident. It was
Cominius who gave the hero his name, and now reports he has
abandoned it. It was Cominius who described him as a thing of blood
before Corioles, a near-supernatural power. But that description
reflected something we had seen; the connection between shadow and
substance was tight. The new Coriolanus, not a 'thing' but a 'nothing',
seems all shadow. His godlike quality is a matter of interpretation and
report, not something we have seen in action; in fact, we have not seen
Coriolanus at all since his meeting with Aufidius. And his resolve to give
himself a new name from the next city he will destroy (we notice that he
still in some sense depends on Rome) is a promise for the future that
will never be fulfilled.

He is challenged by reminders of his old life, his old ties and identity.
Like the arming of Antony, but more unobtrusively, the sequence of
embassies from Rome moves the play towards allegory without
breaking its realistic surface. Cominius, his old general, stands for
friendship and Coriolanus' identity as a Roman soldier. Menenius, who
insists on seeing him after dinner because 'The veins unfill'd, our blood
is cold, and then / We pout upon the morning' (V. i. 51–2), stands –
appropriately, given his earlier role – for the common physical life we
all share. His reaction to Coriolanus' banishment, we remember, was to
ask Volumnia to supper (IV. ii. 49). Less convincingly, he presents
himself as Coriolanus' father (V. i. 3, V. ii. 62). Coriolanus rejects both
these figures with seeming ease, though the fact that he also gives them
letters outlining his surrender terms suggests that the rejection may be
less absolute than it looks. The family makes a far more powerful
appeal. Each of the Roman plays explores some aspect of the private
dimension: friendship in *Julius Caesar*, sexual love in *Antony and
Cleopatra.* In *Coriolanus* the focus is on the family. They approach him,
not in a hierarchical order, but in unexpected relationships that
emphasize their solidity as a group:

> My wife comes foremost; then the honour'd mould
> Wherein this trunk was fram'd, and in her hand
> The grandchild to her blood. (V. iii. 22–4)

Coriolanus fears this appeal more than any other. We sense this when he says of Menenius, 'Their latest refuge / Was to send him' (V. iii. 11–12), refusing to admit to himself that Menenius was far from being Rome's ultimate weapon. Even before they enter, the shout that signals their approach triggers his instinctive recognition of danger: 'Shall I be tempted to infringe my vow / In the same time 'tis made?' (V. iii. 20–1). When he calls himself to order it is with a conscious effort, a sense of strain: 'Let it be virtuous to be obstinate' (V. iii. 26).[17] Richard of Gloucester could declare flatly, 'I am myself alone' (*3 Henry VI*, V. vi. 83). Coriolanus' phrasing is different:

> Let the Volsces
> Plough Rome and harrow Italy; I'll never
> Be such a gosling to obey instinct, but stand
> As if a man were author of himself
> And knew no other kin. (V. iii. 33–7)

The difference lies in two words: 'As if'.

From his exile to the entrance of his family, Coriolanus has seemed a man sleepwalking, acting automatically, betraying a final indifference. Now again his intelligence and his senses are alert as before. His full nature, the nature he has tried to narrow artifically, is coming into play. The difference is that he is no longer defending a position he passionately believes in but one whose underlying falseness haunts him and requires an extra, strained effort betraying deep unease. When he asks Virgilia for 'a kiss / Long as my exile, sweet as my revenge' (V. iii. 44–5), he seems to be trying to redefine his old life in terms of his new one; but we feel also a sharp erotic longing that the embraces of Aufidius could never satisfy. The women appeal not just to his instincts but to his mind: Volumnia tells him how their integrity has been broken; they cannot even pray to the gods, since their prayers for their country and for him, both necessary, are irreconcilable (V. iii. 104–11). Virgilia, referring to his son (whom Coriolanus encounters here for the first time in the play), declares she 'brought you forth this boy to keep your name / Living to time' (V. iii. 126–7). This reminder of the larger movement of time, so characteristic of Shakespeare in general, is a new note for this play, in which the excitements of the moment are paramount. Coriolanus is made to think not just of his family but of the whole network of relationships they are involved in, which includes posterity. He surrenders to the words of his mother, as he has before; but the stage direction, *'Holds her by the hand silent'* (V. iii. 182) – perhaps the most eloquent stage direction in Shakespeare – conveys other levels of meaning. The gesture is an acknowledgement of a physical bond at a deeper level than Menenius can argue for, and silence is the medium of Virgilia, 'My gracious silence' (II. i. 174), who stands not just for marriage but for the withdrawn and secret life we all need, without which we would be incomplete, creatures of our relationships and of nothing else. Our first impression of Virgilia may have been that she is too soft for Rome, indeed ridiculously soft – 'His bloody brow? O Jupiter, no blood!' (I. iii. 38) – but in the face of pressure from Valeria she holds her determination not to leave the house in her husband's absence. The first impression of weakness fades as we sense an inner strength of will. Utterly at odds with Coriolanus' life as a warrior, she presents an image of that private integrity he has tried, and failed, to live by.[18]

In surrendering to his family, Coriolanus is confronting and admitting the truth of his own nature. The ultimate appeal has been, I think, not to his capacity to love but to his honesty, his refusal to play a part. We saw that honesty shaken in the political scenes, and in his first reaction to the family we see him fighting against it. It is worth noting that in all of Volumnia's long speech the barb that finally sticks is

> This fellow had a Volscian to his mother;
> His wife is in Corioles, and his child
> Like him by chance.                    (V. iii. 178–80)

'His child / Like him by chance', with its sarcastic double reality, exposes what the rest of the passage makes implicit: that Coriolanus is living a lie. We have seen him reject the pretence and play-acting required by the gown of humility; we have seen him refuse to be possessed by the harlot's spirit of the actor. But, if he has refused to impersonate someone else, he has always had a dangerous tendency – as Brutus did – to dramatize himself:

>                 Would you have me
> False to my nature? Rather say I play
> The man I am.                       (III. ii. 14–16)

Volumnia retorts that he is overplaying: 'You might have been enough the man you are, / With striving less to be so' (III. ii. 19–20). In the sequence in which he refuses to play-act in the market-place he behaves like a temperamental young star surrounded by anxious handlers.[19] When he comes to Antium and reveals himself to Aufidius, he milks the discovery scene, building to a climactic flourish with the revelation of his name, in a style worthy of Beaumont and Fletcher (IV. v. 55–69). The one kind of play-acting can shade into the other, the overdramatizing of himself leading to a loss of integrity no less deadly than the lies of impersonation. This is what he has done in his attempt to present himself as a lonely dragon, an avenging god, a nameless thing descending on Rome. He has so overdramatized his present state that he has become false to his essential nature. His warning to Virgilia, 'These eyes are not the same I wore in Rome' (V. iii. 38), suggests that he could change himself as he changes costumes. Virgilia's reply, 'The sorrow that delivers us thus chang'd / Makes you think so' (39–40), tells him that only the scene before him has changed. The eyes are the same. He replies:

> Like a dull actor now
> I have forgot my part and I am out,
> Even to a full disgrace. (V. iii. 40–2)

This gives Volumnia her opening, though she is less sure and instinctive than Virgilia in knowing how to exploit it. It is a long time before she hits on the taunt that leads to his surrender. But we can see that surrender coming when Virgilia denies his new identity, and he admits he has been acting.

His old honesty returns, and combines with his new capacity for detachment, in a bleak recognition of the full irony of the situation:

> O mother, mother!
> What have you done? Behold, the heavens do ope,
> The gods look down, and this unnatural scene
> They laugh at. O my mother, mother! O!
> You have won a happy victory to Rome;
> But for your son, believe it, O, believe it,
> Most dangerously you have with him prevail'd,
> If not most mortal to him. But let it come. (V. iii. 182–9)

He knows that he has delivered himself to death at the hands of Aufidius; he has no illusions about his new ally. He senses that they are now all actors in a scene played for the laughter of the gods. The sight of son and mother reconciled is 'unnatural' because Volumnia, who gave him life, has just given him death. But he ends with a quiet acceptance of his fate, resigned to playing his part to the end. This time his awareness of himself as an actor means recognizing not falsehood or exaggeration but destiny: the actor's part is written for him, and its end is inevitable.

He cannot go back to his old life in Rome. For one thing, his acknowledgement of his common humanity means rejecting not just his new role as the inhuman avenger but his old role as the sword of Rome. In Volumnia's first scene she idealized her warrior son by opposing the values of war to the humane values of love and family: 'If my son were my husband I should freelier rejoice in that absence wherein he won honour, than in the embracements of his bed, where he would show most love' (I. iii. 2–5). And, more startlingly,

> The breasts of Hecuba
> When she did suckle Hector, look'd not lovelier
> Than Hector's forehead when it spit forth blood
> At Grecian sword contemning.          (I. iii. 40–3)

In asking him to spare Rome she is implicitly arguing against all the values she herself stood for in this earlier scene, the values she has instilled in him. The incongruity of Volumnia as an advocate for natural humanity is connected with an element of performance in her plea. Like Coriolanus when he wore the gown of humility, she and the other women have dressed for their parts:

> Should we be silent and not speak, our raiment
> And state of bodies would bewray what life
> We have led since thy exile.          (V. iii. 94–6)

As she urged him to do in the market-place, she uses the language of gesture as part of her performance: 'Down ladies: let us shame him with our knees' (V. iii. 169). When Menenius presented himself as Coriolanus' father, there was an element of pose, for he was adopting that role for the first time in the play; so there is an element of pose or at least contrivance in the theatricality of Volumnia's plea. It is a contradiction of everything she has stood for up till now. It tells him a truth about himself by sacrificing a truth about her. This paradox is central to the theatre, which holds the mirror up to nature by using invented images, false in themselves but revealing truth to the viewer. Coriolanus can no more go back and live with Volumnia now than an audience can live in a play, or a viewer can enter, like Alice, into a looking-glass world. It is worth noting that he takes her by the hand, but does not embrace her. He is both making contact and keeping her at arm's length.

Instead he goes back with Aufidius. But there is no real future for him there either. He has just said, in fact, that it will mean his death. Yet moments after that clear insight he says to Aufidius, 'I'll not to Rome, I'll back with you; and pray you, / Stand to me in this cause' (V. iii. 198–9), as though he has forgotten or buried the certainty that Aufidius will kill him. For the rest of the play he seems again to be going through the motions, sleepwalking, acting as though he really could go on living among the Volsces.[20] Does he know he is once again living a lie? Has he suppressed his earlier insight, or actually lost it? Or, now that his end is determined, has he simply stopped caring? Like the Bolingbrokes he is passing beyond our ken. So are the women. The Romans welcome them back with a great flood of noise, in the midst of which they remain silent, leaving us to wonder if they have taken Coriolanus' warning to heart, what they think of it, or whether they even remember it.[21] One thing is certain: Rome, though temporarily united in rejoicing, has not been born again. Menenius' gibe at the tribunes –

> This Volumnia
> Is worth of consuls, senators, patricians,
> A city full; of tribunes such as you,
> A sea and land full. (V. iv. 53–6)

– shows that tomorrow it will be business as usual: class conflict tempered by mockery.

The most remarkable thing about Rome is that at the end of the play it sharply and suddenly disappears, as though it no longer matters or even exists. Coriolanus dies alone in a strange Volscian city, whose own identity seems to shift during the final scene. It seems at first to be Antium, and later (for good reason) Corioles. The stage communities and the characters who inhabit them seem to blur and dissolve before our eyes. Coriolanus' own identity disappears behind mocking images of what he was. Menenius' description of the inhuman avenger takes on an edge of caricature: 'The tartness of his face sours ripe grapes. When he walks, he moves like an engine and the ground shrinks before his treading.' He concludes, 'He wants nothing of a god but eternity, and a heaven to throne in', to which Sicinius replies, 'Yes, mercy, if you report him truly' (V. iv. 17–26). Two scenes earlier this would have been a telling exchange. But we have just seen him surrender to his mother, and we know that all this is out of date. The surrender itself is caricatured by Aufidius:

> At a few drops of women's rheum, which are
> As cheap as lies, he sold the blood and labour
> Of our great action. (V. vi. 46–8)

As they have all through the play, other characters are talking about Coriolanus; but their images of his cruelty and of his mercy are radically opposed, exaggerated, unfixed from reality. Yet what is the reality of Coriolanus now? The speakers seem to be firing past a target we can no longer see. Prospero, when he turns to mercy, can act out that decision for the rest of the play, with a responsive supporting cast. Coriolanus finds no medium in which to do so.[22] What he offers instead in his final scene is a shadowy re-enactment of his first, satisfyingly heroic role as conqueror of Corioles, alone against the city. The echoes are clear. Aufidius strips the new name from him, returning him to what he was for most of Act I:

> Ay, Martius, Caius Martius! Dost thou think
> I'll grace thee with that robbery, thy stol'n name
> Coriolanus, in Corioles? (V. vi. 88–90)

When he tries to reduce him further, calling him 'boy', Coriolanus reacts. Once again the hero is alone to answer all the city. The difference is that this time, as Philip Brockbank puts it, 'The strongest lines express a readiness to die, not a readiness to kill.'[23] He invokes his place in Volscian history, not as a sign of his immortality (this never interests him), but as a way of provoking his death:

> Cut me to pieces, Volsces, men and lads,
> Stain all your edges on me. Boy! False hound!
> If you have writ your annals true, 'tis there,
> That like an eagle in a dove-cote, I
> Flutter'd your Volscians in Corioles.
> Alone I did it. Boy! (V. vi. 111–16)

The solitary figure becomes once more a thing of blood, as '*The Conspirators draw, and kill Martius,*[24] *who falls; Aufidius stands on him*' (V. vi. 130SD). There is no indication that he fights back. His body, on which so much attention has been focused in both war and politics, is now an inert thing on the stage floor, a footstool for Aufidius.

Cleopatra's last performance summed up and fulfilled everything she was; Coriolanus' end seems to be a ghostly echo of his first heroic appearance, replaying the only role in which he has found satisfaction. But the deeds that won Cominius' praise are now recalled again, in a flood of revulsion based not just on the Volsces' natural resentment of an enemy but on a new awareness of how that earlier heroism violated the humane values represented in the ties of family: 'He killed my son! My daughter! He killed my cousin Marcus! He killed my father!' (V. vi. 121–2).[25] His two great moments, both intensely dramatic, have been his conquest of Corioles and his surrender to his family; but the values behind these moments are irreconcilably opposed. Cleopatra could fuse her own contradictions in a single grand performance. The contradictions of Coriolanus simply tear apart the image of the character the play has created, cancelling each other out and leaving us with nothing. He does not even, like Richard II, explicitly recognize his own nothingness. Nor can he make a final appeal, as Richard does, to the meaning bestowed by his office, for he has no office. All he can do is provoke his own death, leaving us to wonder if the provocation is fully conscious or not. He attacks Corioles; he attacks Rome; and finally he tears himself apart. The fact that he does this not through denying his place in the common bond of humanity but through accepting it, 'by his own alms empoison'd, / And with his charity slain' (V. vi. 11–12), is one of the darkest ironies in Shakespeare.

# 9

# *Henry VIII*

Shakespeare used his Roman plays to explore the interplay of greatness and frailty, and of public and private interests, in the free political arena of a republic. Returning to England for his last political play, *Henry VIII*, he continues this exploration but takes it in new directions. Once again we are under the aegis of a monarchy: the political system is fixed, its central office clear. The underlying security of the state is if anything greater than in the earlier history plays, since Henry's right to hold his office is not questioned for a moment. The pressure put on Shakespeare's Plantagenet kings is not put on him. This may help to account for the relaxation, the lack of urgency, the avoidance of conflict, that make this play a striking departure from its predecessors. The high and low views of characters like Julius Caesar, Mark Antony, and Cleopatra, like the views of Coriolanus as wartime hero and peacetime nuisance, were brought into tense opposition, and struck sparks off each other. *Henry VIII* also combines high and low views of its characters, but in a manner that is more eclectic, tolerant and accommodating. The realistic and idealizing manners we have followed through this study shade delicately into each other here.

We can see something of the play's range in the scene in which Anne Bullen pities the misfortunes of her mistress Queen Katherine:

> O, now after
> So many courses of the sun enthroned,
> Still growing in a majesty and pomp, the which
> To leave a thousand-fold more bitter than
> 'Tis sweet at first t'acquire: after this process,
> To give her the avaunt, it is a pity
> Would move a monster! (II. iii. 5–11)

There is a delicate balance here. Anne's pity makes her appear, as she does elsewhere, as the simplified image of a good woman; but we notice

214

that she is preoccupied, more than Katherine herself is, with the earthly pomp the old Queen is losing. This is a good-natured but worldly girl; and when, later in the scene, Henry sends his first rich presents to her she accepts them without demur, in a spirit of 'thanks and ... obedience' (71). On the question of ambition her mild words are countered by the raucous, cynical voice of the Old Lady:

*Anne.*     By my troth and maidenhead,
    I would not be a queen.
*Old L.* Beshrew me, I would,
    And venture maidenhead for't, and so would you,
    For all this spice of your hypocrisy.          (II. iii. 23–6)

We catch echoes of Desdemona and Emilia, echoes that get stronger as Anne declares she would not be Queen 'For all the world' and her companion retorts,

                In faith, for little England
        You'd venture an emballing: I myself
        Would for Carnarvonshire.          (II. iii. 46–8)

'Emballing' plays neatly on two kinds of royal orbs, and suggests the two levels of satisfaction that await Anne as Henry's wife. When the Lord Chamberlain brings Anne the first sign of Henry's favour, the title of Marchioness of Pembroke and £1,000 a year, the Old Lady crows in triumph: 'How tastes it? Is it bitter?' Yet Anne expresses no resentment or indignation at being caught out, and no sense of the incongruity of her position; only a dry, enigmatic, 'Come, you are pleasant' (II. iii. 89,93).

We are allowed to admire Anne's pity for the Queen, and to enjoy her worldly success. The incongruity between them is treated as merely amusing. There is no suggestion anywhere in the play of a conflict between Anne and Katherine: Anne is consistently sympathetic to her predecessor, and Katherine appears not to know that Anne exists. The Old Lady's sarcastic joke about a lady 'That would not be a queen ... / For all the mud in Egypt' (II. iii. 91–2) reminds us of another lady who was a great queen and a great courtesan, and thus underlines the mildness of the portrayal of Anne, whose royalty will consist of standing silent in the midst of pomp, and whose sexual relations with Henry will be kept well away from our eyes, reported only through good-natured gossip. The tolerance of the play's manner is most strikingly illustrated, however, by the Lord Chamberlain's conduct in this scene. He calls Anne's pity for the Queen 'a gentle business, and becoming / The action of good women', and expresses the hope that 'All

215

will be well' (II. iii. 54–6); he then gives Anne her presents. The two gestures are connected only as tributes to Anne's virtue; he makes no acknowledgement that her rise is at Katherine's expense. Speaking aside, the Chamberlain adds to the Old Lady's bawdy jokes about Anne's destiny a more dignified reason for celebration:

> I have perus'd her well;
> Beauty and honour in her are so mingled
> That they have caught the king: and who knows yet
> But from this lady may proceed a gem
> To lighten all this isle. (II. iii. 75–9)

Henry's love is given grace and dignity, and there is a sudden flicker of what will be visionary prophecy in the play's last scene. Through all this Anne retains her solemnity, and her own prophecy is darker and more enigmatic:

> Would I had no being
> If this salute my blood a jot: it faints me
> To think what follows. (II. iii. 102–4)

Her worry may be for the Queen; but it may also be for her herself, as she senses the danger of the world she is about to enter, in which her own fate was to be more grim than Katherine's. She is guarded and cautious, telling the Lord Chamberlain that 'prayers and wishes / Are all I can return' and advising the Old Lady to say nothing to the Queen (II. iii. 69–70, 106–7). As we watch, the scene's perspectives split and multiply: dignity and bawdry, worldly wealth and visionary beauty, celebration and politic caution, a golden future and a dark one. And there is something refracted in the dramatic idiom itself: the characters are realistically observed, yet show an awareness of the future that makes them creatures of theatrical artifice. We are looking at history through a pebbled glass that shows us multiple images.

While Cleopatra's final scene fused the great queen and the witty, sensual woman, Anne's coronation sets the components out separately:

> *2 Gent.* [*Looking at the Queen.*]     Heaven bless thee!
>     Thou hast the sweetest face I ever look'd on.
>     Sir, as I have a soul, she is an angel;
>     Our king has all the Indies in his arms,
>     And more, and richer, when he strains that lady;
>     I cannot blame his conscience.
> *1 Gent.*                         They that bear
>     The cloth of honour over her, are four barons
>     Of the Cinque-ports. (IV. i. 42–9)

We go from worship to chuckling appreciation to a straight reporting of the details of pomp. The sensual exactness of 'strains', the cynical joke about the King's conscience, and the dry voice of a BBC commentator at a royal occasion, all play off each other; yet the overall effect is curiously free of satire. We simply enjoy the variety. The countesses who accompany the new Queen are given similar treatment:

> *2 Gent.*                     These are stars indeed –
> *1 Gent.* And sometimes falling ones.
> *2 Gent.*                     No more of that. (IV. i. 54–5)

The play is concerned with two kinds of falling, Katherine's and Wolsey's on the one hand, Anne's on the other. It also reminds us that those who wear fine clothes and walk in formal processions have sex lives too. Anne's pregnancy, and Henry's action in marrying her while the case of the old Queen is still in question, are suggested in the bawdy energy of the mob in the Abbey:

> Great-bellied women,
> That had not half a week to go, like rams
> In the old time of war, would shake the press
> And make 'em reel before 'em. No man living
> Could say 'This is my wife' there, all were woven
> So strangely in one piece.                     (IV. i. 76–81)

The fusing of the crowd into a single mass has bawdy overtones; Henry has also had some trouble deciding which lady is his wife. In the midst of all this, Anne herself 'kneel'd, and saintlike / Cast her fair eyes to heaven and pray'd devoutly' (IV. i. 83–4). The mob's excitement has been triggered by the sight of her 'opposing freely / The beauty of her person to the people' (IV. i. 67–8); yet she remains separate, enclosed in pious thoughts. We remember Cleopatra's fear of being pawed by the saucy lictors of Rome; here the mob can have its fun and the Queen can keep her dignity, with no strain or unease on either side.

If the play has a central action, it is Henry's exchange of Katherine for Anne. The development of that action, like the moments when we fix on Anne herself, has an eclectic quality, a refracted vision. The two queens are kept carefully apart, and Henry's own feelings about them appear to be in separate compartments. So do his motives:

*Chamb.* It seems the marriage with his brother's wife
    Has crept too near his conscience.
*Suf.* [*Aside*]                            No, his conscience
    Has crept too near another lady.
*Nor.*                               'Tis so;
    This is the cardinal's doing.               (II. ii. 16–19)

The Arden editor marks Suffolk's speech as an aside, and thus makes Norfolk's line more natural as a response to the Chamberlain's. Yet Henry's affair with Anne is also, inadvertently, the cardinal's doing. They meet at his banquet, an occasion whose tone is set by jokes about lay-thoughts, running banquets, and easy penances on a down-bed (I. iv. 10–18). Henry and his fellow masquers appear dressed as shepherds: the range of possible associations goes (as in *The Shepherd's Calendar*) from pastoral love-poetry to public responsibility, from the King as wooer to the King as shepherd of his people. For Shakespeare the associations may include Henry VI's yearning for the simple satisfactions of private life. Henry's infatuation flowers instantly: 'The fairest hand I ever touch'd: O beauty, / Till now I never knew thee' (I. iv. 75–6). The fact that the touch of Anne's hand starts Henry's love evokes its sensual quality; on a similar occasion Romeo began with sight alone. Wolsey gives us a clue to the king's mood when he observes, 'Your grace, / I fear, with dancing is a little heated' (I. iv. 99–100).[1] As the occasion itself is not quite public and not quite private, so Henry, a king dressed as a shepherd, will seek in Anne both private satisfaction and the fulfilment of his public duty to give England an heir.

In Wolsey's plotting, however, Katherine's fall has nothing to do with Henry's desire for Anne. The court gossips accuse him of working against the old Queen to spite her father Charles V, who refused him the archbishopric of Toledo (II. i. 162–4). For a while, Henry seems to be Wolsey's pawn: the scene in which his dependence on the cardinal is clearest and most unhealthy is the scene in which he seeks his advice about the divorce, calling Wolsey 'The quiet of my wounded conscience; / . . . a cure fit for a king' (II. ii. 74–5). At the same time he takes Wolsey's creature Gardiner into his service. We see the King surrounded by Romish prelates, Wolsey, Gardiner, and Campeius – an ominous sight for a Protestant audience. (It is typical of the play, however, that the prelates do not present a united front, as Campeius rebukes Wolsey for his treatment of Gardiner's predecessor – II. ii. 121–35.) Wolsey's own candidate for the next Queen is the French King's sister the Duchess of Alençon, and he says of Anne, 'There's more in't than fair visage' (III. ii. 88). The Lord Chamberlain remarks:

                    All that dare
Look into these affairs see this main end,
The French king's sister.                    (II. ii. 39–41)

The play's diffuseness comes from moments like this: this is one of only two occasions on which this 'main end' is mentioned. As the explanations multiply, Henry invokes his conscience:

                    O my lord,
Would it not grieve an able man to leave
So sweet a bedfellow? But conscience, conscience;
O 'tis a tender place, and I must leave her.     (II. ii. 140–3)

This becomes the main public reason for the divorce. How hypocritical is it? Henry's reference to his own sexuality seems meant to remind us that he has another and even sweeter bedfellow in mind. If that reminder is not enough, Henry's speech ends the scene and Anne enters immediately to begin the next one. Shakespeare has actually rearranged the sequence of events in Holinshed to give precedence to Henry's affair with Anne, so that our memory of it may colour our hearing of the dignified public statements in which he says nothing about her. Yet Henry, like Anne herself, makes no acknowledgement of the incongruity. And there is no logical reason why his scruples and his desire should not be equally genuine. As in *Henry V* and *Antony and Cleopatra*, events appear discontinuous, and we can make what we like of the sequence in which they are ordered. At the trial Henry attributes the proceedings to the promptings of his own conscience, instigated by remarks of the Bishop of Bayonne and by his own brooding on his failure to produce a male heir. He claims to have been encouraged by practically every prelate in the land *except* Wolsey, who, according to Henry, has 'ever / . . . wish'd the sleeping of this business' (II. iv. 160–1). This does not square with what we have seen. Through all this we may wonder if Henry is merely fooling the public or has actually succeeded in fooling himself. Like the Bolingbrokes when they explain themselves, like Coriolanus in his final return to Volsces, he is becoming inscrutable.

There is a further incongruity between the slow, scrupulous process of reflection and consultation Henry describes to the court and the impatience he shows in his asides: 'I abhor / This dilatory sloth and tricks of Rome' (II. iv. 234–5).[2] The first impression that the divorce was drawing him closer to Wolsey is sharply reversed, as he declares, 'These cardinals trifle with me', and looks for the return of Cranmer, using terms like those he had used for Wolsey: 'with thy approach, I know /

My comfort comes along' (II. iv. 234, 237–8). The move that Henry saw as a way of producing a male heir has the unexpected effect of drawing him not only away from Wolsey but away from Rome. As motives appear separate from each other, motives and results are disconnected. The need for a male heir is introduced sideways into the play, in the notion that Buckingham would be king if Henry died without issue (I. ii. 133–5); it obviously weighs with Henry in his public statements; yet Shakespeare calls attention to the fact that Henry's desire in this matter is frustrated, when the Old Lady pretends for a moment that Anne's child is a boy (V. i. 161–70). What Shakespeare does not make clear is Henry's reaction to the news: actors may suggest shock and chagrin,[3] but the lines do not require this, and the Old Lady's complaint that her tip is too small (V. i. 171–6) could reflect her greed as well as Henry's annoyance. Any disappointment he may feel is put right by Cranmer's prophecy of the reign of Elizabeth, which leads Henry to declare, 'never before / This happy child did I get anything (V.iv.64–5). What looked like an ironic and futile end to the affair of the two queens is now seen as Henry's greatest achievement.

Whether we take a cross-section of an individual moment, like Anne's coronation, or try to follow a train of events, like the divorce, we see a mixture of styles and motives, and a pervasive incongruity. Our attention is always being dissipated, pulled in contrary directions. Secondary questions keep getting in the way of the main points: at Katherine's trial, for example, the divorce itself is set aside as the Queen debates with Wolsey over his responsibility for the proceedings and his right to be her judge (II. iv. 66–131). If we compare this with the tight focus on the central question in the deposition of Richard II, the contrast is striking. Instead of shaping and clarifying the political action as he has elsewhere, Shakespeare seems to be deliberately leaving it untidy. Throughout the play he makes it hard for us to keep our bearings. We are just getting used to seeing Wolsey as an extravagant, over-mighty subject when we hear him praised for his generosity: 'Men of his way should be most liberal, / They are set here for examples' (I. iii. 61–2). Henry himself expresses different views of Wolsey's lavish household at different times. As Wolsey's guest, he teases him about it: 'You are a churchman, or I'll tell you cardinal, / I should judge now unhappily' (I. iv. 88–9); later, as his king, he is outraged: 'it out-speaks / Possession of a subject' (III. ii. 127–8). But the real split in our view of Wolsey comes at his fall. We looked to see a villain despatched; but his accusers are so smug and hectoring that we see the justice of his counter-attack – 'Now I feel / Of what coarse metal ye are moulded, envy' (III. ii. 238–9) – and the Lord Chamberlain relents: 'My heart weeps to see him / So little of his great self' (III. ii. 335–6). By the same token, Buckingham appears at first as Wolsey's innocent victim, an honest man destroyed by corrupted witnesses. But even a friendly observer reports, 'All these accus'd him strongly, which he fain / Would have flung from him; but indeed he could not' (II. i. 24–5), opening the possibility that however corrupt the witnesses are there is substance in their charges.[4] Our view of Katherine is split in a variety of ways. She storms out of the court in a blaze of pride and anger, and Henry immediately praises her 'sweet gentleness' and 'meekness saintlike' (II. iv. 135–6). In her next scene she rounds on Wolsey and Campeius like a cornered tigress – 'cardinal sins and hollow hearts I fear ye' (III. i. 104) – only to conclude: 'Come reverend fathers, / Bestow your counsels on me' (III. i. 181–2). Her double relation to them reflects a doubleness in her nationality and religion. Her refusal to let them address her in Latin makes her an honorary Protestant heroine, and her insistence on conducting the interview in English makes her an adopted English-woman (III. i. 40–6). Yet she also regards herself as a stranger in a hostile land: 'can you think lords, / That any Englishman dare give me counsel?' (III. i. 83–4). We see for a moment the sinister side of the royal power the play accepts and celebrates elsewhere. And that England whose miraculous destiny Cranmer will proclaim in his final vision is shown by her in a very different light:

> Would I had never trod this English earth,
> Or felt the flatteries that grow upon it:
> Ye have angels' faces, but heaven knows your hearts.
>
> (III. i. 143–5)

For all the sympathy the play generates for her, her interests are not England's, and she is a necessary sacrifice to the larger good. But she is human enough not to accept this role meekly, and we are allowed for a moment to see her point of view.

The vision in her death scene gives promise of a heavenly reward; but even here her pious acceptance of her fate is not undisturbed. It is not before, but after, her glimpse of heavenly honour that she snaps at a messenger who seems disrespectful, and refuses to accept his apology (IV. ii. 100–8). In her last instructions about the disposal of her body she insists on her worldly dignity: 'although unqueen'd, yet like / A queen, and daughter to a king inter me' (IV. ii. 171–2). Going to his execution, Buckingham describes himself as 'half in heaven' (II. i. 88), and the phrase seems to describe Katherine's condition too: sincerely preparing for heaven, she cannot quite shake her lingering interest in earth. The phrase also describes Buckingham himself, whose gentle, pious farewell is shot through with flickers of resentment: 'Yet I am richer than my base accusers, / That never knew what truth meant' (II. i. 104–5). It also describes Wolsey, whose glad surrender of worldly pomp is cut across, just for a moment, by irritation when he learns that Thomas More has already been appointed his successor: 'That's somewhat sudden, / But he's a learned man' (III. ii. 394–5).[5] One of the clearest and steadiest movements of the play is the movement of fallen greatness to the finer rewards of heaven; but this movement, like that of history, is disturbed by cross-currents. In a complementary touch, Henry imagines that the advantage of being in heaven will be a clear view of England: 'When I am in heaven I shall desire / To see what this child does, and praise my maker' (V. iv. 67–8). Even in heaven, Henry will be half on earth.

Diffused attention is characteristic of this play. As those who are caught in this world find themselves looking towards the next, so Henry imagines that even in heaven his eyes will be fixed on earth. Distraction, we might think, can go no further than this. Spreading and splitting, rather than straight movement, characterize the play's action. In the second scene, for example, Katherine wins a battle with Wolsey over the taxation and loses one over Buckingham. Minor characters proliferate and secondary interests swirl around the main ones. The Prologue offers a mixed bag: there will be something here for 'Those that can pity', those who seek 'truth', and 'Those that come to see / Only a show or two' (5–10). The last promise in particular is amply fulfilled. Its phrasing suggests that the play can be read as a series of detached set pieces, and at several points this seems to be the case. Frustrated at trying to make sense of the action as a whole, we may be tempted to take each moment as it comes, and the Prologue appears to allow this. The set pieces include not only shows but patches of oratory. Henry praises Buckingham as 'a most rare speaker' (I. ii. 111), as though to prepare us for his long farewell. Lapidary inscriptions are a natural mode of speech. Wishing his successor well, Wolsey seems to be writing, in anticipation, an epitaph in his praise:

> May he continue
> Long in his highness' favour, and do justice
> For truth's sake, and his conscience; that his bones,
> When he has run his course and sleeps in blessings,
> May have a tomb of orphans' tears wept on him.
>
> (III. ii. 395–9)

(The glance away from the central business of Wolsey's own fall is also characteristic.) Katherine and Griffith between them construct a balanced obituary for Wolsey, with Katherine outlining his faults and Griffith, after formally asking permission – 'May it please your highness / To hear me speak his good now?' (IV. ii. 46–7) – his compensating virtues. While the Prologue's promise that this will not be 'a merry bawdy play' (14) is a little misleading, even the outbursts of sensual excitement among the lower orders have a certain formality. The accounts of the crowds at the coronation and christening are set pieces of oratory, no less than the long farewells of Buckingham and Wolsey. The christening of Elizabeth is celebrated by a pompous ceremony in the palace and what sounds like group sex in the streets: 'Bless me, what a fry of fornication is at door! On my Christian conscience this one christening will beget a thousand, here will be father, godfather, and all together' (V. iii. 34–7). Each celebration stands on its own, making its own independent statement. The Porter and his man have orders to keep the crowd away from the great folks, and though it is an effort it seems they finally succeed.

Given the lavish spectacles the play requires, the Prologue's promise of 'a show or two' sounds like an understatement. But the spectacle may seem more lavish than significant. The wands, purses, processional crosses, pillars, canopies, and rich robes do not have in themselves the specific symbolic value for the play of the spectacles in *The Tempest*: the vanishing banquet and the harpy, the water-nymphs and harvesters, the rainbow and the goddesses. Compared with that of the final romances, the spectacle of *Henry VIII* is a display of cost more than a use of symbolic language; it is not spectacle of the theatre, but spectacle in the theatre. Nor can it really be called ceremony, for the actual ceremonies, the actions that achieve something – the coronation and the christening – take place offstage. We see only the processions that accompany them, and the spectators at the coronation seem more interested in the pedantic reporting of details of protocol, 'those that claim their offices this day' (IV. i. 15), than in the inner significance of the occasion itself. The same interest is reflected in the stage directions throughout. We do not always feel a direct connection between the spectacles and the private lives of the main characters, and many of the figures who crowd the stage are otherwise unknown to us. But the shows are in a general way 'images of order',[6] signs of the power and majesty of the state. The spectators' disinclination to analyse them implies familiarity and acceptance. The three most lavish punctuate three key moments in the public action: Katherine's trial, Anne's coronation, Elizabeth's christening. In each case the necessary business of England is being done. The spectacles thus balance the long orations given to Buckingham and Wolsey, who are swept away by history and seek private satisfaction in thoughts of another world. The public occasions and the private ones have appropriately contrasting languages. (Katherine's death scene combines the two, since she is granted both a vision and a long farewell.) And not all the figures we see are there only to swell a progress; they also start a scene or two. Characters like Surrey, Norfolk, and Gardiner lead double lives, figures in the pageant and actors in the drama, reminding us that there is a connection after all. Finally, a broader view suggests that there are relationships between one spectacle and another. The most obvious is between Anne's earthly coronation and Katherine's heavenly one, which appear in adjacent scenes. The process, as Edward I. Berry has pointed out, is 'one not of antithesis but of refinement'.[7] More subtly, Katherine's 'Saw you not even now a blessed troop / Invite me to a banquet . . . ?' (IV. ii. 87–8) may recall the worldly banquet at which Henry met Anne. The idea of the banquet seems, interestingly, to be Katherine's own; it is not suggested in the stage directions for the vision. Heaven for her is a palace.

The play opens with a description of spectacle at its worst: the heavy, pointless, almost obscene display of the Field of the Cloth of Gold, dispersed by a tempest and celebrating a league that is already broken as we hear the description (I. i. 87–99). This spectacle is kept offstage, I think, not just for reasons of budget but so that Norfolk's language, working against his own overt admiration of the scene, can tell us what to think, and there is no chance of our being impressed against our better judgement:

> To-day the French,
> All clinquant all in gold, like heathen gods
> Shone down the English; and to-morrow they
> Made Britain India: every man that stood
> Show'd like a mine. Their dwarfish pages were
> As cherubins, all gilt: the madams too,
> Not us'd to toil, did almost sweat to bear
> The pride upon them, that their very labour
> Was to them as a painting. (I. i. 18–26)

While Enobarbus' description of Cleopatra's barge had a smooth flow that made the art sound easy, this speech suggests heaviness, disproportion, and blasphemous pride.[8] Above all, it is competitive, while the healthier spectacles that follow are communal. It suggests the folly of foreign entanglements, a suggestion made more lightly in the complaints about Frenchified English courtiers (I. iii). All this is preparation for Henry's choice of an English queen.[9] The Field of the Cloth of Gold is there, I think, not to make us suspicious of the other spectacles but to defuse possible criticism of them as mere display. Having seen (or rather heard) what the wrong kind of spectacle looks like, we can appreciate the dignity and decorum of the English occasions.

The spectacles and other set pieces are a clue to the method of the play – apparent diversity, underlying control. As we look at the seemingly fussy details of the widely dispersed action, we can see its various elements connecting. Wolsey's taxation is to finance the King's war with France, the ironic upshot of the Field of the Cloth of Gold (I. ii. 59–60). Cranmer appears not just to christen Elizabeth and suggest the future of Christianity in England, but to play a part in the King's divorce (III. ii. 71–3). Spotting Gardiner in Anne's coronation procession, the spectators predict the trouble he will cause for Cranmer (IV. i. 99–107). One action is always opening out into another. The actions are also juxtaposed so as to bring out the underlying principles of rise and fall. The Second Gentleman, watching Buckingham's last moments, predicts 'an ensuing evil, if it fall, / Greater than this' (II. i. 141–2), namely the fall of Katherine. The same character, at Anne's coronation, reminds his fellows that they last met at Buckingham's execution: 'that time offer'd sorrow, / This general joy' (IV. i. 6–7). As he and his fellows wait for the new Queen they spare a thought for the old one, and so bring them together in our minds: 'Alas good lady. / The trumpets sound: stand close, the queen is coming' (IV. i. 35–6). It is in moments like this, not in their own persons, that the two queens confront each other. The result, compared with the relations of Richard and Bolingbroke or Hal and Hotspur, is a reduction to pure pattern.

The play's diffuseness and its tendency to split judgements suggest at first a realistic reporting of history. But the more closely we look, the more we see that everything is being subsumed to a grand design. In the service of that design, individuals tend to blur and disappear. Buckingham's combination of angry vigour and pious submission pulls the character apart. He himself sees his own fall as the illustration of a principle: he and his father were both betrayed by servants (II. i. 107–31). Losing his individuality, he seems detached from the action that follows except on the level of pattern. He is simply our first example of the fall of greatness. He is recalled as Wolsey falls (III. ii. 254–69), and Henry warns Cranmer that he too could be set on by corrupted witnesses: 'such things have been done' (V. i. 133). Though much of the action hinges on her, Anne is lightly characterized and in the last of her three scenes she is glimpsed briefly as a silent figure surrounded by the spectacle of the court. She disappears into gossip and rumour, as though the court has in some way reduced and absorbed her. One of the technical oddities of the first scene is that the two kings on whom the spectacle centres are never named; they too seem hidden by the pomp, and part of Henry's development early in the play is an emergence from anonymity. The Prologue refers to 'The very persons of our noble story'(26) but does not identify them; there is no indication even of the period or country in which the action is set. The Epilogue declares that the play's best hope lies in 'The merciful construction of good women, / For such a one we show'd 'em' (10–11), but there are three possible candidates for that one position, Katherine, Anne, and Elizabeth. The general category 'good woman' has so absorbed the individuals that we cannot be sure which is meant. Patterning and control affect the audience as well as the characters. While the Chorus of *Henry V* enlists our creative participation, the Prologue to this play is more coercive: 'Be sad, as we would make ye'(25). The common people, who in earlier plays have been awkward, disruptive, and therefore invaluable in extending the range of the political analysis, are reduced here almost as thoroughly as they are in *Antony and Cleopatra*. The populace, Pierre Sahel observes, 'uses rumour as a means of expression and communication, being too weak to voice its concerns and grievances differently'.[10] Apart from the silent crowd that accompanies Buckingham they never appear. Katherine speaks for them on the question of taxation (I. ii); elsewhere they express approval and disapproval *en masse*. The Second Gentleman says of Wolsey:

> All the commons
> Hate him perniciously, and o' my conscience
> Wish him ten faddom deep: this duke as much
> They love and dote on; call him bounteous Buckingham,
> The mirror of all courtesy – (II. i. 49–53)

At the christening they are compared to the tide (V. iii. 17). In that tide we glimpse a familiar figure: 'there is a fellow somewhat near the door, he should be a brazier by his face, for o' my conscience twenty of the dog-days now reign in's nose' (V. iii. 38–41). This is obviously a descendant of the late Lieutenant Bardolph; unlike his ancestor he is kept offstage, reduced to a comic report and not allowed to speak for himself.

The actions of the central characters are also flattened and simplified. A recurring device is significant mime: Henry enters '*leaning on the* CARDINAL'S *shoulder*', so that when Wolsey '*places himself under the*

*King's feet on his right side'* (I. ii. SD) we see that the appearance of deference is deceptive. At Katherine's entrance *'she kneels.* KING *riseth from his state, takes her up, kisses and placeth her by him'* (I. ii. 8SD). On three occasions Cranmer kneels before Henry, who raises him (V. i. 89–92, 115; V. iv. 9). Henry's growing political authority is signalled when he appears *'at a window above'* (V. ii. 18SD), looking down on the Council. The cumulative effect is to reduce the action to a few significant vertical moves. Characters are absorbed into recurring plot patterns, of which the most obvious is the fall of greatness. Seen this way, they begin to look alike: Buckingham and Wolsey, antagonists and opposites in life, are surprisingly similar in their pious and otherworldly ends.[11] Katherine extends the pattern, resembling Wolsey in particular in the care she takes to provide for her followers; and she reconciles herself with her old enemy across the barrier of death. Wolsey's fall, as he himself sees it, is not particularly his own:

> This is the state of man; to-day he puts forth
> The tender leaves of hopes, to-morrow blossoms,
> And bears his blushing honours thick upon him:
> The third day comes a frost, a killing frost,
> And when he thinks, good easy man, full surely
> His greatness is a-ripening, nips his root,
> And then he falls as I do.           (III. ii. 352–8)

As in the final songs of Spring and Winter in *Love's Labour's Lost*, the vicissitudes of individual lives are absorbed into the workings of nature.

Submission and absorption are at once the process of the play and one of its principal subjects. Buckingham's words, 'Hear what I say, and then go home and lose me' (II. i. 57), suggest a willingness to be lost in the larger pattern that we hear in various ways from other speakers. His words on his arrest, 'The will of heav'n / Be done in this and all things: I obey'; (I. i. 209–10), are echoed and extended moments later by Abergavenny, on whom the same net has fallen: 'The will of Heaven be done, and the king's pleasure / By me obey'd' (I. i. 215–16). Submission to the King in particular ironically unites Katherine and Anne. Katherine's principal defence of her conduct as Henry's wife is that she has been

> At all times to your will conformable,
> Ever in fear to kindle your dislike,
> Yea, subject to your countenance, glad or sorry
> As I saw it inclin'd.           (II. iv.22–5)

227

Anne accepts the King's favour in the same spirit: 'Vouchsafe to speak my thanks and my obedience, / As from a blushing handmaid' (II. iii. 71–2). Moments after hearing that Wolsey has found 'the blessedness of being little', Katherine orders her attendant, 'Patience, be near me still, and set me lower' (IV. ii. 66, 76). Katherine's Patience, unlike Antony's Eros, is an invention. The virtue she stands for is also Cranmer's guide as he waits for the Council to dispose of him: 'their pleasures / Must be fulfill'd, and I attend with patience' (V. ii. 17–18). Worldly pomp, as we have seen, is part of the play's language of celebration. But when Sir Nicholas Vaux orders that Buckingham's barge be prepared for his last journey 'with such furniture as suits / The greatness of his person' he replies, 'Let it alone; my state now will but mock me' (II. i. 99–101). In a similar vein, Wolsey disposes of the wealth that has helped to bring him down: 'There take an inventory of all I have, / To the last penny, 'tis the king's' (III. ii. 451–2). The great individuals who in earlier plays have tried to shape their own natures and destinies – Richard of Gloucester, Hal, Brutus, Coriolanus – give way here to a group of characters who are relatively passive, who accept what the action of the play brings to them, and who in the process begin to look alike. There is no self-fashioning, there are no grand assertive soliloquies. Wolsey is the key example: his career of power is reported through the blurred and diffuse idiom of the play's early scenes. His one great scene, the one in which he totally dominates the stage, is the scene in which he gives his life away.

In the laments of *Richard III* characters were crushed by artificial language to fit a formal design. Here they voluntarily take their places in that design, which is created by the accumulation of individual moments, realistic in themselves, that allow the key ideas to emerge by repetition. One of those ideas, as we have seen, is a final deference not just to heaven but to the King, and it helps to take the play beyond the Prologue's announced subject, the fall of greatness. The victims of Henry's justice are united in blessing his future. Buckingham wishes he may live 'Longer than I have time to tell his years' and exemplify an ideal virtue so that at the end 'Goodness and he fill up one monument' (II. i. 91, 94). Katherine combines this wish with a surrender of herself, praying that Henry may

> ever flourish,
> When I shall dwell with worms, and my poor name
> Banish'd the kingdom. (IV. ii. 125–7)

This deference seems directed to Henry himself, not to his sacred office, as though Shakespeare is implicitly acknowledging that the strength of the Tudors came from their own remarkable personalities. Yet for the most part Henry himself does not parade his strength or authority. As in the Roman plays, the importance of the King is shown through other characters: his effect on them, their view of him, and – particularly in the early scenes – their behaviour when his power is inoperative. The Wolsey–Buckingham feud is a 'private difference' (I. i. 101), like the Gloucester–Winchester feud in *Henry VI*. Buckingham could have been a public critic of Wolsey, appealing to the King for the good of England; but he and the King never make contact, and he is destroyed. The effect, as in *Henry VI*, is that the King stands back while his subjects attack each other in a private contest whose only rule is survival of the fittest. The contrast with the Cranmer–Gardiner conflict is striking. Gardiner is Wolsey's creature and successor; he shares his master's hostility to Anne (V. i. 20–3), and he seems poised to destroy Cranmer as Wolsey destroyed Buckingham. But this time the King and the chosen victim make contact, and Henry, having promised, 'They shall no more prevail than we give way to' (V. i. 143), keeps his word. At the window, watching Cranmer's disgrace, he remarks grimly, 'Is this the honour they do one another? / 'Tis well there's one above 'em yet' (V. ii. 25–6), and he descends, a *rex ex machina*, to impose his will. He makes it clear that the unity he creates in the Council is for his good as well as theirs: 'As I have made ye one lords, one remain; / So I grow stronger, you more honour gain' (V. ii. 214–15). A united people means a strong monarchy, and vice versa. Henry speaks not as the Lord's anointed but as an executive whose strength is measured in human relationships. His descent to the main stage, unlike Richard II's, is a sign not of his fall but of his determination to do business.

His rescue of Cranmer is related in various ways to the fall of Wolsey, and both actions reflect on him as King. There are echoes, both verbal and visual. As the Lord Chamberlain tells Wolsey's accusers, 'Press not a falling man too far; 'tis virtue' (III. ii. 333), so Cromwell warns Gardiner not to be too hard on Cranmer: ''tis a cruelty / To load a falling man' (V. ii. 110–11). Though Gardiner and the Chancellor take the lead, Norfolk, Suffolk, Surrey, and the Chamberlain are also implicated in the attack on Cranmer, and we remember that they pulled down Wolsey. There is an element of sheer chance (or is it Providence?) in both episodes: Wolsey just happens to put incriminating documents in a packet for the King; Dr Butts just happens to pass by and see the Council's shabby treatment of Cranmer. More significant, however, is the fact that the virtues Wolsey gains in his fall are the virtues Cranmer exemplifies throughout. Cranmer's ready forgiveness of his enemies leads Henry to quote a proverb about him: 'Do my lord of Canterbury / A shrewd turn, and he's your friend for ever' (V. ii. 210–11). The same Christian values are urged by Wolsey on Cromwell: 'Love thyself last, cherish those hearts that hate thee' (III. ii. 443). Wolsey also charges his servant to 'fling away ambition' (III. ii. 440), and Cranmer admonishes Gardiner, 'Love and meekness, lord, / Become a churchman better than ambition' (V. ii. 96–7). Wolsey's virtue develops in private after his fall; in state affairs he is proud, ruthless, and cynical. His career seen in isolation makes virtue and public involvement look incompatible. And Henry worries about Cranmer: 'Now by my holidame, / What manner of man are you?' (V. i. 116–17). To encounter such meekness in public life is a new experience for Henry, and he is not sure what to make of it; throughout the sequence he shows an amused appreciation of the fact that his Archbishop of Canterbury actually behaves like a Christian. But he feels bound to warn him of his danger:

> Ween you of better luck,
> I mean in perjur'd witness, than your master,
> Whose minister you are, whiles here he liv'd
> Upon this naughty earth?             (V. i. 135–8)

In the end Henry uses his own worldly power to save Cranmer; it is the King's business to ensure a place for Christian virtue in this naughty earth. The fall of Wolsey shows the ruin of worldly pride, with private Christian virtue coming out of it. The rescue of Cranmer shows Henry not only taking on a new and better clerical servant but giving virtue a place in the state, guaranteed by the royal prerogative. In return he gets from Cranmer, as Elizabeth's godfather, a prophecy of the golden reign to come.

Throughout the sequence the focus is at least as much on Cranmer as on Henry; his kingship is examined, not in the direct spotlight that is put on earlier kings, but sideways, through the career and character of one of his principal subjects. And in fact the growth of Henry's strength as the play advances is less dramatic and obvious than we might have expected. This may be because in the early scenes his weakness is not shown directly, like that of Henry VI, but suggested by default in the theatrical and political dominance of Wolsey. As in the first tetralogy, stage authority and political authority go together. In the description of the Field of the Cloth of Gold, Henry goes unnamed for the entire scene; but the organizer is identified as 'the right reverend Cardinal of York' (I. i. 51). In a typical twist of interest, the scene turns from the relations of England and France to the dominance of Wolsey in English public life.

His relations with Henry are caught in Buckingham's words:

> I wonder
> That such a keech can with his very bulk
> Take up the rays o'th'beneficial sun,
> And keep it from the earth. (I. i. 54–7)

Later, a repentant Wolsey makes this good by calling Henry 'That sun I pray may never set' (III. ii. 415). It is in his relations with Wolsey, not in his own person, that Henry (like Richard II and Henry V) becomes a sun-king. Wolsey also presents a threat at a deeper level, by his self-sufficiency. Norfolk comments, with a mixture of admiration and distaste:

> There's in him stuff that puts him to these ends;
> For not being propp'd by ancestry, whose grace
> Chalks successors their way, nor call'd upon
> For high feats done to th'crown, neither allied
> To eminent assistants, but spider-like,
> Out of his self-drawing web, O, gives us note,
> The force of his own merit makes his way.
> (I. i. 58–64)

Like Richard of Gloucester and Coriolanus he is author of himself (Richard, we remember, was also called a spider). Even in his bounty he remains a bit aloof: '*A small table under a state for the* CARDINAL, *a longer table for the guests*' (I. iv. SD). He is set in opposition to the communal life celebrated elsewhere: in the Abbey crowd, 'woven / So strangely in one piece' (IV. i. 80–1),[12] and in Henry's final instruction to his people to make holiday: 'This day, no man think / 'Has business at his house' (V. iv. 74–5). His self-centredness makes him a threat, not just to the community, but to the King who should preside over that community. Buckingham determines to warn Henry that the cardinal 'Does buy and sell his honour as he pleases, / And for his own advantage' (I. i. 192–3). Pleading against Wolsey's taxation, Katherine tells the King:

> That you would love yourself, and in that love
> Not unconsider'd leave your honour nor
> The dignity of your office, is the point
> Of my petition. (I. ii. 14–17)

The taxation threatens not just the subjects' financial welfare but their loyalty: 'Tongues spit their duties out, and cold hearts freeze / Allegiance in them' (I. ii. 61–2).

231

Henry is moved by this plea, and his rebuke to Wolsey adds another factor:

> Things done without example, in their issue
> Are to be fear'd. Have you a precedent
> Of this commission? I believe, not any.
>
> (I. ii. 90–2)

It is always reassuring to hear a ruler speak against taxes. The special reassurance Henry adds is that of conservatism: he stands not just for the welfare of the subject but against dangerous innovation. This is ironic in view of the historical Henry's role as the king who changed the face of England for ever; but that king is not quite Shakespeare's. As Wolsey is a social upstart, he is also an innovator; on both grounds Henry has an interest in keeping him down. It is a sign of Henry's relative weakness at this point that he does not know what is going on in his kingdom: 'Taxation? / Wherein? and what taxation?' (I. ii. 37–8). But we do not see him so at a loss again. When he finally strikes Wolsey down, he emphasizes his own part in raising him (III. ii. 161–2) and finds his private wealth unbecoming a subject (III. ii. 127–8). It is the business of Henry V to lead his nation on a great adventure; it is the business of this new Henry, as Shakespeare conceives him, to keep things as they are, with himself at the centre. Subjects are to make their careers only by his grace and favour, and under his control. Seemingly unaware of the incongruity, Wolsey, having declared, 'O how wretched / Is that poor man that hangs on princes' favours' (III. ii. 366–7), urges Cromwell to make his career in the King's service (III. ii. 412–21). Cast off by the King, Katherine commends her daughter and her attendants to him (IV. ii. 129–51).

And yet, as we have seen, Henry's central political role is not quite reflected theatrically. The sustained attention that is fixed on Richard II and Henry V is not fixed on him. He does not indulge in the self-assertive role-playing of the earlier kings or the central Roman heroes; he is touched neither by the light of divine office nor by the glamour of heroic achievement. His energy comes in short bursts: 'Who am I? Ha?' (II. ii. 66); 'By holy Mary, Butts, there's knavery' (V. ii. 32). He seems most vivid in private moments, when he is jocular, irritable, or anxious – as when, waiting for news of Anne's delivery, he tells Suffolk, 'Charles, I will play no more tonight, / My mind's not on't' (V. i. 56–7). As a king he seems mostly a manager of men and a dispenser of patronage. R. A. Foakes has observed his 'lack of definition', which makes him less a character than 'a representative of benevolent power acting upon others'.[13] As part of the play's tendency to reduce itself to pattern, we are made to see the general function and significance of kingship, rather than given a vivid portrait of a king. Finally, Henry's most important feat is performed in Anne's bed: he gives England Elizabeth. This is hardly a feat which can be dramatized on stage, nor one for which Henry can claim much personal credit. Like other characters in the play, he is fulfilled in the end, paradoxically, by absorption into a larger pattern, ensuring not only the continuity of the monarchy but the provision of an even better monarch than himself.

Elizabeth's reign, as described in Cranmer's prophecy, is a striking contrast to Henry's. While he has kept control, more or less, of a fractious and troubled state, she will preside over an England as idealized as Gaunt's. While he went unnamed in the play's first scene, its last scene begins – appropriately, for it celebrates a christening – with the naming of Elizabeth. In a formal sense, that gives her a sharper reality than Henry enjoys. Yet we may wonder, as we do in *Richard II*, about the relations between the vision and the world we have to live in. Cranmer's language is more abstract than Gaunt's, and his prophecy is, for the characters on stage, a future that 'few now living can behold' (V. iv. 21). For the theatre audience it is the past, lost and idealized like York's memories of the Black Prince. For neither party is it a living reality.[14] But Cranmer's vision, though the characters will not see it come to pass, does not stand out in splendid isolation from the rest of the play. For one thing, Buckingham, Wolsey, and Katherine have already accustomed us to the idea of wishing others a worldly happiness one will never see oneself. And Cranmer is not, like Henry VI, the only character in the play with the special gift of seeing the future. Minor figures, the Lord Chamberlain and the Duke of Suffolk, anticipate his inspired vision of Elizabeth (II. iii. 75–9, III. ii. 50–2). The gift of prophecy is in the air, something generally available. Whereas *3 Henry VI* showed a sudden and temporary breakthrough of prophecy into the dark world of history, this play has a subtle and pervasive air of inspiration throughout, and a consequent suspension of normal reality. When, in Shaw's *Saint Joan*, Warwick and Cauchon talk of Nationalism and Protestantism, they become not twentieth-century men in medieval dress but medieval men with a twentieth-century understanding of their position – creatures, in other words, of an artifice peculiar to the play. The same is true of the prescient characters in *Henry VIII*; and the reduction of history to simple recurring patterns is part of that artifice.

At the same time the play has shown real historical problems, and Cranmer's vision deals with them too. Gaunt's England, Canterbury's commonwealth of bees, and Menenius' body politic were all placed early in their respective plays, open to challenge and criticism by the ensuing action. Cranmer's vision is placed at the end, in a future no one in the play can question. They may doubt, but he insists their doubts will be satisfied: 'the words I utter / Let none think flattery, for they'll find 'em truth' (V. iv. 15–16). More to the point, Cranmer's speech, being placed at the end, can gather up and resolve problems from earlier in the play. England has suffered from extortionate taxation, in enforced contributions to the Field of the Cloth of Gold, by which many have 'so sicken'd their estates that never / They shall abound as formerly' (I. i. 82–3), and in Wolsey's taxation for the ensuing French wars, which forces employers to lay off their men (I. ii. 30–7). In Elizabeth's days,

> every man shall eat in safety
> Under his own vine that he plants, and sing
> The merry songs of peace to all his neighbours.
>
> (V. iv. 33–5)

It sounds like an idealized version of the party in Shallow's orchard, with no messengers from London to disrupt it. And peace is here, as it was not in *Coriolanus*, an unequivocally pleasant state. Earlier in the play we have seen not civil war but bitter sectarian battles between Cranmer and his accusers, who attack him for spreading heresy (V. ii. 49–65). In Elizabeth's reign 'God shall be truly known' (V.iv.36). Wolsey has built his own independent career, as an over-mighty subject. Elizabeth's counsellors will also be 'new men', but dependent on the favour and example of the monarch:

> those about her
> From her shall read the perfect ways of honour,
> And by those claim their greatness, not by blood.
>
> (V. iv. 36–8)

Cranmer's speech may seem at first to float free of the political realities of England; but it is shaped by the problems and anxieties of the history we have seen.

It has also more to offer the Jacobean theatre audience than the dream of a lost golden past that never was. Cranmer extends the vision into the reign of James. At first the relation between the two monarchs is one of simple continuity:

> Peace, plenty, love, truth, terror,
> That were the servants to this chosen infant,
> Shall then be his, and like a vine grow to him.
>
> (V. iv. 47–9)

Once again, monarchy appears to be a principle, independent of individuals. (James, like Henry at the start of the play, is not actually named.) But the reference to the current ruler is also bound to make the audience aware of itself. This too is nothing new for the play. The Prologue has done this by discussing the different expectations we may bring. Cromwell, when he declares, 'Bear witness, all that have not hearts of iron, / With what a sorrow Cromwell leaves his lord' (III. ii. 424–5), is alone onstage with his master and must therefore be calling on us. The crowd at the christening includes apprentices, 'the youths that thunder at a playhouse, and fight for bitten apples' (V. iii. 59–60); the joke seems to be aimed into the auditorium. Finally, when Cranmer tells his contemporaries, 'Our children's children / Shall see this, and bless heaven' (V. iv. 55–6), he is referring to the audience. At the end of *Richard III*, Richmond appeared to be warning the Elizabethan spectators that the golden future he offered would depend on continued vigilance against treason. Cranmer is more complacent, telling his audience that the golden age is still with them, complimenting the living monarch as well as the dead one.

But the audience's awareness of its own present life, once triggered, can operate in a variety of ways. Those who knew the court of James might smile a little wryly, though the play offers no direct encouragement to do so. Those who knew their history might think of the troubled years that lay ahead for Cranmer and his contemporaries, of his own fate and those of Anne and Cromwell, apparently secure at the end of the play.[15] The last scene does not encourage such thoughts directly; but Katherine has reminded us that she has a daughter (IV. ii. 131–8), though she does not name her – she is named elsewhere by Henry (II. iv. 173) – and it is not always possible in watching a dramatization of historical characters to forget what we know of them just because the play does not show it. How far this should affect our reception of the last scene is debatable; but Shakespeare does unquestionably trouble the golden vision once, in a very simple way:

> She shall be, to the happiness of England,
> An aged princess; many days shall see her,
> And yet no day without a deed to crown it.
> Would I had known no more; but she must die,
> She must, the saints must have her; yet a virgin,
> A most unspotted lily shall she pass
> To th' ground, and all the world shall mourn her.
>
> (V. iv. 56–62)

Cranmer's voice hesitates for a pulse-beat before resuming its normal tone of exultation. He may be taking us out of history as we normally experience it, but not out of life altogether. Elizabeth joins Richard II, Henry V, and the other monarchs who become time's subjects in the end. She also joins Katherine, whose fall made her own life possible; a single image unites them. Katherine declares:

> like the lily
> That once was mistress of the field and flourish'd,
> I'll hang my head and perish.             (III. i. 151-3)

This is the ultimate pattern, the one that includes us all.

We should also consider the stage picture before us as Cranmer speaks. Elizabeth's perfect England is juxtaposed with Henry's imperfect one, in a collision of word and picture. While Gaunt speaks only to a few hearers (in the Folio, only to York), Cranmer speaks to a full stage; Henry's world is solidly present throughout. This alerts us to the difference between Cranmer's simplified vision and the complex, devious pattern of history we have just seen these characters engaged in. Ideal patterning and the reporting of untidy reality, delicately balanced throughout the play, are held in suspension to the end. Elizabeth too is present – as a baby in a christening dress. When we hear of her death, her life seems, theatrically, to be a circle that closes in a moment. What we do not see, of course, is what Heywood had already shown in the two parts of *If You Know Not Me, You Know Nobody* – the adult Elizabeth as a living presence on stage. We see a baby, and we hear of a golden queen. The radical split between these images, combined with the low-key portrayal of Henry, leaves monarchy as a principle, an idea; we have not seen an individual who can really embody it. What we see instead is a communal experience, a general agreement to celebrate, the focus of that celebration being, as at Christmas, a helpless infant: 'This little one shall make it Holy-day' (V. iv. 76). The disproportion is touched at once with mystery and with mild amusement. The focus on the community is in line with the play's historical action, in which a wide variety of characters, often inadvertently, often with little sense of what they are really doing, have contributed to the destiny of England. The Roman plays focus on great individuals, but the breaking of Coriolanus seems to leave Shakespeare disillusioned with that ideal. When he turns back to the group, the community, he treads a little warily, as though fearing disillusionment there too. The reduction of the characters to figures in a pattern, grim and dehumanizing in the first tetralogy, is seen here in a more benevolent light, but reservations are admitted. In *Coriolanus* the communal rejoicing that heralded the salvation of Rome was shot through with savage irony, for Volumnia saved Rome by killing her son. *Henry VIII* is gentler, but also shows the sacrifice of individuals to the common good. The communal rejoicing that hails the destiny of England is delicately touched by reminders that history is usually more untidy than this, and that the greatest of us are mortal. The play as a whole shows that we are members one of another, not in a simple golden world but in a life that even at its best demands sacrifice, subjects us to injustice, exposes our littleness, and leaves us with no virtue higher than that of graceful surrender.

# Conclusion

Shakespeare's treatment of politics is exploratory rather than prescriptive. He is by our standards little concerned with the practical implications of political life. The carriers of *Henry IV* grumble about the rise in the price of oats, but do not blame anyone for it or look for a solution. The plebeians in *Coriolanus* are given the corn they demand at the outset, but we are told this only in passing and we are not told how the decision was made. If Shakespeare had had our interest in political solutions for economic problems, he would have made some connection between the election of the tribunes and the distribution of corn; he does not. His interest is not in examining what political structures best serve the general good, but in watching how people behave within the structures they have. Politics for him is not a search for solutions to social and economic problems but a search for power and authority by the politicians themselves. This is not just because Shakespeare is cynical or because the quest for power makes better drama (though it does). He is not just a man of his profession but a man of his time. According to Christopher Morris, Tudor Englishmen found it difficult to think of politics 'except in terms of persons. They talked more of the monarch than of the monarchy, more of the sovereign than of sovereignty.'[1] At a time when the average citizen's ability to participate in public life was limited or non-existent, it was natural that instead of thinking about political structures and functions people would be more inclined to watch the pageantry of greatness, the rise and fall of the very few who had power.

That is the business, though far from the whole business, of *Henry VI*. Power here is crudely measured and crudely won: it comes with aggressiveness in civil life and success on the battlefield. There is a simple relation between political authority and theatrical panache – as we see, for example, in the career of Richard of York. But the game of power is also constricted and inhuman, and, while at first there seems

238

little to choose between the sides, the pageantry of violence is gradually shaped into a fantasy like that of a morality play as Richard and Richmond confront each other, polarized images of good and evil. Right triumphs, but only at the cost of leaving history behind for the sake of a stylized myth. As if in reaction to this, *Richard II* tests two myths – Gaunt's England and Richard's divinely appointed kingship – against a more open, complex, and pragmatic vision of political life. Here we see no decisive battle of good and evil, and no simple equation of theatrical and political authority. Richard gains theatrical strength not as he comes up in the world but as he goes down. Richard of Gloucester consciously creates his own myth of himself as a super-Machiavel, the play's world shapes itself around that myth, and Richard himself believes in it almost to the end. Richard II creates a myth of himself as the Lord's anointed, or rather tries to use a myth that the political traditions of his land have created for him; but he never quite believes it himself, and it is not usable currency in the world he lives in. Yet he *is* the Lord's anointed, and when he is killed England becomes desanctified. It falls to Prince Hal to restore confidence, not in the kingship but in himself, by creating his own myth: the prodigal prince who reforms and becomes a national hero. He knows how to fight, but his real political instrument is his reputation, and the real battlefield is not Shrewsbury or Agincourt but the minds and imaginations of his countrymen, and of the audience.

There is, then, a shift in emphasis between the two tetralogies, from the appearance of power to the power of appearance. This carries over into the Roman plays. In *Julius Caesar* as in *Henry V*, the principal character sets out to impress by performing a great deed; but, while Henry wants to impress his countrymen and posterity, Brutus, to a dangerous extent, seems to be trying to impress himself. Henry's achievement is gradually eroded by time. In the case of Brutus and Caesar, there is a sharper, more immediate conflict between the image of greatness and the mortal frailty beneath. This motif, which began with our double view of Talbot, at once heroic and pragmatic, reappears in *Richard II* in the contrast between the royal icon and the petulant man. It runs through the Roman plays: the noble Brutus and the posturing political failure, the triple pillar of the world and the strumpet's fool, the thing of blood and the boy of tears.

The final three plays bring into particularly sharp focus the problems of relating the heroic to the human, the private to the public. In *Antony and Cleopatra* there is a fusion of different elements that other plays have kept apart: by the time we come to Cleopatra's death we can no longer distinguish, as we did very clearly in the case of Talbot, between the heroic image and the mortal body. Shadow and substance, person and performance, are one. The private life of self-indulgence that was so firmly cut away in *Henry IV* is absorbed into Cleopatra's final assertion of her royalty. In *Coriolanus* there is a sharp reaction. Heroism and humanity, fused in Cleopatra, are irreconcilably opposed here, with fatal consequences for the hero. As Hal, having rejected Falstaff, goes on to public glory and achievement, Coriolanus, having accepted his mother's plea, goes to his death alone in an alien city. These are reverse images, both equally painful, of the irreconcilable opposition of heroic achievement and full humanity. *Henry VIII* heals the wounds, not by the daring fusion of *Antony and Cleopatra*, but by a new, relaxed tolerance. Private pleasure and the interests of the state can both be served, but this seems to be made possible more by a happy accident or by the working of a hidden, benevolent comic principle than by the imaginative power and will of a single character, of the sort we see in Cleopatra. *Henry VIII* is touched by grace but not by heroism. Like *Henry VI* it presents a panoramic view of the state, of the rise and fall of greatness. But the motives that drive its characters are more complex and divided, the relations of cause and effect are haphazard, and the myth that emerges is not a stylized conflict of good and evil but a slightly wistful vision of a peaceful golden state we can never quite see. Once again, as in the first tetralogy, history has generated a benevolent myth; but the relations of history and myth are more delicately handled, and the final satisfaction is tinged with a certain ruefulness. In Cleopatra's victory we celebrate a human achievement enacted before our eyes; Elizabeth's golden age is something that goes beyond the will of any individual, and is only talked of, not seen.

Through all this runs Shakespeare's concern with political life as something that has to be shaped imaginatively. His business as a playwright is to find a pattern in the untidy events of history. The business of his characters – and from Richard of Gloucester onwards they are quite conscious of this – is to shape their own natures into effective performances that will allow them to impress their fellows and achieve their own ends. They are like actors trying to make an effect, win applause, get the strongest position on stage. Many of them do it brilliantly. But after a certain point the analogy breaks down, for a real actor's responsibility begins and ends with giving the best possible performance, and a political figure's does not. It matters to Richard of Gloucester – as it would not matter to Richard Burbage when he played him – that the performance involves a suppression of his full humanity, an outrage to larger values whose importance he finally recognizes. This matters so much to Coriolanus that unlike Richard he publicly

240

throws his part away. We may wonder how much it matters to Hal; one of the things we find disturbing about him, as prince and king, is that we are not sure he is really aware of what he has lost. Only in Cleopatra do person and performance become one; for the others, the actor's ability to sharpen and make vivid, and to change shapes at will, involves a reduction of full humanity and a loss of authenticity. It is an image, in distinctly theatrical terms, of the loss of self that always threatens those in public life, as they do what the pressures on them, including their own ambitions, demand. We see a positive view of this when Henry V talks of the stream of his own life mingling with the state of floods, the larger life of the nation. Even Coriolanus is happiest when doing what is expected of him as the sword of Rome. But this willingness to surrender is always in conflict with the desire to save a corner of life for oneself – if only one could be sure what that self is. The recurring fantasy of Shakespeare's English kings that the peasants are free and happy suggests that they can no longer imagine domestic peace in their own lives; to find it they would have to be quite different people. Only Brutus in his quiet scene with Lucius seems to achieve that peace before our eyes, and it is a temporary achievement of whose value he himself seems not fully aware.

In plot terms, the great men work towards climatic achievements – gaining a crown, winning a battle, killing an enemy. But this shaping too has a double effect, producing both excitement and irony. The stylization and foreshortening of the theatre can create distance, making the actions of the great look petty and absurd. We see this in the civil conflicts of *Henry VI* and the political scenes of *Antony and Cleopatra*. Theatre itself is peculiarly time-bound and temporary. The action must always change and develop; it cannot freeze at a single moment of achievement, in the manner of a heroic statue or a triumphal arch. Neither the Battle of Agincourt nor the killing of Caesar can be an end; each is undone and swept away by time. A ruler who wants his achievements celebrated had better turn to a painter or sculptor than to a playwright. The theatre's immortality, such as it is, consists not in permanence but in repetition, and no two performances are quite alike. Of all the characters who are aware of time and try to grapple with it, it is Cleopatra who comes closest to success, by living for the moment and by repeating herself. Hal, who tries to give his career a controlled development through time, finds that time will not altogether co-operate. In the end he is wasted by time, as are Richard II, Henry IV, and Hotspur. When Gaunt speaks of an ideal England, he takes it out of time altogether.

The passages that seem frozen and still, that seem to escape from

241

time, are the passages that give a reduced and stylized vision of the state. It may be an image of order, like Canterbury's speech on the bees' commonwealth; or it may be an image of pain and ruin like the Towton allegory. Theatre reduces and simplifies in order to clarify; and Shakespeare is able not just to accept the reduction of full humanity this involves but to make it part of his point – as he does in *Henry IV*, where the shaping artifice of Hal, like that of Falstaff, is placed against a larger world and its narrowness stands revealed. At the same time, these reduced images have considerable power, and haunt the imagination. Even the ending of *Richard III*, being outside history, makes the idea of suppressing treason applicable to the present state of England. In that case the image of pure order, free of time, works directly on the audience. In *Henry VIII* it works within the play, as Cranmer's prophecy of Elizabeth seeps backwards through the action, colouring and shaping the untidy history of Henry VIII's reign.

It is more characteristic of the political play, however, to submit to the usual conditions of time. Free of the formal expectations of comedy and tragedy with their decisive endings, it can register something of the open, unfinished quality of life. This is especially true of the English plays, whose action generally trails a past behind it and ends with less than a full resolution. Characters' fates may be resolved but the nation goes on. And, while a character's end may be known, his full nature is sometimes hidden from us, as though involvement in public life, demanding as it does the manipulation of appearances, leaves the character's inner self somewhat concealed from us, and perhaps even from him. Hence the difficulty we have interpreting Henry IV, Hal, Coriolanus in his later scenes, Henry VIII at Katherine's trial. This unresolved quality both in character and in action leaves us with a sharper awareness of our own responsibilities and problems as audience: the need to interpret, to do some shaping of our own (to make sense of the contradictory messages we get in *Henry V* and *Antony and Cleopatra*, for example); the need to be aware of past and future events that help us judge what we see before us; and the need to admit at times · the limits of our knowledge. As the characters cannot fully control their lives, so Shakespeare cannot fully express them and we cannot fully know them.

Artists express their power over life by creating imaginative structures; and Shakespeare's politicians express their power in the same way. In neither case is the achievement final. Bottom's account of his dream insists, comically and in the end movingly, on his inability to describe it. Prospero, having tested the strengths and limits of his art, gives it up. In contrast, Richard of Gloucester and Coriolanus try to impose their wills absolutely, each attempt involving a denial of humanity. Richard goes dead and Coriolanus breaks apart. Other characters accept their limits more readily. Henry IV dreams of cleansing England, and himself, by a crusade; but he learns in the end that he can cleanse England only by dying, and he no longer seems to want anything for himself. Henry V settles for a temporary achievement in France and leaves it to his unborn son to conquer the Holy Land. But the most positive act of Henry VI has been to look forward, as Henry VIII does, to a better ruler than himself. Brutus and Cassius kill Caesar and then invoke him to give meaning to their own deaths, needing him after all. Stubbornly egocentric in life, Caesar in death finds his identity through Brutus. For Antony and Cleopatra, full achievement depends on political defeat and the surrender of life itself. Coriolanus ends by giving away a sure victory and then virtually demanding to be killed; *Henry VIII* presents image after image of graceful surrender.

But surrender does not always have to be graceful, nor is it always a sign of weakness. The key figure here is Richard II, who defines his kingship most brilliantly when he gives it away, and thus gains a power over Bolingbroke he never had as a ruler. We have our sharpest sense of him as king when he places his own hands on the crown and removes it. The paradox reverberates through other plays. The ultimate achievement of Shakespeare's political characters is not to order and rule their own worlds but to move and impress the theatre audience, not in victory but in defeat. The authority of Henry VI as critic and prophet is never greater than in his death scene. Henry V's victory is exciting not in spite of its elusiveness but because of it; time swept it away and the play itself cannot contain it. Judged as an attempt to save the republic, the murder of Caesar is a total failure; yet of all the events Shakespeare depicts in his political plays it is probably the most famous, and the play dwells on this. Cleopatra in her own way turns political failure and death into personal triumph. Historical drama deals naturally in ending, loss, failure. The most impressive characters in Shakespeare's political world are not the winners but those who have confronted and absorbed the experience of loss, whose achievement is not to order a state but to assert themselves against inevitable ruin. This is the political thinking of a playwright. It will not help us to control the economy, achieve social justice, win or prevent war. But it tells us something about human power and the endless fascination it has for us in the face of our own mortality.

# Notes

*PREFACE*

1 We see the result in Stephen Greenblatt's 'Invisible bullets: Renaissance authority and its subversion, *Henry IV* and *Henry V*', in Jonathan Dollimore and Alan Sinfield (eds), *Political Shakespeare: New Essays in Cultural Materialism* (Ithaca, NY, and London: Cornell University Press, 1985), pp. 18–47. I single this essay out because I find it powerful and impressive, the work of a first-rate critic. And it seems to me limited, as Tillyard is limited, by the sheer power of its myth, which produces a single-minded reading.
2 According to Marie Axton, drama was 'by virtue of its form and social ambience, ideally suited to *question* the validity of any conceptual explanation of human behaviour': *The Queen's Two Bodies: Drama and the Elizabethan Succession* (London: Royal Historical Society, 1971), p. x.
3 Quoted from Gāmini Salgādo (ed.), *Eyewitnesses of Shakespeare* (New York: Barnes & Noble, 1975), p. 16.
4 Quoted from the Arden edition of *Henry VIII*, p. 180.
5 Alexander Leggatt, 'Dramatic perspective in *King John*', *English Studies in Canada*, 3 (1977), 1–17.
6 See, for example, G. K. Hunter, 'Shakespeare's politics and the rejection of Falstaff', *Critical Quarterly*, 1 (1959), 234–5.

*1 HENRY VI*

1 The Arden stage direction at l. 45, '*Exit Funeral*', is I think, premature: ll. 62–4 suggest that Shakespeare wants the effect of bad news pouring in while Henry's corpse is still onstage.
2 In the 1962 printing (subsequently corrected) Arden reads 'I know not what I am' – an interesting mistake, and I restore the Folio reading with some reluctance.
3 I have restored the Folio punctuation, which affects the meaning.
4 On the staging of the scene and its connection with the Auvergne scene that follows, see Alan C. Dessen, 'The logic of Elizabethan stage violence: some alarums and excursions for modern critics, editors, and directors', *Renaissance Drama*, 9 (1978), 65–6.
5 Emrys Jones has explored the theatrical implications of the scene in *The Origins of Shakespeare* (Oxford: Clarendon Press, 1977), pp. 146–7. His reading is valuable, but his emphasis on the importance of the imagination is not, I think, the final emphasis of the scene and would be more appropriate

245

to a reading of *Henry V* or *Antony and Cleopatra.*

6 The Countess's picture, which has not prepared her for the reality, evidently shows a physically imposing Talbot, exaggerated to correspond with his legend. Cf. Lucy's words to the French after Talbot's death: 'Were but his picture left amongst you here, / It would amaze the proudest of you all' (IV. vii. 83–4). Shakespeare's interest in the shadow–substance theme at this period can also be seen in *The Two Gentlemen of Verona,* IV. ii, iv.

7 On the similarity, see Elizabeth Longford, *Wellington: Pillar of State* (New York: Harper & Row, 1972), p. 415.

8 See A. C. Hamilton, *The Early Shakespeare* (San Marino, Cal.: Huntington Library, 1967), p. 17.

9 See Preface, p. xi.

10 See J. P. Brockbank, 'The frame of disorder – *Henry VI* ', in John Russell Brown and Bernard Harris (eds), *Early Shakespeare* (London: Arnold, 1961), p. 76. Brockbank points out that the list of titles comes from Talbot's tomb at Rouen – an interesting case of documentary detail contributing to a stylized effect. He also draws the analogy with the effect of a Tudor tomb: 'Beneath the effigy of the complete man in, as it were, painted marble finery, lies the image of the rotten corpse.' Shakespeare returns to this idea in *Troilus and Cressida,* where Hector kills a man in splendid armour and finds inside a corpse that has already putrefied.

11 David Riggs points out that the French use artillery while 'the English . . . seem scarcely aware that gunpowder has been invented'. See *Shakespeare's Heroical Histories: Henry VI and its Literary Tradition* (Cambridge, Mass.: Harvard University Press, 1971), p. 102.

12 See Edward I. Berry, *Patterns of Decay: Shakespeare's Early Histories* (Charlottesville: University of Virginia Press, 1975), p. 10.

13 E. M. W. Tillyard, *Shakespeare's History Plays* (London: Chatto & Windus, 1944; repr. Harmondsworth: Penguin, 1962), p. 169.

14 On the irony of the rose symbolism, see F. W. Brownlow, *Two Shakespearean Sequences: Henry VI to Richard II and Pericles to Timon of Athens* (London: Macmillan, 1977), p. 21. On the arbitrariness of the symbols, see Sigurd Burckhardt, *Shakespearean Meanings* (Princeton, NJ: Princeton University Press, 1968), p. 92.

15 Burckhardt, op. cit., pp. 54–5. Burckhardt, however, applies this principle more broadly to the trilogy as a whole than I would do.

16 Christopher Morris, *Political Thought in England: Tyndale to Hooker* (London: Geoffrey Cumberlege, Oxford University Press, 1953), p. 103.

17 The Arden stage direction is based on the Quarto, in which Clarence changes his mind onstage after conversing with Richard. The Folio suppresses even this explanation, as Clarence enters with his mind evidently made up, after a change we never see.

18 See Jones, op. cit., p. 175.

19 ibid., p. 189.

20 That is the reduced cast of the Folio version; the Quarto also has Montague and Hastings but gives them no lines.

21 See Raymond V. Utterback, 'Public men, private wills, and kingship in *Henry VI, Part III* ', *Renaissance Papers 1978* (Durham, NC: Southern Renaissance Conference, 1979), p. 49.

22 John W. Blanpied, *Time and the Artist in Shakespeare's English Histories*

(Newark: University of Delaware Press, 1983), p. 68. For Blanpied's general discussion of this quality in the play, see pp. 64–70.

23  M. M. Reese, *The Cease of Majesty* (London: Arnold, 1961), p. 126.

24  See John Wilders, *The Lost Garden* (London: Macmillan, 1978), p. 17. The Folio gives two versions of the Father's entrance. In one, he and the Son come on together from different doors; in the other, the Father enters just before he speaks. The second version is also found in the Quarto, and is preferred by the Arden editor; but the first would increase the visual shock following Henry's speech, and is in keeping with the general stylization of the scene. It is more likely to represent Shakespeare's second thoughts about the staging.

25  See Tillyard, op. cit., p. 151.

26  A reviewer of a Victorian production reports: 'He died boldly, like a courageous rebel of the true English type, and won our respect even in his fall': *Athenaeum*, 30 April 1864; quoted in Gāmini Salgādo (ed.), *Eyewitnesses of Shakespeare* (New York: Barnes & Noble, 1975), p. 88.

27  See Wilders, op. cit., p. 16.

28  Edward I. Berry accuses the King of 'sublime ignorance of the psychology of symbolism' (op. cit., p. 25).

29  The analogy is drawn by Holinshed. See Geoffrey Bullough (ed.), *Narrative and Dramatic Sources of Shakespeare*, vol. 3 (London: Routledge & Kegan Paul, 1960), p. 210. On the relations between this scene and the Passion sequences in the mystery plays, see Jones, op. cit., pp. 54–6.

30  See Michael Manheim, *The Weak King Dilemma in the Shakespearean History Play* (Syracuse: Syracuse University Press, 1973), p. 110.

31  See Michael Manheim, 'Silence in the *Henry VI* plays', *Educational Theatre Journal*, 29 (1977), 71.

32  See Philip Edwards, *Threshold of a Nation* (Cambridge: Cambridge University Press, 1979), p. 124.

33  See Robert Ornstein, *A Kingdom for a Stage* (Cambridge, Mass.: Harvard University Press, 1972), p. 58.

34  Stephen Greenblatt, *Renaissance Self-Fashioning: From More to Shakespeare* (Chicago: University of Chicago Press, 1980), *passim.*

35  In the John Barton adaptation *The Wars of the Roses* (Royal Shakespeare Company, 1963) the dying Henry (David Warner) planted a bloody kiss on the forehead of Richard (Ian Holm). The gesture of forgiveness later became a curse; in *Richard III* Henry's ghost kissed Richard again, and Richard went into his final battle wearing the mark of Cain.

36  The Quarto text includes (after l. 79) the words 'I had no father, I am like no father.' In view of Richard's earlier admiration for his father, this makes his rejection of his own humanity even more startling.


## 2 *RICHARD III*

1  See Bernard Beckerman, 'Playing to the crowd: structure and soliloquy in *The Tide Tarrieth No Man*', in J. C. Gray (ed.), *Mirror up to Shakespeare* (Toronto: University of Toronto Press, 1984), pp. 128–37.

2  Emrys Jones has even suggested that Richard seems to be making these characters up as he goes along; see *The Origins of Shakespeare* (Oxford: Clarendon Press, 1977), p. 201. But Richard does not initiate their entrances;

he reacts to them. The distinction is important, since it suggests the final limits of Richard's authority.

3 Ralph Berry, '*Richard III*: bonding the audience', in Gray (ed.), op. cit., p. 121.

4 As is frequently pointed out, the joke about christening Clarence in the Tower anticipates his being drowned in a butt of malmsey. See, for example, Wolfgang Clemen, *A Commentary on Shakespeare's Richard III*, English version by Jean Bonheim (London: Methuen, 1968), p. 14.

5 See Thomas F. van Laan, *Role-Playing in Shakespeare* (Toronto: University of Toronto Press, 1978), p. 139.

6 Hall explains the rotten armour as designed to create an air of unexpected crisis. See Geoffrey Bullough (ed.), *Narrative and Dramatic Sources of Shakespeare*, vol. 3 (London: Routledge & Kegan Paul, 1960), p. 267. No such expanation is offered in the play.

7 In the great mass of commentary on Richard's failure as king, one theatrical image stands out. In the early scenes of Bill Alexander's 1984 Royal Shakespeare Company production, Antony Scher played Richard on crutches, giving him a speed and variety of movement unavailable to any other character. As soon as he became king he was carried everywhere in a portable throne, all his movements dependent on the servants in charge of it. He was literally the prisoner of his office.

8 When at the end of III.vii Buckingham acclaims the new King, the Folio text has '*All*' say 'Amen' (240); in the Quarto only the Mayor does. The Quarto reading is tempting, and even if the Folio is preferred the quality of that 'Amen' is still up to the citizens.

9 See Anne Barton, 'The king disguised: Shakespeare's *Henry V* and the comical history', in Joseph G. Price (ed.), *The Triple Bond* (University Park and London: Pennsylvania State University Press, 1975), pp. 93–8.

10 In Robin Phillips's 1977 production at Stratford, Ontario, Richard's first entrance as king was a magnificent spectacle, with attendants carrying great banners. As soon as he spoke his first words, the stage was suddenly empty of all but himself and Buckingham.

11 See Nicholas Brooke, *Shakespeare's Early Tragedies* (London: Methuen, 1968), p. 57.

12 Waldo F. McNeir, 'The masks of Richard the Third', *Studies in English Literature*, 11 (1971), 173.

13 Richard's dream of being set upon by the ghosts of his victims is not unlike Clarence's dream in I.iv. He has also admitted a certain resemblance to his mother: 'Madam, I have a touch of your condition, / That cannot brook the accent of reproof' (IV.iv.158–9). While there is no acceptance of conventional values here, Richard is compromising his earlier rejection of all family likeness, and the joke may be more against himself than he suspects.

14 At the end of the wooing scene in Robin Phillips's production Anne (Martha Henry) touched Richard's crippled hand as though it held an erotic fascination for her. One thought of De Flores's remark about Beatrice-Joanna: 'Some women are odd feeders.'

15 Murray Krieger, 'The dark generations of *Richard III*', *Criticism*, 1 (1959), 38. See also H. M. Richmond, *Shakespeare's Political Plays* (New York: Random House, 1967), p. 85.

16 See Bullough (ed.), op. cit., pp. 265–7.

17 In Robin Phillips's production Margaret (Margaret Tyzack) was equipped

with a hidden microphone that made her voice echo, setting her apart from the other characters.

18 One reason why Cibber's adaptation held the stage so long may be that in cutting Margaret he removed a major threat to the leading actor. See George C. D. Odell, *Shakespeare from Betterton to Irving*, vol. 2 (repr. New York: Dover, 1966), pp. 269–71.

19 In Laurence Olivier's film, Edward's sentimental delight at the reconciliation is contrasted with the obvious lack of enthusiasm the courtiers show as they embrace.

20 See Brooke, op. cit., p. 51.

21 On the significance of All Souls' Day as the setting for the last movement of the play, see Jones, op. cit., pp. 227–9.

22 See Antony Hammond, Introduction to the Arden edition, p. 110.

23 See Krieger, op. cit., p. 43.

24 F. W. Brownlow, *Two Shakespearean Sequences: Henry VI to Richard II and Pericles to Timon of Athens* (London: Macmillan, 1977), p. 63.

25 Richmond, op. cit., p. 96.

26 This corresponds roughly to the actual Tudor practice of resting their claim on God's will, shown in the outcome of the Battle of Bosworth. See G. R. Elton, *The Tudor Constitution* (Cambridge: Cambridge University Press, 1960), pp. 1–2. Hall describes Richmond as 'of no great stature' but 'so formed and decorated with all the gyftes and lyniaments of nature that he semed more an angelical creature than a terrestrial personage' (Bullough (ed.), op. cit., p. 294).

27 See Wilbur Sanders, *The Dramatist and the Received Idea* (Cambridge: Cambridge University Press, 1968), p. 93.

28 Robert B. Pierce, *Shakespeare's History Plays: The Family and the State* (n.p.: Ohio State University Press, 1971), p. 96.

29 'Your country's fat' is perhaps tactless in its suggestion of the spoils of victory, but the rest of the speech controls the image, emphasizing the *earning* of reward. Hall's version (Bullough (ed.), op. cit., p. 295) is much more tactless.

30 See Sanders, op. cit., p. 72.

31 M. M. Reese, ' 'Tis my picture: refuse it not', *Shakespeare Quarterly*, 36 (1985), 254.

## 3 *RICHARD II*

1 See John R. Elliott, Jr, 'History and tragedy in *Richard II*', *Studies in English Literature*, 8 (1968), 261.

2 Wilbur Sanders, *The Dramatist and the Received Idea* (Cambridge: Cambridge University Press, 1968), p. 186.

3 See Paul Gaudet, 'The "Parasitical" counsellors in Shakespeare's *Richard II*: a problem in dramatic interpretation', *Shakespeare Quarterly*, 33 (1982), 142–54.

4 See H. R. Coursen, *The Leasing Out of England: Shakespeare's Second Henriad* (Washington, DC: University Press of America, 1982), p. 19.

5 See Allan Bloom, '*Richard II*', in John Alvis and Thomas G. West (eds), *Shakespeare as Political Thinker* (Durham, NC: Carolina Academic Press,

1981), p. 53.

6 See Ernst H. Kantorowicz, *The King's Two Bodies: A Study in Medieval Political Theology* (Princeton, NJ: Princeton University Press, rev. 1981), pp. 24–86. In the days following the execution of Charles I, his ordeal was compared in some quarters to the Crucifixion. See C. V. Wedgwood, *The Trial of Charles I* (London: Collins, 1964), pp. 207–8.

7 Michael McCanles, *Dialectical Criticism and Renaissance Literature* (Berkeley, Los Angeles, and London: University of California Press, 1975), p. 167.

8 For an analysis of this moment, see Brents Stirling, 'Bolingbroke's "decision" ', *Shakespeare Quarterly*, 2 (1951), 31–2.

9 Phyllis Rackin points out that, in challenging the theatre audience as well as the onstage characters, Richard is like Christ in a Crucifixion pageant; Christ's accusations embrace the spectators as well as the other characters in the play. See 'The role of the audience: Shakespeare's *Richard II* ', *Shakespeare Quarterly*, 36 (1985), 270–1.

10 In the 1964 Royal Shakespeare Company production (jointly directed by John Barton, Peter Hall, and Clifford Williams) as soon as Bolingbroke (Eric Porter) touched the crown Richard (David Warner) turned it upside down.

11 In IV.ii of *King John* John's act in having himself crowned twice produces what looks at first glance like disproportionate resentment from the barons. On reflection one can see their point: in suggesting that the ceremony did not 'take' the first time, John is devaluing it. Richard, on the other hand, insists that the efficacy of a coronation does not wear off; it has to be removed by formal reversal – if indeed it can be removed at all. Richard repeats his gesture of reversing a ceremony when he bids his Queen farewell: 'Let me unkiss the oath 'twixt thee and me' (V.i.74).

12 See M. L. Ranald, 'The degradation of Richard II: an inquiry into the ritual backgrounds', *English Literary Renaissance*, 7 (1977), 188. Ranald shows (pp. 191–4) that Richard's deposition has some points of contact with established ceremonies of degradation. The whole article is extremely valuable as background for the play.

13 Stephen Greenblatt, *Renaissance Self-Fashioning: From More to Shakespeare* (Chicago and London: University of Chicago Press, 1980), pp. 78–9.

14 Michael Goldman, *Acting and Action in Shakespearean Tragedy* (Princeton, NJ: Princeton University Press, 1985), p. 64.

15 C. L. Barber, *Shakespeare's Festive Comedy* (Princeton, NJ: Princeton University Press, 1959; repr. Cleveland and New York: World Publishing Company, 1963), p. 193.

16 See Philip Edwards, 'Person and office in Shakespeare's plays', *Proceedings of the British Academy*, 56 (1972 for 1970), 100. Ranald (op. cit., p. 172) reports a ceremony for degrading a knight which includes a mock-baptism, removing the knight's original name, and giving him the new name 'traitor'. Richard pins this name on himself at IV.i.247–8.

17 David Warner broke the mirror with his hand, which was then seen to be covered with blood. In fact there is nothing in the original texts to indicate how Richard breaks the glass; but Theobald's direction that he hurls it to the ground is convincing and is generally followed.

18 Stirling, op. cit., p. 34.

19 When David Garrick was considering reviving the play, George Steevens

wrote to him requesting that 'proper regard be paid to old *puss in boots*, who arrives so hastily in the fifth act': quoted in Arthur Colby Sprague, *Shakespeare's Histories: Plays for the Stage* (London: Society for Theatre Research, 1964), p. 29. On the comedy of the Aumerle sequence, see Sheldon P. Zitner, 'Aumerle's conspiracy', *Studies in English Literature*, 14 (1974), 239–57.
20 In the 1964 Royal Shakespeare Company production, Hotspur (Roy Dotrice) did not at first recognize Bolingbroke and sat down beside him on a crate of supplies, elbowing him out of the way.
21 See Alvin B. Kernan, 'The Henriad: Shakespeare's major history plays', *Yale Review*, 59 (1969), 17.
22 See Stanley Wells, *Royal Shakespeare: Four Major Productions at Stratford-upon-Avon* (Manchester: Manchester University Press, 1977), p. 76.


## 4 HENRY IV

1 Derek Traversi, *Shakespeare from Richard II to Henry V* (Stanford, Cal.: Stanford University Press, 1957), p. 3.
2 See Dain A. Trafton, 'Shakespeare's Henry IV: a new prince in a new principality', in John Alvis and Thomas G. West (eds), *Shakespeare as Political Thinker* (Durham, NC: North Carolina Academic Press, 1981), p. 85.
3 In Peter Moss's 1979 production at Stratford, Ontario, Douglas Rain delivered the entire speech from this point on as a whisper.
4 Arthur Colby Sprague, *Shakespeare's Histories: Plays for the Stage* (London: Society for Theatre Research, 1964), p. 53.
5 See James Black, '*Henry IV*: a world of figures here', in Phillip C. McGuire and David A. Samuelson (eds), *Shakespeare: The Theatrical Dimension* (New York: AMS Press, 1979), p. 168.
6 Jason Robards, in Michael Langham's 1958 production at Stratford, Ontario, delivered much of the speech to the letter itself, which he had reduced to a crumpled ball of paper on the floor.
7 The tendency to revise the past is speeded up in Part 2 by Morton, who describes Hotspur as able to inspire even his dullest followers, only to contradict himself a few lines later in order to build up the Archbishop of York (I.i. 112–15, 192–200).
8 Robert Hapgood, 'Shakespeare's thematic modes of speech: *Richard II* to *Henry V*', *Shakespeare Survey*, 20 (1967), 43.
9 John F. Danby, *Shakespeare's Doctrine of Nature: A Study of King Lear* (London: Faber & Faber, 1961), p. 90.
10 See, for example, Hardin Craig, *An Interpretation of Shakespeare* (Columbia: Lucas Brothers, 1948), p. 137; Irving Ribner, *The English History Play in the Age of Shakespeare* (London: Methuen, rev. 1965), p. 170.
11 See Donald Stauffer, *Shakespeare's World of Images* (New York: W. W. Norton, 1949), p. 96.
12 See John Dover Wilson, *The Fortunes of Falstaff* (Cambridge: Cambridge University Press, 1943), pp. 17–25.
13 Samuel Johnson, *Johnson on Shakespeare*, ed. Walter Raleigh (London: Oxford University Press, 1908), p. 114.
14 See Walter Kaiser, *Praisers of Folly: Erasmus, Rabelais, Shakespeare* (Cambridge, Mass.: Harvard University Press, 1963), p. 225.

15 Norman Rabkin, 'Rabbits, ducks, and *Henry V*', *Shakespeare Quarterly*, 28 (1977), 281.
16 We may contrast this with the hero of *The Famous Victories of Henry the Fifth*: 'heres such adoo now adayes, heres prisoning, heres hanging, whipping, and the divel and all: but I tel you sirs, when I am King, we will have no such things, but my lads, if the old king my father were dead we should be all kings.' Quoted from Geoffrey Bullough (ed.), *Narrative and Dramatic Sources of Shakespeare*, vol. 4 (London: Routledge & Kegan Paul, 1962), p. 312, ll. 453–7.
17 Stephen Greenblatt, 'Invisible bullets: Renaissance authority and its subversion, *Henry IV* and *Henry V*', in Jonathan Dollimore and Alan Sinfield (eds), *Political Shakespeare* (Ithaca, NY, and London: Cornell University Press, 1985), p. 36.
18 Harold Jenkins, *The Structural Problem in Shakespeare's Henry the Fourth* (London: Methuen, 1956), p. 26.
19 I have restored the simpler stage direction of the Quarto, and removed the knocking which most modern editions give but which is not in the original texts. The sound effect is tempting, but I suspect Shakespeare does not want to over-use it. He saves it for Part 2, when Bardolph announces that 'A dozen captains' have come looking for Falstaff (II. iv. 369), and when Pistol interrupts the party in Shallow's orchard with news from London (V.iii.68).
20 See Brian Vickers, *The Artistry of Shakespeare's Prose* (London: Methuen, 1968), p. 117. In his last soliloquy Richard III also assumes he is alone, and thus triggers our awareness that we are watching and judging.
21 Henri Bergson, 'Laughter', quoted from Wylie Sypher (ed.), *Comedy* (New York: Doubleday, 1956), p. 190.
22 See Robert Ornstein, *A Kingdom for a Stage* (Cambridge, Mass.: Harvard University Press, 1972), pp. 155–6. Sherman H. Hawkins observes that there are scene-for-scene parallels between the two parts early in Part 2 but that the parallels fade as the play goes on. See '*Henry IV*: the structural problem revisited', *Shakespeare Quarterly*, 33 (1982), 298–301.
23 Quoted from *The Seagull and Other Plays*, tr. Elisaveta Fen (Harmondsworth: Penguin, 1954), p. 20.
24 James Winny, *The Player King* (London: Chatto & Windus, 1968), p. 109.
25 I have restored the punctuation of the Quarto, or rather removed the punctuation of Arden, which puts a comma after 'right' and so weakens the line.
26 Jonas A. Barish calls Henry's declaration 'self-mutilating'. See 'The turning away of Prince Hal', *Shakespeare Studies*, 1 (1965), 10.
27 James L. Calderwood observes, 'To require Falstaff to reform in the interests of decorum is literally to kill him off as a comic character': *Metadrama in Shakespeare's Henriad: Richard II to Henry V* (Berkeley, Los Angeles, and London: University of California Press, 1979), p. 102.
28 Vickers, op. cit., p. 124, points out that Shallow's 'questions concerning the present are shrewd and direct'.
29 See A. C. Bradley, *Oxford Lectures on Poetry* (London: Macmillan, 1909), pp. 258–9.
30 The process continues in I.i of *Henry V*, where the two bishops have contradictory theories about the relation between the King's present character and his Eastcheap days (25–37, 60–6).

Notes

5 *HENRY V*

1 In Laurence Olivier's film version, Harcourt Williams delivers this speech with a shudder of superstitious dread.
2 Jamy's loyalty in particular is a striking contrast to the traditional enmity of 'the weasel Scot' (I. ii. 170) which concerns Henry in the first council scene.
3 The power of the speech was shown in Michael Langham's 1956 production at Stratford, Ontario: Gratien Gelinas, who played the French King as a bewildered invalid confined to a chair, rose to his feet during the speech and began unsteadily to walk, electrifying his court and the audience.
4 In the preface to his Great War book *In Parenthesis* David Jones complains, 'I have been hampered by the convention of not using impious and impolite words, because the whole shape of our discourse was conditioned by the use of such words' (New York: Viking Press, 1963), p. xii.
5 See Geoffrey Bullough (ed.), *Narrative and Dramatic Sources of Shakespeare*, vol. 4 (London: Routledge & Kegan Paul, 1962), p. 380.
6 Anyone who has seen Tony Church's brilliant reading of the speech in the LWT series *Playing Shakespeare* knows it is possible – if only just – for a skilled actor to capture both qualities.
7 Introduction to the Oxford edition of *Henry V* (Oxford: Oxford University Press, 1982), p. 65.
8 Robert Ornstein, *A Kingdom for a Stage* (Cambridge, Mass.: Harvard University Press, 1972), p. 188.
9 T. J. B. Spencer, *Shakespeare: The Roman Plays* (London: Longmans, Green, 1963), p. 16.
10 See Michael Goldman, *Shakespeare and the Energies of Drama* (Princeton, NJ: Princeton University Press, 1972), p. 59.
11 One of the most attractive touches in the Olivier film is the mutual liking of the two men, which creates a separation between their private feelings and the business they have to do.
12 Herbert Whittaker, reviewing the 1956 Stratford, Ontario, production, wrote, 'In this last scene, [Christopher] Plummer held his audience … in the hollow of his hand, capping an evening of slowly-mounting triumph': 'French, English-speaking actors are united', *Globe and Mail*, 18 June 1956.
13 See William Babula, 'Whatever happened to Prince Hal? An essay on *Henry V*', *Shakespeare Survey*, 30 (1977), 55–6.
14 In this scene in the 1964 Royal Shakespeare Company production, jointly directed by John Barton, Peter Hall, and Clifford Williams, Henry (Ian Holm) was kneeling and trying to pray; Fluellen (Clive Swift) was at his elbow, distracting him.
15 In the Royal Shakespeare Company's 1975 production, directed by Terry Hands, the wall that represented Harfleur sank down to reveal Katharine standing on the stage. See Gary Taylor, *Moment by Moment by Shakespeare* (London: Macmillan, 1985), p. 118.
16 Ian Holm allowed a flicker of pain to show on his face and turned aside to cross himself, seen only by the audience. Douglas Rain (in Michael Langham's 1966 production at Stratford, Ontario) pointedly showed no recognition, though the body of Bardolph was dumped at his feet. In Adrian Noble's 1984 Royal Shakespeare Company production, Henry (Kenneth Branagh) was forced to watch in growing discomfort as Bardolph was

slowly garrotted before his eyes; the extravagance of the effect made one appreciate the economy of Shakespeare's version. Alan Howard, who played Henry in the 1975 Royal Shakespeare Company production, said of the execution of Bardolph, 'That he doesn't do that coldly, and without a struggle, can be seen in the ramblings, the indecision, the contradictions of his speech to Montjoy immediately after Bardolph's death': quoted in Sally Beauman (ed.), *The Royal Shakespeare Company's Production of Henry V for the Centenary Season at the Royal Shakespeare Theatre* (Oxford: Pergamon Press, 1976), p. 57. The use of Bardolph's death to show Henry's commitment to justice may go back to the fact that it was in a dispute over Bardolph that Hal struck the Lord Chief Justice.

17 See Marilyn L. Williamson, 'The episode with Williams in *Henry V*', *Studies in English Literature*, 9 (1969), 277.

18 See Ann Barton, 'The king disguised: Shakespeare's *Henry V* and the comical history', in Joseph G. Price (ed.), *The Triple Bond* (University Park and London: Pennsylvania State University Press, 1975), p. 101.

19 See Philip Edwards, 'Person and office in Shakespeare's plays', *Proceedings of the British Academy*, 56 (1972 for 1970), 104.

20 See Norman Rabkin, 'Rabbits, ducks, and *Henry V*', *Shakespeare Quarterly*, 28 (1977), 287.

21 See Ornstein, op. cit., p. 202.


## 6 *JULIUS CAESAR*

1 According to Aristotle, a tyrant should not allow schools, for there men learn to trust each other. See *The Politics*, tr. T. A. Sinclair, rev. Trevor J. Saunders (Harmondsworth: Penguin, 1981), p. 345.

2 See Julian Markels, *The Pillar of the World: Antony and Cleopatra in Shakespeare's Development* (n.p.: Ohio State University Press, 1968), p. 82.

3 As Edward Pechter points out, Brutus' phrase 'that which is not in me' shows that he 'clings to a self, a "me" ': '*Julius Caesar* and *Sejanus*: Roman politics, inner selves and the powers of the theatre', in E. A. J. Honigmann (ed.), *Shakespeare and his Contemporaries: Essays in Comparison* (Manchester: Manchester University Press, 1986), p. 62.

4 Plutarch, *Life of Brutus*, tr. Thomas North; quoted from Geoffrey Bullough (ed.), *Narrative and Dramatic Sources of Shakespeare*, vol. 5 (London: Routledge & Kegan Paul, 1964), p. 93.

5 See Adrien Bonjour, *The Structure of Julius Caesar* (Liverpool: Liverpool University Press, 1958), p. 48.

6 There may be a sly irony on Shakespeare's part here, as the defender of the republic slips unthinkingly into political imagery drawn from monarchy.

7 See Ralph Berry, '*Julius Caesar*: a Roman tragedy', *Dalhousie Review*, 61 (1981), 334. I am less convinced than Berry that the text is correct and the caricature intentional, but I think he is right about the effect of the text as it stands.

8 In Trevor Nunn's 1972 Royal Shakespeare Company production, Brutus (John Wood) threw a tantrum and physically attacked the poet, while Cassius (Patrick Stewart) merely laughed.

9 There is admittedly a quality of display in Titinius' words before his death: 'Brutus, come apace, / And see how I regarded Caius Cassius' (V. iii. 87–8).

But there is no such quality in Cassius' last speech, which is remarkably matter-of-fact (V. iii. 36–46).

10 See Maurice Charney, *Shakespeare's Roman Plays* (Cambridge, Mass.: Harvard University Press, 1961), p. 13.

11 See Berry, op. cit., p. 335.

12 See H. B. Charlton, *Shakespeare, Politics, and Politicians* (London: English Association, 1929), p. 21.

13 See T. J. B. Spencer, 'Social assent and dissent in Shakespeare's plays', *Review of National Literatures*, 3 (1972), 29.

14 In that way his death resembles the Crucifixion: 'into thy hands I commend my spirit' (Luke 23: 46) and 'It is finished' (John 19: 30) emphasize the death as Christ's own willed act. E. A. J. Honigmann sees in the conspirators' ironic fawning on Caesar a parallel to the soldiers' mockery of Christ. See *Shakespeare: Seven Tragedies: The Dramatist's Manipulation of Response* (London: Macmillan, 1976), pp. 39–40. The view of Caesar's death as an event equivalent in the secular sphere to the Crucifixion is clearest in Dante, where Brutus and Cassius are punished alongside Judas Iscariot, endlessly gnawed by the Devil.

15 Sir Thomas Elyot, *The Book Named the Governor*, ed. S. E. Lehmberg (London: Dent, rev. 1962), pp. 178–9.

16 Michael Langham's 1955 production at Stratford, Ontario, ended with Antony and Octavius glaring at each other across an empty stage.

17 In John Barton's 1968 production for the Royal Shakespeare Company, Antony covered Brutus' corpse with Caesar's bloodstained mantle. See J. C. Trewin, '*Julius Caesar*', *Birmingham Post*, 5 April 1968.

18 See John Palmer, *Political and Comic Characters of Shakespeare* (London: Macmillan, 1964), p. 59.


## 7 *ANTONY AND CLEOPATRA*

1 See T. J. B. Spencer, *Shakespeare: The Roman Plays* (London: Longmans, Green, 1963), p. 36.

2 See Robert Ornstein, 'The ethic of the imagination: love and art in *Antony and Cleopatra*', in John Russell Brown and Bernard Harris (eds), *Later Shakespeare* (London: Arnold, 1966), p. 35.

3 Julian Markels, *The Pillar of the World: Antony and Cleopatra in Shakespeare's Development* (n.p.: Ohio State University Press, 1968), p. 21.

4 Maynard Mack, '*Antony and Cleopatra*: the stillness and the dance', in Milton Crane (ed.), *Shakespeare's Art: Seven Essays* (Chicago: University of Chicago Press for George Washington University, 1973), p. 81.

5 See Janet Adelman, *The Common Liar: An Essay on Antony and Cleopatra* (New Haven, Conn.: Yale University Press, 1973), p. 14; David Kaula, 'The time sense of *Antony and Cleopatra*', *Shakespeare Quarterly*, 15 (1964), 215.

6 Margery M. Morgan, 'Your crown's awry: *Antony and Cleopatra* in the comic tradition', *Komos*, 1 (1968), 131.

7 George Bernard Shaw, *Three Plays for Puritans* (repr. Harmondsworth: Penguin, 1946), p. xxx.

8 Harley Granville-Barker, *Prefaces to Shakespeare*, vol. 1 (Princeton, NJ: Princeton University Press, 1946, repr. 1952), p. 454. Antony's courtesy to Lepidus is one sign that, while Octavius seems a logical extension of the

Octavius we saw in *Julius Caesar*, Antony is esentially a new character.

9 See Adelman, op. cit., p. 137.

10 In Peter Brook's 1978 Royal Shakespeare Company production, the scene was played on a carpet, which during the dance was hooked on to ropes and drawn up to the flies. The great men tumbled over each other like toys tipped out of a box.

11 H. A. Mason, *Shakespeare's Tragedies of Love* (London: Chatto & Windus, 1970), p. 242.

12 See Maurice Charney, *Shakespeare's Roman Plays* (Cambridge, Mass: Harvard University Press, 1961), pp. 96–107.

13 See Paul A. Cantor, *Shakespeare's Rome: Republic and Empire* (Ithaca, NY: Cornell University Press, 1976), pp. 136–7.

14 See William Blissett, 'Dramatic irony in *Antony and Cleopatra*', *Shakespeare Quarterly*, 18 (1967), 158.

15 Here it may be worth recalling a general remark of Clifford Leech: 'The Elizabethan way of writing is to put things together, the Jacobean way is to fuse': *The Dramatist's Experience* (New York: Barnes & Noble, 1970), p. 159.

16 Derick R. C. Marsh, *Passion Lends them Power: A Study of Shakespeare's Love Tragedies* (Sydney: Sydney University Press, 1976), p. 182.

17 See Margaret Lamb, *Antony and Cleopatra on the English Stage* (London and Toronto: Associated University Presses, 1980), pp. 180–5.

18 See Michael Goldman, *Acting and Action in Shakespearean Tragedy* (Princeton, NJ: Princeton University Press, 1985), p. 113.

19 Janet Adelman reminds us, 'Popular tradition associated the serpent with his tail in his mouth with the cosmos and with eternity' (op. cit., p. 62).

20 See ibid., pp. 153–4.

21 I have accepted the traditional emendation here; the Folio reads 'Antony', as do some editors.

22 Susan Snyder, 'Patterns of motion in *Antony and Cleopatra*', *Shakespeare Survey*, 33 (1980), 117.

23 Richard Griffiths, who played the Clown in Peter Brook's production, displayed an exaggerated fear of the worm, putting slippers on his hands before opening the basket. But the basket was seen to be empty, and the Clown then produced asps from all over his body.

24 In Michael Langham's 1967 production at Stratford, Ontario, Zoe Caldwell gave a jealous pounce on the word 'my' and snatched another asp from the basket.

25 Duncan S. Harris, ' "Again for Cydnus": the dramaturgical resolution of *Antony and Cleopatra*', *Studies in English Literature*, 17 (1977), 227.

26 See Martha Tuck Rozett, 'The comic structure of tragic endings: the suicide scenes in *Romeo and Juliet* and *Antony and Cleopatra*', *Shakespeare Quarterly*, 36 (1985), 162.

8 *CORIOLANUS*

1 See Michael Goldman, *Shakespeare and the Energies of Drama* (Princeton, NJ: Princeton University Press, 1972), pp. 111–12.

2 There is also a simplicity about sex roles in the opening war sequence, very different from the blurring and even exchanging of sexual identities in *Antony and Cleopatra*. While the men are off fighting, the women '*set them*

*down on low stools and sew'* (I. iii. SD), then go to visit another woman who 'lies in' (I. iii. 77).

3 The Arden edition gives the line to the soldiers. Most editors follow the Folio, which gives it to Coriolanus.

4 See Norman Rabkin, '*Coriolanus* : the tragedy of politics', *Shakespeare Quarterly*, 17 (1966), 203–4.

5 Northrop Frye, *Fools of Time* (Toronto: University of Toronto Press, 1967), p. 56.

6 Richard S. Ide, *Possessed with Greatness: The Heroic Tragedies of Chapman and Shakespeare* (Chapel Hill: University of North Carolina Press, 1980), p. 189.

7 See Una Ellis-Fermor, *Shakespeare the Dramatist* (London: Methuen, 1961), p. 66.

8 The similarity between the two scenes is pointed out by Harley Granville-Barker, *Prefaces to Shakespeare*, vol. 2 (Princeton, NJ: Princeton University Press, 1947, repr. 1951), p.213.

9 In a similar vein Octavius scorns Antony and Cleopatra for appearing enthroned 'I' the market-place' (III. vi. 3).

10 Eugene M. Waith, *The Herculean Hero* (New York: Columbia University Press, 1962), p. 138.

11 Anne Barton, 'Livy, Machiavelli, and Shakespeare's *Coriolanus*', *Shakespeare Survey*, 38 (1985), 117. Barton contrasts the Roman populace with the Volscian commoners who 'constitute a miniature herd' (p. 125).

12 See Brian Vickers, *Shakespeare: Coriolanus* (London: Arnold, 1976), p. 36.

13 As Paul A. Cantor points out, mediators are much more successful in this play than they are in *Antony and Cleopatra*. See *Shakespeare's Rome: Republic and Empire* (Ithaca, NY: Cornell University Press, 1976), pp. 48–9.

14 See Ide, op. cit., p. 177.

15 Samuel Johnson, *Johnson on Shakespeare*, ed. Walter Raleigh (London: Oxford University Press, 1908), p. 179.

16 'I banish you' may also echo John of Gaunt's proposal that Bolingbroke treat reality as relative: 'Think not the king did banish thee, / But thou the king' (*Richard II*, I. iii. 279–80).

17 See M. W. MacCallum, *Shakespeare's Roman Plays and their Background* (London: Macmillan, 1910), pp. 618–19.

18 According to Una Ellis-Fermor, Coriolanus' tribute to Virgilia's silence represents his 'longing for the balancing silences, graces, and wisdom banished from the outer world but vital to the wholeness of life' (op. cit., p. 74.)

19 The analogy is made by Michael Long, *The Unnatural Scene* (London: Methuen, 1976), p. 75; Long compares Menenius to a 'harrassed PR man'.

20 As Brian Vickers (op. cit., pp. 51–2) points out, in his self-defence on his return to the Volsces, Coriolanus talks for the first time like a tricky politician, putting his actions in the best light.

21 E. A. J. Honigmann discusses the possibilities for the actress playing Volumnia in V.v, concluding, 'the text provides no clue and we can make of it what we will'. *Shakespeare: Seven Tragedies: The Dramatist's Manipulation of Response* (London: Macmillan, 1976), pp. 188–9.

22 The play is usually dated 1608, but could be as late as 1610 (see Introduction to the Arden edition, pp. 24–9). This would place it not just before the final

romances, where we usually think of it, but in the midst of them, around the same time as *The Winter's Tale* and a year before *The Tempest*. In any case its treatment of a family reunion and its consequences makes it an ironic counterweight to the romances.

23 Introduction to the Arden edition, p. 64.

24 The Folio reads *'Draw both the Conspirators, and kils Martius'*. If the stage direction is authorial, then Shakespeare, who specified '*3 or 4 Conspirators*' earlier in the scene, may have been uncertain of the resources available at this moment, or uncertain how he wanted them used. In any case, after the effect of Aufidius' rousing a whole stage full of people against Coriolanus, for him to be killed by two men, with neither Aufidius nor himself striking a blow, is anticlimactic. Editors and directors alike want a more spectacular end, and revise accordingly. But the anticlimax may well be deliberate, marking a sudden reduction in the hero's stature.

25 'He killed my daughter' is a startling accusation, suggesting the sort of atrocities Henry V threatened at Harfleur. There is no other hint in the play that Coriolanus kills civilians as well as soldiers. The line should probably be read symbolically, not literally, showing Shakespeare's concern not with particular deaths but with the fundamental violation of humanity involved in all killing.

## 9 HENRY VIII

1 At this point in George McCowan's 1961 production at Stratford, Ontario, Henry's hands were on Anne's breasts.

2 See Lee Bliss, 'The wheel of fortune and the maiden phoenix of Shakespeare's *King Henry the Eighth*', *ELH*, 42 (1975), 7.

3 This was done, for example, in Paul Barry's 1985 production at the New Jersey Shakespeare Festival and Brian Rintoul's 1986 production at Stratford, Ontario.

4 Holinshed, while expressing pity for Buckingham, makes his guilt much clearer than Shakespeare does: 'Such is the end of ambition, the end of false prophesies, the end of evill life, and evill counsell': quoted from Geoffrey Bullough (ed.), *Narrative and Dramatic Sources of Shakespeare*, vol. 4 (London: Routledge & Kegan Paul, 1962), p. 463.

5 Douglas Rain (in George McCowan's 1961 production) delivered the first part of the line as a flash of anger, then showed Wolsey regaining his control.

6 David Bevington, *Action is Eloquence: Shakespeare's Language of Gesture* (Cambridge, Mass.: Harvard University Press, 1984), p. 139.

7 Edward I. Berry, '*Henry VIII* and the dynamics of spectacle', *Shakespeare Studies*, 12 (1979), 239.

8 See Howard Felperin, 'Shakespeare's *Henry VIII*: history as myth', *Studies in English Literature*, 6 (1966), 234–5.

9 When Henry comes to Wolsey's banquet, he and his fellow masquers pretend they can speak no English, and Wolsey asks the Lord Chamberlain to welcome them in French (I. iv. 57); but no foreign language is actually spoken, and, when Henry takes Anne's hand, his aside – his first speech in the scene – is, of course, in English.

10 Pierre Sahel, 'The strangeness of a dramatic style: rumour in *Henry VIII*', *Shakespeare Survey*, 38 (1985), 148.

11 See Eugene M. Waith, *The Pattern of Tragicomedy in Beaumont and Fletcher* (New Haven, Conn.: Yale University Press, 1952), pp. 121–2.
12 See G. Wilson Knight, *The Crown of Life* (Oxford: Oxford University Press, 1947; repr. London: Methuen, 1965), p. 304.
13 Introduction to the Arden edition, p. lxiii.
14 See Frank V. Cespides, 'We are one in fortunes: the sense of history in *Henry VIII*', *English Literary Renaissance*, 10 (1980), 436.
15 See Berry, op. cit., pp. 241–2.

*CONCLUSION*

1 Christopher Morris, *Political Thought in England: Tyndale to Hooker* (London: Geoffrey Cumberlege, Oxford University Press, 1953), pp. 1–2.

# Index

261